THE APPRENTICESHIP OF
ABRAHAM LINCOLN

Also by Olivia Coolidge

Olivia Coolidge

The Apprenticeship of
Abraham Lincoln

Charles Scribner's Sons / New York

Printed in the United States of America
Library of Congress Catalog Card Number 74–11713
ISBN 0–684–14003–9 (RB)

Contents

Introduction

———◄◉►———

A MARBLE EFFIGY OF ABRAHAM LINCOLN sits enthroned in
Washington, gazing over the heads of his visitors with an air
of grave reflection. The building which shelters him has a
classical design, recalling aptly the order and balance of the
United States Constitution. His chair, decorated with the
symbols of imperial power, is so vast that a man of lesser
stature would be diminished. Lincoln's huge hands rest easily
on its wide arms, his long legs appear in proportion, and his
magnificent head dominates its setting. Here sits the man
acquainted with grief who bore the nation's burden in its
most tragic era. The hollow eyes, the melancholy furrows on
the cheeks, the brooding solemnity of the face demand that
people approach him quietly. This is the President who in
four years and a few weeks engraved his image in the annals
of his countrymen forever.

This is the President, but there was also another Lincoln
in Washington during those years who never fitted the presidential chair as though it had been made specially for him.
There is nothing in this impressive marble figure to remind
us of the man who went into his secretaries' office in his
nightshirt to share a joke with them, "utterly unconscious
that he with his short shirt hanging about his long legs, and
setting out behind like the tail feathers of an enormous os-
trich, was infinitely funnier than anything in the book he was

laughing at." We do not see the ugly man with the leathery, yellowish skin and untidy hair. We miss the beanpole figure, rounded shoulders, and clumsy movements. We cannot hear the high-pitched voice and the twang in his speech. We are not horrified, as his graver contemporaries were, to discover that the President's stories could be coarse, provided always that they were funny. The truth is that if we want to see the real man who became a great President, we should go not to Washington, but to Indiana and Illinois, and in particular to Springfield.

Abraham Lincoln was fifty-two when he came to Washington to be President for the remaining few years of his life. During his half-century of preparation for this great task, no remarkable teacher inspired him, no college educated him in its traditions. His learning, such as it was, had been gained by private reading or the actual practice of law. His political wisdom was acquired from newspapers and day-to-day experiences. In fact, so dependent was his development on that of Illinois and its surrounding states that Carl Sandburg with considerable poetic insight depicts him as a folk-hero, gaining some sort of mystical strength from physical contact with the soil and the people. Yet this view of Lincoln is no more a complete picture than is the memorial in Washington. Essentially Lincoln was not a folk-hero, but an individual with a highly distinctive personality.

It is natural for a man so dependent on the forces which shaped his society to adopt without question its ethical standards. We ought not to be surprised when we see that the "spoils system" was an accepted part of political life as Lincoln understood it. It is perfectly characteristic that he should insist after his election that "Something has to be done for Carl Schurz" and should acquiesce in the appointment of that notorious revolutionary as ambassador to Spain—a nation ruled by the least progressive and perhaps most snobbish monarchy in Europe. When we look at Lincoln's personal character, however, we discover that his honesty was always considered unusual. Although not a reformer, he made his personal virtue seem remarkable by the manner in which he expressed its importance to him. It was this individual quality in Lincoln which kept him a stranger in Washington. In many respects he had marvelous powers of adapting to new situations. He could put on dignity like a coat, yet shirtsleeves remained his natural costume. Sophistication broadened but did not change him. In the White House, as in his father's log cabin, his personality stood out from his surroundings.

Fundamentally there was something mysterious about Lincoln which nothing that happened to him ever destroyed. No man enjoyed company more or could be more garrulous. His Secretary of War complained that Lincoln could not keep secrets. Yet if he chose to be reserved, it was futile to pressure him. Any question, no matter how direct, would remind him of a story which enabled him to change the conversation. In particular, he was a man who said little about himself. After his death, people recalled how funny he had been, how sad he had looked, how individual his acts and manners were. But they could not entirely explain him—and nobody can to this day. Recognizably, however, the man in Washington was the very same person whom his friends had known in Springfield. He was not an awesome figure there, and they had not needed to walk quietly around him.

1
Childhood

THE BIRTH OF A SON to Thomas and Nancy Lincoln on February 12, 1809, aroused little interest in anybody for about sixty years. By the time that Lincoln's law partner, William Herndon, began to collect tales of the great President's childhood, nearly everybody who had known him as a baby was dead. There was, however, a cousin called Dennis Hanks, nine years older than Lincoln, who had been living a couple of miles away with Thomas and Betsy Sparrow, aunt and uncle to himself and Nancy Lincoln.

According to Dennis, Tom Lincoln had dropped by the Sparrow cabin on that long-ago Sunday to let them know that the baby was born and was a boy. Betsy Sparrow went up to wash the child and dress him in the unbleached homespun petticoats Nancy had ready, while Dennis followed out of curiosity. He found Nancy lying under a bearskin on the bed built into a corner of the cabin. Next morning when Betsy went again, Dennis got up his courage to ask to hold the baby, who promptly started screaming. Disconcerted, Dennis thrust him back, saying, "Aunt, take him! He'll never come to much!"

This prophecy of Dennis Hanks' sounds rather too apt to be convincing and is chiefly worth retelling because it illustrates how little we know for certain about Abraham Lincoln's early years. Dennis Hanks in his seventies was a jovial, uneducated fellow, happy to oblige with a good story, partly out of sheer good nature, partly in hopes that there might be profit in it, and partly perhaps out of the sense of humor which was his chief family likeness to Lincoln. It amused Hanks, and seems to have amused others, to see how much inquirers would swallow. Thus, though a great deal of genuine information was collected both from Hanks and other companions of Lincoln's boyhood, the most obviously authentic comment was that of a man who knew him in his early twenties and explained, "At that time I had no idea of his ever being President therefore I did not notice his course as close as I should of."

This lack of certainty about many incidents of Lincoln's boyhood extends also to his ancestry. Most people are curious to know what happy combination of family strains has produced a remarkable character. Research has connected Thomas Lincoln with earlier New England Lincolns who produced a number of able citizens, but no other great ones. Of Nancy Hanks Lincoln we can only say that she was the daughter of Lucy Hanks and probably illegitimate. In any case, nothing definite is known about her father. Even what his contemporaries thought of as the conspicuous ugliness of Lincoln is hard to trace to either of his parents. Thomas Lincoln appears to have been thick-set, round-faced, and of middle height, resembling his famous son chiefly in the shock of ill-kempt hair which covered his head. Nancy Lincoln was dead so long before anyone cared to recall her that descriptions of her appearance differ widely.

The pioneer farmers who built Kentucky, Indiana, and Illinois left their dead behind them as they moved on, generally finding little to say to their sons about their forebears. It happened, however, that Thomas Lincoln had a dramatic memory of his father. This earlier Abraham Lincoln belonged to a branch of the family which had drifted southward through Pennsylvania to Virginia. He was a connection of Daniel Boone, by whom he had been encouraged to move into Kentucky about 1782. Some four years later he was killed by an Indian as he was working on his farm. Thomas, then about ten years old, was with his father. The Indian snatched up the boy and was making off with him when he was killed by a bullet fired from the cabin by the eldest son, Mordecai.

Had Abraham Lincoln lived, his large land claims in Kentucky might have made him prosperous. His death soon sent off the older boys to make their own way in the world. Lincoln met both his uncles while he was growing up, but the families were not generally in touch. Thomas Lincoln, who had drifted with his mother and two sisters to various places, only picked up enough education to sign his own name and read a very little. By trade he was for a while a carpenter. In 1803, however, he was able to pay a hundred and eighteen pounds for a farm near Elizabethtown, county seat of Hardin, Kentucky. This fairly large sum probably represented his share of his father's estate. In Kentucky, Thomas was well respected by his neighbors, among whom he was considered prosperous. At different times he was chosen by church or community to perform jobs which he discharged satisfactorily. He was interested in public affairs, calling himself in politics a Democrat, in religion a Baptist with an anti-slavery bias. This last was probably due to the competition of slave labor, which was felt by the artisan and farming groups to which he always belonged. Personally, Thomas was a rough, humorous man, not lazy, yet rather ineffective, apt to postpone jobs and often preferring hunting to the heavy labor of clearing a farm. He was free, however, from all tendency to drunkenness, the familiar vice of his time.

In 1806, Thomas Lincoln married Nancy Hanks, who is said to have been able to read in the Bible, though this seems unlikely, as she could not sign her name on documents. Since

Thomas's mother and other relatives were living on his farm, he built a log cabin for himself and his wife in Elizabethtown, where he worked at his trade. Their daughter Sarah was born here in 1807, two years and two days before Abraham Lincoln. In 1808, Thomas moved to a second farm eighteen miles out of town on Nolin Creek, where he built another log cabin with the usual dirt floor and stick chimney lined with mud. Here his second child Abraham was born. Unfortunately, the Nolin Creek land was poor; so that in the spring of 1811, the Lincolns bought yet a third farm on Knob Creek, where the soil was more productive and the situation less remote. By their door passed the Cumberland Trail from Louisville to Nashville, along which during the summer moved peddlers, preachers, and other itinerants, bringing gossip with them.

The Lincoln family stayed three years on Knob Creek, which was the earliest home that Abraham Lincoln remembered. A couple of miles away was a log schoolhouse where Sarah and he were sent to learn the rudiments of reading, writing, and arithmetic at such seasons as their work was not needed on the farm. This schooling was paid for by the Lincolns, probably in farm produce, and is evidence that they were not destitute. Thomas Lincoln's second wife, who should have known, said that he was ambitious for his children's education. Tradition, on the other hand, states that he thought book-learning a waste of time and that it was Nancy who seized every chance to send her children to school. However that may be, Abe Lincoln's schooling at Knob Creek amounted merely to a few weeks in the year, since Thomas, whatever his desires, was seldom able to do without two extra pairs of hands. In these "blab" schools, all the children learned lessons by heart and out loud, which made it easy for the master to tell who was studying and who was not. The reading primer was moral and religious in tone, by no means calculated to amuse a child, but well adapted, if he had any turn that way, to making him think. Some say that after these scattered weeks of primitive schooling, Abe could read the Bible to his mother. If so, he could presumably do no more than spell out verses already known, or nearly known, by heart.

Land claims in Kentucky had been casually staked out; surveys were inaccurate and disputed ownership was exceedingly common. In 1814, when Tom Lincoln sold his first farm he got eighteen pounds less for it than he had given, since it turned out to be thirty-eight acres smaller than he had thought. He lost a lawsuit over the ownership of the Nolin Creek farm and at least for a time got nothing back on his investment. Finally, suit was filed by a claimant to Knob Creek. Meanwhile, across the Ohio lay Indiana, where the wilderness had been laid out by government survey, so that a man could buy a clear, indisputable title.

Thomas Lincoln traded his interest in Knob Creek for twenty dollars in cash and ten forty-gallon barrels of whisky. He is generally supposed to have built himself a flatboat, loaded it with his whisky, tools, iron plowshare, seed corn, and other bulky objects, and floated it down the creek into the Salt River, which in turn flowed into the Ohio. Crossing to the Indiana side, he left his belongings with someone there and walked sixteen miles inland through what was later known as Spencer County. Here he marked off a quarter-section of land, one hundred and sixty acres, on Little Pigeon Creek, notching trees with his axe and clearing away some brush to prove his claim.

Returning to Knob Creek, he probably mounted his family on a couple of horses which he then owned, horses that also had to carry kitchen utensils and whatever else he had left behind with Nancy. In this fashion, riding or walking to spare the laden beasts, Nancy and Thomas Lincoln set out with their children on a roundabout journey of a hundred miles, though the actual distance which they moved was about fifty if measured in a straight line. Once across the Ohio they must have hired a wagon in which to carry their goods, hacking a path for it through grapevines and underbrush growing so thickly that Abraham Lincoln, newly promoted to handling an axe, remembered that journey as one of the hardest experiences of his life.

Tom's first concern on arrival was to put up some sort of shelter. Pioneer families seldom started to move until their harvest was in, with the result that winter was on them almost as soon as they reached their new home. Thomas Lincoln threw up a half-faced cabin, a lean-to looking south made out of poles and chinked with mud and grass. On the open side a fire was kept burning day and night. It has been said that the Lincolns passed the whole winter in this rude structure, but this was not the case. Log cabins were of simple construction and not infrequently went up within a week, especially as helpers would come from many miles to settle a new family in. Thomas Lincoln was a carpenter and had already built three cabins. Young Abe, now seven years old, was big enough to clear the undergrowth or top off branches. Nancy and Sarah could help with chinking and caulking, which seems to have been an endless job because the mud and hay used for the purpose washed out in winter rains no matter how tightly wooden shingles were rammed between the logs.

Certainly by February, 1817, the Lincolns were in their cabin because Abraham remembered that a few days before he was eight a flock of wild turkeys came over and that he, standing inside, poked the family rifle through an uncaulked crack between the logs and brought one down. Instead of feeling excited, he decided he did not like killing and never again pulled a trigger on large game. This is the first time that we have a glimpse of young Abraham as anything but the typical son of a pioneer farmer. Thomas Lincoln must have been pleased that the boy was not eager to waste precious powder and shot, for these articles were among the very few he had to purchase.

We cannot be sure what Thomas Lincoln did with his barrels of whisky or the cash which he got for his three farms. Perhaps he had gone in debt to buy the later ones and had little left after their sale. He certainly had to stock his Indiana farm with cows, hogs, and sheep, and eventually with chickens. Abraham Lincoln later said that the family practically never saw cash, while any which they could lay their hands on was earmarked for the "Land Office" as payment for their farm. Actually, however, Thomas Lincoln paid two installments, amounting to eighty dollars in 1817, which made one-fourth of the purchase price of his tract. Ten years later he took advantage of a provision by which land could be re-surrendered to the government for credit. Thus by getting rid of the least productive half of his claim he was able to make up the purchase price of eighty good acres without paying anything further. In addition he had acquired by cash or barter twenty acres from a neighbor, making up a farm of a hundred acres of which he eventually had fifteen or more under cultivation.

Towards the end of 1817, Betsy and Thomas Sparrow with Dennis Hanks moved in near the Lincolns, occupying for a time the half-faced cabin. But in the summer of 1818, a disease called the "milk-sick" appeared in the area. It is said to have been caused by cattle eating wild snakeroot, a plant which has more or less died out now that the land is cleared and open. Cattle got the "trembles" and died, but not before they had passed on the poison in their milk to human beings. Thomas and Betsy Sparrow fell ill and died in a few days. Tom Lincoln made their coffins and buried them, while Dennis Hanks moved into the Lincoln cabin. This was still unfloored, but

there was a half-attic into which Abe and eighteen-year-old
Dennis climbed to their beds by a ladder of pegs driven into
the log wall. Only a week after the death of her uncle and
aunt, Nancy Lincoln also fell sick of the milk disease and died
on October 5, 1818, when her son Abraham was nine years old.

There followed a year of squalid living. Eleven-year-old
Sarah was not equal to the cooking, soapmaking, mending,
spinning, and other chores which made up the endless toil of
a pioneer woman. She had three males to look after whose
rough outdoor work soon wore out buckskin shirts and
breeches, which shrank when they got wet and then dried
hard. Winter shoes were birch bark with hickory bark soles
strapped on over yarn socks which Sarah had to spin and knit
and keep mended. Her best was not good enough; and after
the harvest of 1819, Thomas Lincoln left the children to fend
for themselves while he took a trip to Elizabethtown.

There could not have been much letter-writing between
the almost illiterate Thomas and his connections in Elizabethtown; but southern Indiana was filling up fast with folk from
Kentucky who brought news. There was a widow in Elizabethtown called Sarah Bush Johnston, nearly eleven years
younger than Thomas Lincoln, but with three children, the
eldest a girl about Sarah Lincoln's age. She was the sister of
Isaac Bush, who owed Thomas Lincoln a little money as the
result of the suit over the Nolin Creek farm. It is said, though
without convincing evidence, that Thomas had courted Sarah
Bush before she married Johnston. At all events, he and
Nancy had known her well and, if he called on Isaac Bush to
pick up his money, he would soon have learned she had been
left badly off. Thomas went into Elizabethtown to propose
marriage without wasting precious time on a long courtship.
He stated his business bluntly, was accepted, discharged a few
debts that Sarah owed, presumably with the money received
from her brother, and borrowed a four-horse wagon from his

sister's husband to carry Sarah with her possessions and children into Indiana. It is noticeable that in the few years which had elapsed since his own migration, passable trails had developed for this wagon journey.

Sarah and Abraham Lincoln, who had not been told their father's errand, had the shock of their lives when he reappeared with a new "Mama" together with a four-year-old brother and two sisters. Sarah Bush Lincoln was a big, strong, steady woman who took to Tom's children as though they had been her own and soon developed a special affection for Abraham, whom she later liked to describe as the best boy she ever knew and one who never spoke a cross word to her. Moreover Sarah was used to small-town living and had brought with her such comforts as a black walnut bureau, a clothes chest, a table and chairs, knives, forks and spoons, and a feather mattress. Under her influence Tom Lincoln was induced to floor the cabin and to mend the roof so that snow did not drift through it onto the beds of the boys who slept in the attic.

There were now eight people living in the Lincoln cabin; but crowding was not unwelcome in pioneer families, since it meant more hands to do the work. As the neighborhood became settled, wool was spun and flax cultivated; jeans and cowhide boots gradually took the place of bark and buckskin. Cabbage was grown as well as corn; eventually a barrel of molasses replaced the occasional wild honey which was the only sweetening of the early pioneers. "We felt as if we was gitting along in the world," said Dennis Hanks, remembering the delights of salt pork, corn dodgers, and boiled greens. Young Abe expressed his confidence and well-being in a different fashion. When Sarah had the cabin ceiling whitewashed, he held up some small boys to make muddy footmarks right across it and laughed heartily at his stepmother's astonishment. Sarah entered into the joke, and Abe redid the ceiling, perfect harmony reigning between them. Naturally not all changes for the better came at once, nor were they all due to the influence of Sarah; but the day that her wagon drew up at the Lincolns' door marked their beginning.

Little Pigeon Creek did not develop into a community center, but within a mile radius of the Lincolns there were shortly nine families with forty-nine children among them. In the slack seasons of the farmer's year there were schools which Abe attended in the usual irregular fashion, receiving a total of less than one year of instruction, including that which he had already had in Kentucky. In other words, his education was about average for a boy in that time and place. It was what he did with it which made Dennis Hanks remark that there was always something "peculiarsome" about Abe. His stepmother, Sally Bush Lincoln, noted that when grown-ups came calling, Abe listened to their conversation in silence. As soon as they had gone, however, he wanted to know exactly what they had meant down to the smallest detail. He would repeat a discussion in his own words until he understood the sense of it to his satisfaction, by which time it was fixed in his memory, apparently forever.

He used the same slow, tenacious method in digesting his lessons, starting with the one-syllable sentences in Dillworth's Speller which informed him, "No man may put off the law of God." It was not enough to read the words correctly. He had to puzzle over the sense and start discussions on topics which his fellow pupils never thought of. He would spend his evenings doing sums by firelight or trying to express the ideas behind his lessons in short compositions written on a wooden shovel for lack of paper. When he had covered this, he shaved it clean and began again.

At about twelve Abe had already learned to read and write. He began devouring all the books that he could manage to borrow. Luckily people who took the trouble to add a book

to their portable possessions were likely to want one which
gave them something to think about. Abe mulled over the
ideas in *Aesop's Fables*, *The Pilgrim's Progress*, *Robinson Crusoe*,
and *The Autobiography of Benjamin Franklin*. Weem's *The Life
and Memorable Actions of George Washington* presented in vivid
terms the great ideals for which the Revolution was fought
and the country founded.

It is impossible to say where this boy, who seemed in other
ways to fit so easily into family life, had acquired his study
habits. Even allowing for a natural gift, Abe's concentration
in the midst of people who must have been tripping over his
big feet or making a good deal of noise is quite remarkable.
It is tempting to wonder whether Nancy Lincoln, pondering
over difficult sayings which she had picked up from preachers, had started her son off on a way of thinking which he
found congenial. When, however, many years later, Lincoln
remarked that he owed everything that he had become to his
mother, it is hard to be certain whether he meant anything
more than that he did not inherit his powers from his father.
It is clear that Thomas Lincoln had no idea what went on in
his son's mind, though Sally maintained that he was proud of
the boy's learning, and that if Abe was reading, his father
would do a chore himself rather than interrupt him. It seems
that Thomas liked to boast of a boy who could write letters
for the whole neighborhood, but there is no indication that
he thought Abe needed any more knowledge than would be
generally useful to a farmer. In later life, Lincoln's devotion
to Sally was greater than his affection for Thomas.

By the time Abe was fourteen, he was big and strong
enough to be hired out to neighboring farmers, among whom
he won the reputation of being lazy. It was admitted that he
could do a hard day's work; but when people came on him
taking a lunch break under a tree with his feet up, a piece of
corn pone in one hand and a book in another, it looked pretty

much as if he were taking a nap. Abe himself remarked that his father had taught him to work, but not to like it. Apparently, from his earliest years he was determined to be something more than a dirt farmer. What made him acceptable in that rough community was his physical strength and his good nature. It seemed as though he would never stop growing. He had the longest legs, the biggest hands and feet that anybody had ever seen. His movements looked clumsy, but his strength matched his height; and he could outrun any boy of his age in the district. No one ever saw him lose his temper; he liked to be obliging; and he grew up to tell a funny story even better than his father.

"We lived just like the Indians," said Dennis Hanks, recalling his early pioneer life, " 'ceptin we took an interest in politics and religion." A couple of years after Thomas Lincoln had moved into Little Pigeon Creek, a comparatively wealthy man called James Gentry, who had settled on a thousand acres, established a store at his house, a mile and a half from the Lincoln cabin. This soon became the nucleus of a small village called Gentryville, containing a blacksmith, a well-digger, a butcher, and other tradesmen. All the neighborhood went to Gentryville for articles like gunpowder, cotton cloth, or even tea. Once there, they hung around waiting for repair jobs at the blacksmith's, or simply passing the time at Gentry's store. Another center was the mill where people took their corn to be ground, often waiting as much as a day for their turn. Naturally when men came together they talked of the weather and the crops, laughed at crude jokes, or gossiped. They also discussed land-office affairs or what the government should be doing to help the settler. They passed around news of roads or mail deliveries. When mail came regularly to Gentryville in 1825, it brought occasional newspapers, most especially at election times. People discussed candidates; and since national, state, and local elections were all held at different intervals, there was nearly always a political contest coming up. One summer about harvest time when everybody was working at full stretch, a candidate came around asking for votes and wanted people to gather and listen to a speech. Young Lincoln made one in answer which was agreed to be as good as the real thing. An argument like that was something worth listening to, so that everybody was pleased except the owner of the field, who wanted his work finished.

Other arguments took place at the county courthouse about fifteen miles away, where one could also see clapboard houses. Both Abe and Dennis Hanks were among those who walked over when the circuit court came round, especially if there was a murder case or something exciting. It did a man good to hear what the lawyers made of it.

Nancy and Thomas Lincoln had belonged to a small Baptist congregation in Kentucky, but they did not affiliate with the nearest group in Indiana. Only after some years was a meeting-house erected about a mile from the Lincoln cabin. Thomas, as carpenter, supervised the building and did the difficult parts. Abe, at fourteen, was given the caretaker's duties, filling the woodbox, checking on the stock of candles, and sweeping out the dirt which was trodden in. Thomas and his family presumably went to some religious meetings during the early years; but once he and Sarah became full members of the new church, they would take their family whenever a preacher came over. Sermons gave a thoughtful boy yet more to puzzle about. Revival meetings, however, which satisfied a craving for excitement in many a dull life, did not appeal to Abe's cautious habit of thought. It is not significant that he never joined the church as a full member, since only heads of households customarily did so. The surprising thing is that, looking around for a focus for his vague ambitions, he never seems to have considered aspiring to be a preacher. The nearest he got to this was a habit of retelling sermons, partly in mimicry and partly for the pleasure of explaining their ideas. There seems to have been at least a period when Thomas and his son were at odds. This may perhaps have been connected less with his reading than with his keeping other people from their work.

Such were the discussions, political and religious, which molded Dennis Hanks and his like. Briefly summarized, they suggest considerable, if informal influence on Lincoln's intellectual development. It is easy, however, to exaggerate this. We need to give proper weight to Lincoln's own later statement that there was absolutely nothing to excite ambition for education in Indiana. It may be granted that Abe got more from his opportunities than Hanks did. It may even be admitted that Lincoln's interest in politics and law followed naturally from the climate to which he had been exposed in his boyhood. We must realize, however, that real intellectual challenge was rare, that nobody around young Lincoln had ambitions to be more than a successful farmer or tradesman. Among the few things, however, that Lincoln said of himself in later life was that he had always prided himself on sticking to his purpose. The more he read, the more he realized how unfit he must be for a learned profession, yet he persevered in reading. This would have been less surprising if he had been in the conventional sense a brilliant child, or even if he had been in open rebellion against uncongenial surroundings; but he was neither of these things. Everyone commented on his easiness and good temper and also on the slowness and pains with which he tackled learning problems. It is hardly possible to see any signs of greatness in young Abe at this stage. It was far too early for that, but he was an unusual child without any question.

2
Adolescence

YOUNG ABE LINCOLN was soon developing into a strange, contradictory fellow. At times he would be so deep in his book that he had to be roused and reminded when it was his turn to bring in logs or a bucket of water. Yet nobody had a greater craving for company than he. At the end of a long day's work on the farm, he would walk over to Gentry's store with Dennis Hanks and stay there swapping yarns long after Dennis was imploring him to come on home to bed. It was not that he wanted to show off his learning, though he was always obliging if anybody wanted a paper written. Abe was simply a wonderful mimic who liked a good laugh and seemed to get one out of his own stories just as well as out of new ones. When he decided that he did not want to be a farmer, it was not because he despised the simple folk at Gentry's store. What he seems to have disliked about this way of life was the lack of company just as much as the lack of mental challenge. People did not have much chance to talk while they were plowing, grubbing out tree roots, or splitting fence rails.

Luckily for Abe, in 1823, a cousin, John Hanks, came up from Kentucky to join the Lincolns, with whom he spent the next four years. There were thus three grown men to do the work of one farm as well as Abe and young John Johnston, now eight years old. Thomas found it profitable to hire Abe out to other farmers who were more pressed for labor, par-

ticularly as a boy's earnings belonged to his father until he
was twenty-one.

In the summer after he turned sixteen, Abe was working
on the farm of one James Taylor, at the mouth of Anderson
Creek where it joined the Ohio, and where Taylor ran a ferry
for anyone wanting to cross the river. By this time there were
steamboats on the Ohio, some of which stopped at Troy by
the mouth of the creek to take on wood. In consequence, Troy
was a rough little town full of transients of every sort—land
speculators, traders, hunters, gamblers, preachers, and many
more. They nearly all had three things in common: they were
tough, they carried whisky jugs, and they went armed. Besides the steamboats there were the flatboats, essentially log
rafts drifting downstream with loads of farm produce for
southern markets. They generally tied up at night, and the
crew would get talking with people on the shore. Flatboats
were broken up when they reached the end of their journey;
but there were other, more permanent craft which fought
their way back upstream with gunpowder, lead for bullets,
iron plowshares, pots and pans, even crockery and cheap
cotton goods to satisfy the growing needs of farmers like Tom
and Sally Lincoln. Abe liked the ferrying which fell to his
share because it made him a part of all this movement and
adventure. He had, moreover, a considerable shock when a
couple of travelers whom he rowed out to midstream to catch
a steamboat each threw him half a dollar as they went aboard.
So astounded was he at the possibility of being paid on this
princely scale for a half hour's work that he dropped one of
his precious coins in the river.

It was not surprising that a couple of years later Abe built
himself a boat about a mile and a half downriver at Bates
Landing, where the steamboats did not put in but would halt
in mid-river to take up passengers. On the Kentucky side of
the Ohio at this point were a pair of brothers called Dill who

operated a licensed ferry and were indignant at young Abe's interference with their trade. It was easy enough for them to beckon him across; but when they got a good look at the size of him, they dropped their plan of throwing him into the river and breaking up his boat. It seemed more prudent to take him before a justice of the peace and swear out a warrant. Abe went willingly enough, uncertain of Kentucky law, but ready to swear that he had put no one across the river, having merely rowed passengers out to midstream from the Indiana side. The judge dismissed the case, and Abe was interested enough to cross the river again to listen to him deciding other cases. Tom Lincoln's neighbors would surely have agreed that he was a lazy fellow.

1828 was a year of change. It started with sorrow, for in January Abraham's only sister Sarah died in childbirth. She had been married just over a year before to Aaron Grigsby, son of a prosperous farmer, and was generally thought to have done very well for herself. There was a certain condescension in the attitude of the Grigsbys toward the Lincolns which Abe was quick to resent. He seems also to have suspected that his sister's death was due to carelessness or neglect. Not long after, two Grigsby brothers held a double wedding. Liquor flowed and there was a good deal of rough joking, amid which Abe took a prominent part in introducing the wrong bride-groom to the wrong bride's bed in the dark. The exchange was discovered just in time, but Abe composed a satirical poem celebrating the incident in mock-Biblical language which was sniggered at all around the neighborhood. It was a fairly crude revenge for the slights he had resented, but he was still a crude young man with much to learn.

1828 was the year in which John Quincy Adams stood for the Presidency against Andrew Jackson. Adams called himself a "National Republican," but the name of the party was fairly soon altered to "Whig." William Jones, Gentry's storekeeper, took the *Louisville Journal,* a staunchly Whig paper, and possibly others as well. These featured in particular the speeches of Henry Clay, Kentucky's great statesman, life and soul of the Whig party for many years. As a matter of course small farmers like the Hankses and as far as we know Thomas Lincoln, were Democrats, standing for Andrew Jackson, for small holdings and the independence of the pioneer farmer. But David Turnham, to whom Abe had been hired out to work sometimes, was a bigger man, justice of the peace and possessor of a difficult book on the laws of Indiana which he had lent to Abe.

David Turnham was a Whig, as was William Wood, another of Abe's employers, who lent him temperance tracts and liked an article Abe wrote about them so well that he sent it in to a temperance paper in Ohio, where tradition says it was printed. These were the kinds of people Abe would like to resemble, and they talked convincingly about stable currency, which would make a man's wages worth their nominal value. They talked about transportation developed at public expense to get the farmers' hogs to market. It was probably in 1828 or thereabouts that Abe turned Whig, apparently to the indignation of his family. Dennis Hanks at least tried to talk him out of it, but Abe's slow mind was very tenacious. He never changed back.

Some months after Sarah's death, Abe was hired by James Gentry to help his own son Allen pilot a flatboat clear down the Mississippi to New Orleans, a distance of about twelve hundred miles. A great deal of the storekeeper's business was done by barter, so that he had farm produce on his hands which he could only turn into cash down south by way of the great rivers. Abe and Allen began after harvest to build the boat, which was about sixty-five feet long and eighteen wide with a cabin to protect them from the worst of winter weather. Flatboating was an agreeable way of seeing the world. One moved at about four miles an hour with the current and tied up at night to a bank. The boat was steered by a heavy rudder and a couple of big sweeps. It needed a good deal of skill and strength to pilot its unwieldy length around the bends of the Mississippi, but in between crises there was plenty of time for a flatboatman to sense the vastness of the country and the variety of life and customs in it.

Allen Gentry, who had made the voyage earlier with his father, understood that trading began along the Mississippi, so that the cargo with which they reached New Orleans was not necessarily the same as that with which they had started. But Mississippi river towns were larger and tougher than Troy; there were pirates on the river; and plantation owners were used to driving hard bargains. In Louisiana, Abe and Allen were attacked one night by a gang of seven Negroes who intended to kill them, take their cargo, and sink the boat. Armed with nothing more lethal than clubs, the boys laid into the intruders to such effect that they fled howling.

New Orleans was like nothing a country boy had ever seen. It was all the roistering river towns of the Mississippi rolled into one with flatboats tied up five deep along the levees. It was a great deep-sea port with tall ships unloading cargo from France, from Holland, from the West Indies, above all from England, and loading on sugar or cotton. Wagons clattered over cobblestones; and sailors of every race and color sought entertainment in low dives, jabbering drunkenly in a dozen languages. New Orleans was also a city of gracious living, of cool stucco houses with iron balconies, of carriages driven by liveried coachmen containing ladies in silk or fine muslin whose ivory pallor had never felt the sun. The town was one of the great marts of the slave trade where one could see fettered gangs brought in from Maryland or Virginia for sale to the cotton planters of the South. It is said that the boys from the backwoods went to look at a slave auction and came away indignant. The anti-slavery opinions of Thomas Lincoln had been more economic than humanitarian, but actual contact with the institution aroused warmer feelings in his son.

Abe had only a few days in which to take New Orleans in. Before this river journey, he had hardly seen more than four or five clapboard houses in a row in his life. A good-sized town had been a place of a couple of dozen log cabins which might perhaps shelter a hundred and fifty people. The sheer noise of the big city must have stunned him. But the cargo was soon disposed of and the flatboat sold for firewood. Ahead lay the exciting experience of going back up the Mississippi by steamboat. We may be sure that Abe disembarked with great reluctance to walk back from Anderson Creek to the family cabin, a traveled man with twenty-four dollars for Thomas Lincoln, less any modest expense incurred on the journey.

He was nineteen when he left in December, 1828. He was twenty when he returned to one more year of dull chores for his father. But in 1829 great decisions were being taken by the Lincoln family. By this time both Sally Lincoln's daughters were married, the elder to Dennis Hanks, the younger to Squire Hall, a half-brother of Dennis, come up from Kentucky. John Hanks had drifted on to Illinois, whence he was writing glowing letters about the richness of the virgin soil and urging his relatives to come and join him. The Hanks and Hall couples were eager to go. After all they were not heirs to Thomas Lincoln and had their way to make. Sally Lincoln was anxious not to lose touch with her daughters and still young enough to face fresh years of struggle.

Thomas Lincoln, who was over fifty, seems to have been running out of energy. But if Abe would not stay and work the farm with him, he and Sarah would have no one to help them in old age, unless it was John Johnston, who was turning out to be no great lover of work. While the matter was being debated, there was an outbreak of the milk-sickness in the herd belonging to Dennis Hanks, who was ill himself of the disease, but recovered. This frightened everyone and made Dennis swear to get out of that country.

The upshot was that Thomas Lincoln sold his farm to one of the Grigsbys for $125 in early 1830. It had cost him eighty dollars in cash and another eighty in credit, not to mention what he had paid to his neighbor for twenty acres. He had lived on it fourteen years and had brought maybe twenty acres under cultivation, cutting the trees, clearing the under-brush, fencing a good deal for stock, raising corn, oats, and a little wheat. He had built a cabin for himself and other cabins for the young couples, who by now had children of their own. Yet all he had done was depreciate the value of the land from two dollars an acre to one and a quarter. This is surely a commentary on farming methods as well as on the almost unlimited supply of virgin soil. Luckily Sally still owned a lot and cabin in Elizabethtown which she was able to sell for $123, thus doubling the Lincoln's supply of cash.

Of course they sold their stock. Hogs multiply fast; Dennis had his herd of cows as did Thomas Lincoln. Hall would have his own animals too. They took seed corn, but there was much to dispose of. It was not easy to sell farm goods for cash, but the family scraped together sufficient to feel that they need not wait till harvest. In the early spring they moved, having spent part of the winter building wagons, one for each of the three families, two to be drawn by two yoke of oxen and one by four horses.

With his parents went Abraham Lincoln, to whom the decision to move must have been unwelcome. He had no interest in breaking virgin soil, in repeating the experiences of his first years in Indiana. He was twenty-one and indepen-dent, but without any trade or particular purpose. But the family, absorbed by its immediate problems, was incapable of understanding his ambitions. He laid in a peddler's stock of pins, needles, buttons, and other precious oddments to sell to cabins along the way. He doubled his money, but it cannot have been very much. There could be no question of getting any more formal education, nor did he know what he would do with it.

John Hanks was waiting for them on the banks of the Sangamon near Decatur, where he had already assembled logs to build a cabin. It went up quickly with five grown men to do the work. A good deal of the new land was open prairie, not needing to be cleared of trees but terribly matted with roots. By tremendous efforts, they actually cleared and fenced about twelve acres in time to plant their corn. Abe and John Hanks hired themselves out to split three thousand rails for the local sheriff and an extra thousand for two other neighbors. A good axeman like Abe could split about four hundred rails in a day.

Things went on well during the summer, but toward the end of it, most of the party came down with "fever and ague," or in other words with malaria. This, like the milk-sick, was reckoned to be a local affliction, so that the best cure lay in moving on. They stayed, however, through the winter, which proved to be one of the worst in Illinois records with snow three feet on the level and drifting heavily, overlaid by a crust of freezing rain. This was followed by a northwest gale driving ice-splinters in literal clouds through the air. For nine weeks it is said families were marooned in their cabins. Stock froze to death; wolves ran down deer who had broken through the crusted surface of the snow. Men had to get wood somehow, keep fires going, and dig out buried fodder. It was hard on everybody, but worst on the new arrivals, whose supplies and comforts were naturally lowest.

As soon as the floods of the spring thaw were over, the Lincoln party moved again, but Abraham did not go with them. He seems to have had no idea what to do with himself, unless vaguely he thought of engaging in trade, which at least would mean meeting people. Some time before the disastrous winter set in, John Hanks and he had made the acquaintance of a man named Denton Offutt, who had plans to take a flatboat down the Sangamon and thence to New Orleans by way of the Illinois and Mississippi. John Hanks was an experienced flatboatman, and Abe was eager for another voyage. They easily persuaded Abe's stepbrother, young John Johnston, to come along. Thus while the rest of the tribe piled back into their wagons, the three young men bought a canoe in which they paddled downriver to a point near Springfield, where they had arranged to meet Offutt. In this fashion Abraham Lincoln first entered Sangamon County, which he was to make famous.

He was a young man of six feet four inches tall with long thin legs and arms, at the end of which dangled feet and hands of conspicuous size. His neck was thin, his face leathery and sallow and disfigured by a large mole on one side above his mouth. His voice was high, at times positively squeaky. The features which look so impressive in later photographs were seen by his fellows untouched-up, and also in motion. Motion of any sort in Abraham Lincoln was clumsy. Nor were his looks improved by a thatch of hair which might be combed down for a moment, but which was generally sticking up at all angles, though without managing to conceal his prominent ears. He was narrow-shouldered and stooped a little, as very tall people often do. He was dressed in blue homespun with his pants tucked into rawhide boots and his sleeves inevitably too short. His hat was a shapeless felt which had started black and was now by his own admission "sunburned till it was a combine of colors." This was Abraham Lincoln at twenty-one —with vague ambitions, but no assets save physical strength, a sense of humor, a habit of reflection, and a quite uncomplicated liking for people, whom he was ready to take pretty much as he found them. He was drifting, and the river had brought him into Sangamon County.

3
New Salem

DENTON OFFUTT WAS NOT at the meeting-place which he had appointed, but was discovered at the Buckhorn Tavern in Springfield, then a town of five hundred and seventy, drinking and boasting. Offutt was prepared to assemble a cargo but had made no plans for a flatboat. He offered the young men ten dollars a month to build one eighty feet long and eighteen wide, which took over four weeks of hard work. They cut their trees on government land and floated them downriver to a sawmill in order to get the planks. By the time the boat was built and loaded with pork, corn, and live hogs, the spring floods had receded from the Sangamon, which near Springfield was not a very big river. All the same it had enough water for the flatboat until the voyagers got to a small place called New Salem, where there was a dam across the stream to work a sawmill and gristmill. Some water was still flowing over this; but the laden flatboat, coming down with the current, slid about halfway across and stuck with her bow in the air and her stern shipping water. Naturally the cargo slid toward the downward end, forcing it lower.

The citizens of New Salem, a town of about fifteen log cabins, came out to watch the excitement. No one had any idea what to do except an immensely tall young stranger "with his trousers rolled up about five feet," who started a movement to unload cargo until the boat righted itself somewhat. Borrowing an auger and choosing his spot with care, he drilled a hole to let water out. Soon the stern floated higher and drained out yet more water. Some of the cargo was reloaded in the bow, and presently the boat slid over the dam after the young man had pegged his hole. The operation had taken most of the day, but the boat went successfully on its way, leaving the people of New Salem impressed. They liked a man to show resource, and they had been anxious lest the flatboat tear a hole in their mill-dam.

Denton Offutt, engaged no doubt in pacifying the mill-owners, had liked the look of New Salem, which he thought was a town with a future. Central Illinois was beginning to be opened up, and it required no genius to know that the difficulty about the area was transport. If the Sangamon could be made navigable as far as Springfield, it would make all the difference to the farmers of the region. Denton Offutt's flatboat, loaded with farm produce for the New Orleans market, was intended to show the way. But Offutt had also in mind a Sangamon River deepened here and there, straightened out around bends and cleared of obstructions, which could be navigable for steamboat traffic bringing up the store goods which every farmer needed. If this ever happened, New Salem would be the center of a whole new district in no time.

Quick to seize a chance, Offutt had already discovered that the mill's owners would be glad to rent it to him and that a lot on which he could build a store would cost only ten dollars. He could run the mill himself, while young Abe Lincoln was just the man to keep a popular store. Offutt had taken a fancy to young Abe, whose inexperience was dazzled by this talk of frontier opportunities. An agreement between them was quickly made before Offutt dropped off the boat at the mouth of the Sangamon. John Hanks, who had not expected the long delay in starting, got off in St. Louis to get home in time to plant his corn. John Johnston and Abe Lincoln took

the boat to New Orleans and were back again in July. Young
Johnston headed home, while Lincoln went to New Salem to
take up his job.

Offutt had rented the mill, but he so far had done nothing
about stocking a store, quite possibly because his credit was
not sufficient without the profits from the flatboat. At all
events, Lincoln hung about town doing odd jobs for a month
and getting acquainted. New Salem was Gentryville all over
again, but a little larger and far more hopeful of growth. Its
cabins were built of roughly squared logs, which made caulking easier; and its roofs were generally shingled. There was
glass in many of the windows. Most chimneys were of stone,
which made it safe to construct a small back room, slightly
warmed by the fireplace and convenient for storage and sleeping. Lincoln had a bed in the room behind Offutt's store and
boarded around or took his meals at the tavern. When the
store opened, he had a fellow clerk, young Bill Greene of New
Salem, which made it possible for them to spell each other if
an errand had to be done or if Lincoln was needed by Offutt
at the mill. Lincoln's pay was fifteen dollars a month, which
was enough to feed him, buy an occasional shirt or pair of
pants, and leave a bit over.

He made his mark in New Salem easily. There was a group
of cabins outside town at a place called Clary's Grove, where
the settlers, mostly related, were a rough lot. They came
constantly into New Salem to hang out around a saloon
which was just about opposite Offutt's new store. Perhaps
Offutt had been afraid that they might damage his goods for
a lark when they were drunk because he had boasted that his
new clerk would be the equal of any of the boys if it came to
a fight. As a natural result, Jack Armstrong, biggest and
strongest of the Clary's Grove boys, challenged Abe to a wrestling match. Bets were laid and the townsmen turned out to
watch. Some say the result was a draw and others call it a

victory for Lincoln. At all events, a slight hesitation among the Clary's Grove boys was ended by Armstrong himself, who came forward to shake Abe by the hand. From this time on young Lincoln, who did not drink, engage in cruel sports or harmful mischief, was accepted as a leader by those who did. They boasted of his strength and laughed at his stories and used him as an umpire in their matches. If he hung back from a spree, they did not hold it against him, but allowed that he had a right to please himself.

It took longer to win the respect of New Salem's intellectuals. A short time after Lincoln arrived, Dr. John Allen, a graduate of Dartmouth who had moved out into the wilderness for his health's sake, settled in New Salem. Surprisingly, there was a second doctor in the place. The part-owner of the mill and proprietor of the tavern, James Rutledge, was an educated man in terms of the frontier. The schoolmaster, Mentor Graham, about ten years older than Lincoln and coming from fairly near Abe's Indiana home, was a man dedicated to his profession. His teaching, though limited in scope, was founded on principles of thoroughness and logic. Even a local ne'er-do-well called Jack Kelso turned out to be a devotee of Shakespeare and Burns. Young Abe's ambition to learn was soon asserting itself strongly because the atmosphere of the little town was more encouraging than any place he had hitherto known. Mentor Graham put him in the way of borrowing a good grammar, and he began a systematic study of the subject. Graham helped him when he became confused, and young Bill Greene was happy to take the book and ask him questions when there were no customers in the store. Abe swallowed grammar and embarked on a fuller study of mathematics.

Dr. Allen had not been long in the community before he founded the New Salem Debating Society, which met regularly to discuss subjects of general interest. Lincoln's atten-

dance seems to have occasioned mild surprise. People still
chiefly knew him as the man who wrestled Jack Armstrong
and had a limitless repertory of funny stories. Nobody realized how often he had mimicked the preacher or the amateur
politicians of Gentry's store to get a laugh. When Abe finally
rose to his feet in the debating society, he had mastered his
subject in his usual thorough way and made his points so
clearly that James Rutledge remarked in surprise to his wife
that Abe was already a fine speaker, lacking nothing but culture to get ahead.

Denton Offutt, unfortunately, was one of those people who
have bright ideas but do not like steady work. No one at that
time ran a general store without selling liquor by the quart.
As owner of a store Offutt had access to all the liquor he liked
without the necessity of paying cash for it. His consumption
made inroads on the store's profits, but he was not the sort of
man to worry about that. Since he had not the capital to clear
the Sangamon or demonstrate that it was navigable, both he
and New Salem were really gambling on hope. There were
now four stores in the place; and though new settlers like Dr.
Allen had appeared during the summer, a fair number had
also moved on somewhere else. As long as the good weather
lasted, Lincoln and Greene got their share of the trade of
farmers who came to the blacksmith's shop or to the mill. In
winter such people stayed at home and consumed their piled-
up stores. The gristmill had no work and the sawmill very
little, since most of the time the river was frozen.

By the spring of 1832, Offutt, drinking heavily, was losing
his interest in New Salem in favor of other more tempting
speculations. He hung on, however, because New Salem
might be on the threshold of greater things. A speculator was
actually preparing to run a steamboat up the Sangamon
River. He had one of light draft named the *Talisman* at
Beardstown on the Illinois River waiting until the ice went
out.

Meanwhile, Abraham Lincoln, accepted by now at every social level in the New Salem neighborhood, had taken the decision to go in for politics. This had the advantage of being a career which did not need special education, while it opened up vistas for the ambitious. Greatly daring, he was aiming at the state legislature. This was easy enough to do because political parties were at the time in a state of flux. It was not necessary to get the support of local committeemen, since no such groups existed. All that Lincoln needed was to publish his candidacy in the *Sangamo Journal* of Springfield, together with a statement of his position on various current topics. Chief of these was naturally the opening to navigation of the Sangamon, which he was certain could be done by straightening some of the bends, thus allowing the river to cut a deeper channel and sweep away driftwood. Railroads he dismissed for the time as too expensive. He favored education, but without making any suggestions on how to improve it. He was anxious for a law prohibiting high interest rates, since Illinois was a country where settlers were badly in need of capital. Modestly he promised to do his best if elected. "But if the good people in their wisdom shall see fit to keep me in the background, I have been too familiar with disappointments, to be very much chagrined."

Candidate Lincoln did his best to help open up the Sangamon, traveling down the river with a group of men to clear the channel and break up the ice jam at its mouth. The little *Talisman* came puffing upstream, responding to the cheers of tiny settlements with toots on its whistle. To everybody's delight it got clear up to Portland Landing, only seven miles from Springfield, whose citizens staged the biggest celebration that the town had hitherto experienced. Hardly had the echoes died away than it was perceived that the river, which had been running high in the spring floods, was falling. Evidently the channel had not proved deep in spots, because there was immediate hurry to take the boat back down before it was stranded. Rowan Herndon of New Salem was engaged as a pilot with Abe Lincoln, who had taken a flatboat downriver, as his assistant. The *Talisman* stuck on the New Salem dam, so that part of it had to be torn down to let her pass. From there, however, she managed to reach Beardstown successfully.

Lincoln and Herndon were paid off with forty dollars apiece and tramped back home, struggling, no doubt, with a sense of anticlimax. The *Talisman's* owner was a speculator much like Denton Offutt, with ideas but insufficient cash. He was deep in debt for the *Talisman*, whose single voyage had simply proved that work on the Sangamon was necessary before she could make a regular run. One of the first to take the hint that New Salem was doomed was Denton Offutt, who was soon up to his ears in speculation in cottonseed and corn from Tennessee and had not even the cash needed for restocking his New Salem store. Lincoln was very nearly out of a job when employment of a different sort presented itself with startling suddenness.

The opening up of Illinois had pushed Indian tribes back across the Mississippi, compressing them into an area which they found insufficient. Black Hawk, the leader of the Sauks and Foxes, considered that he had been tricked into ceding the lands of western Illinois. In 1832 he recrossed the river at the head of a band of several hundred, giving out that they came to plant corn. There were still only scattered settlements north of New Salem, and panic in the area was widespread. It would be impossible to say who started the shooting, but war was not slow in breaking out. There was a small detachment of U. S. regulars on the frontier, but the governor found it necessary to call out the state militia. This organization embraced nominally every man between eighteen and forty-five. Duties were discharged by an annual muster, at which people supplied their own arms and elected their captains. The governor's proclamation did not propose to call out militia on quite this wholesale scale, but it made a strong appeal for volunteers. New Salem, because of its northerly position in the settled part of the state, might consider itself threatened. Abe Lincoln was to all intents and purposes out of a job, had no dependents, and could borrow a horse from a patriotic citizen. He went off in a contingent dominated by the Clary's Grove boys, who elected him captain with Jack Armstrong as his first sergeant. He was never so proud and pleased at advancement in his life.

Everybody finally assembled at Beardstown, where the companies were formed into some sort of a mounted brigade. They did a bit of drill, during which Captain Lincoln found himself leading his men twenty abreast straight up to a narrow gate. He could not for the life of him remember the command which would turn his platoon endways in order to file through it. Desperately he yelled, "Halt!" and gave the order: "This company will break ranks and re-form immediately on the other side of that gate."

He got away with it that once, but the life of a captain was not, he found, easy. In the first place, the boys did not like to be ordered about and had no hesitation in telling him to go to the devil. In the second place, amateur soldiers were not used to marching, to baggage wagons bogging down in mud, to their horses being stolen by others who had lost theirs, or to camping in tents that were almost wetter than the rain. Owing to poor organization they went three days without provisions. It is not surprising that some of Lincoln's company raided the quartermaster's liquor and got drunk. Their captain was condemned to wear a wooden sword for a couple of days.

They had only joined up for thirty days; and by the time these were over, the single Indian they had seen was an old one who came into camp with a safe-conduct and whom Lin-

coln had trouble saving from the boys because they took the
view that the only good Indian was a dead one. The company
broke up, and most went home. Abe Lincoln signed up for
another twenty days as a private in a company which was
pretty well made up of officers like himself whose men had
been discharged. They were rushed across the state to rescue
Galena, which proved to be in no danger. After the twenty
days were up, Lincoln re-enlisted for another thirty, during
which he got closer to action, being detailed to help bury five
men who had been killed and scalped in a skirmish.

He was finally mustered out on July 10, at which point
somebody stole his horse. The other men of his company
were good about walking and riding by turns until they all
got to Peoria. Here Lincoln and a friend bought a canoe and
paddled to Havana, whence they walked across country to
New Salem. The future leader of a great war had completed
the only military apprenticeship he was to know. Like every
other experience in his life, it was not wasted. He did learn
a little about a private soldier's life; and he made friends.

By the time that Lincoln got back to New Salem, Denton
Offutt had decamped, leaving his creditors to get what they
could out of his store and its contents. Even more impor-
tantly, it was a couple of weeks before the election for the
state legislature, for which Abe Lincoln was standing. He had
only this short time to show himself to Sangamon voters,
which he did by traveling around on foot from one farm to
another, helping out in the fields, joining loungers at country
stores, and dining in rural cabins where he bedded down on
the floor in the informal fashion of guests in those parts.

In Pappsville, where a crowd was gathered for an auction,
Lincoln was called upon for a speech. He got up on a box and
willingly started, when he saw that his friend Rowan Herndon had been set on by a group of men who had a grudge
against him. Descending, he grabbed the leader by the neck

and the seat of the pants and tossed him aside. The fight stopped abruptly, while Lincoln got back on his box and went on speaking. He was wearing a calico shirt and an old straw hat. His pants, which were at least six inches too short, hung from a single suspender. His appearance seemed to a good many people not quite appropriate for the state legislature, though this organization was not inclined to be particular. In spite of his clothes, he made such a good impression that he polled a very nearly unanimous vote in the New Salem precinct. In the rest of the county, where he was unknown, he did less well, so that he ran eighth out of thirteen candidates for four places. His reputation as a veteran had helped, but not enough. He was not discouraged, for he had found his vocation.

What Abe needed immediately was a job, but opportunities were not unlimited in so small a town as New Salem. He considered apprenticing himself to a blacksmith. The trade was a good one for a strong man, but it did not lead anywhere that would satisfy him. One of his friends from the Black Hawk campaign had been a young Springfield lawyer called John Stuart, also with political ambitions. He had suggested Lincoln study law, but on examining the notion, Lincoln concluded that he had not enough education to be successful. More tempting was the chance of an opening in one of the New Salem stores. Lincoln's own experience in Gentryville and New Salem had impressed on him that the storekeeper was the center of his community, presiding over what amounted to the local club. A politician would have real advantages in such a position.

In the summer of 1832, after the failure of Offutt, New Salem still possessed three stores, the most prosperous of which was Samuel Hill's, though the Herndon Brothers did a good trade. Early in the summer, James Herndon had departed with his family for Texas, hiring Abe to pilot his flatboat of household goods down the fast-dwindling Sangamon and intending to float his family down the Mississippi. Rowan Herndon, left in need of a partner, had accepted William Berry, whose father was a farmer and circuit preacher living near New Salem. Young Berry had been in Lincoln's original company during the Black Hawk War, had been mustered out after thirty days, and was anxious to establish himself. Perhaps his father, whose eldest son he was, had put up some money. At all events, William Berry, aged twenty-one, had bought the partnership with Rowan Herndon.

Much has been said to the discredit of Berry by Lincoln admirers, but there is little evidence to show why Rowan Herndon was anxious to get out of partnership with him. Berry lacked experience, but he came of a strait-laced family and could hardly have been the alcoholic that he is accused of becoming later. Lincoln was happy to go into partnership with Berry, while Rowan Herndon was willing to sell to him for whatever cash he might possess, taking his note for the rest. Lincoln, to whom a grateful government owed a hundred and twenty-five dollars whenever it got around to paying him, might look forward to paying over this sum, while he naturally hoped to pay the rest out of profits. Apparently he gave Herndon a note for $250, either directly or made out to a Springfield merchant to whom Herndon owed money. At all events, by late in 1832, Lincoln and Berry were partners in New Salem's second store.

The third New Salem store, that of Sinco and Rutledge, was in financial trouble. Sinco had sold out, and Rutledge was anxious to dispose of the stock. It seemed sensible to Berry and Lincoln to buy it and have one competitor the less. Unluckily the goods were left-overs which were difficult to sell at a profit. Conspicuous among these was liquor, which was not worth much, since nearly all the farmers made their own. Selling by the drink, Berry and Lincoln might do well; but this involved getting a license and being classed as a "grocery," that is to say a "groggery" or "saloon." To a non-drinking man like Lincoln such a prospect was unwelcome.

Not long after the establishment of Berry and Lincoln, Reuben Radford set himself up in yet another store financed by Springfield connections. New Salem was still growing, but its momentum was slowing down as it became doubtful if boats would ever navigate the Sangamon. Three stores might easily prove one too many. Berry and Lincoln did not have the connection with the mill, which must have sent customers into the store of Denton Offutt. Nor did they have the post-office, which was at Hill's and naturally attracted such people as expected mail.

Reuben Radford was tactless enough to get into a quarrel with the Clary's Grove boys, who got drunk and wrecked his place. This made him so angry that he sold out at once. Berry and Lincoln thought it advisable to buy his stock, too. In principle they may have been right, but the chance came at a moment when the cash they had in hand was the $125 which Lincoln had probably intended to pay to Rowan Herndon, plus a little more than as much again, presumably taken in by the store. So hard were they pressed that Berry threw in his horse and bridle to make up the price, while in addition, they assumed another debt of considerable size. By this time they were getting involved in still more debts because it was hard to avoid going surety for customers whose goodwill they needed. It should perhaps be remembered that Lincoln had served his apprenticeship as clerk to Denton Offutt, a man of risky speculations. Offutt had vanished, leaving debts unpaid; but then Offutt drank, which Lincoln did not. It is probable that the young man had learned too much from Denton Offutt, and yet in another way not quite enough.

The Lincoln and Berry store, in Lincoln's phrase, "winked out." It is usually said that Berry drank away profits, while

Lincoln instead of keeping store had his head in a book. Both statements seem doubtful, at least insofar as they affected the life of the store. Why should not Lincoln read in between customers? Berry was elected constable and registered in college twenty-five miles away, which he presumably attended. These are actions which do not suggest drunkenness. It may well be that Berry lost interest, while Lincoln was too casual in closing the store while he did errands or took odd jobs for cash. We may remember, moreover, that Lincoln kept the store during a period when many transactions still involved barter. How much tea should a storekeeper sell for a pair of knitted stockings, or what is the worth of a plowshare when paid in salt pork? The answer depends on how clever the storekeeper is in disposing of the articles he takes in. Profits depend on a sharp eye for a bargain, which Lincoln never showed any sign of possessing. Nor was he the man to handle the problem which puzzles country storekeepers to this day —namely, when to give credit to a neighbor.

Records are fragmentary and memories uncertain, so that we cannot be quite sure when the store closed or when the partnership broke up. Two brothers called Trent bought up the stock, gave Berry and Lincoln a note in payment, and absconded, leaving them without either goods or money. In January, 1835, Berry died, leaving just about enough to pay the doctor who had attended him. There seems no trace of any special debts run up by Berry unknown to Lincoln or unjustified by the terms of their partnership, except for the suggestion that Berry had consumed a good deal of the liquor. Lincoln shouldered the obligations of the firm and, according to his law partner William H. Herndon, was still paying them off as late as 1848.

Herndon surely should have known, and yet no records of New Salem debts or Lincoln's financial position in Springfield suggest that this could have been the case. More important to our estimate of Lincoln is the fact that he made serious errors of judgment, proving that he was not cut out for business. His honesty has never been questioned, either at the time or since. Indeed Lincoln's honesty was even then almost proverbial, not so much because it was of an especially rare sort, but rather because his unconventional manner gave it at times a dramatic quality. After serving one farmer's wife, for instance, he discovered that he had let her go off with two ounces of tea instead of the four she had paid for. She lived ten miles out of town; but Lincoln wrapped up a two-ounce packet and walked out to give it to her that very evening. This is really no more honest than waiting till a convenient occasion to make good; but it is an episode which lingers in the mind. No doubt Lincoln got a meal, a conversation, and possibly a shake-down for the night out of his walk. Not improbably he chose this method of making restitution because he enjoyed such human contacts. All the same, it is not surprising that his neighbors trusted him to pay in full.

As early as the beginning of 1833, Lincoln was looking around for fresh sources of income. By May, he had worked on his friends to have him made postmaster instead of Samuel Hill. This in itself was a minor miracle, since the appointment was a political one and in the hands of Democrats. Only its utter unimportance made it possible to get it for a Whig. Mail came in once a week, at first by rider, and in 1834 by stagecoach on its way to Springfield. People paid for their mail when they picked it up. There was no delivery, but Lincoln was thoughtful about taking letters with him on errands, usually folding them inside his hat. His pay, calculated on the amount of mail received, amounted only to about a dollar a week. It was understood, however, that the postmaster might read any newspapers which were subscribed to before he passed them on to their owners. Lincoln thus acquired the habit of regularly reading newspapers, which laid

the foundation of his vast practical knowledge of politics and
local opinions.

The postmastership by itself was not a living, while the
store was too deeply in debt to supply cash. During 1833,
Lincoln was not above earning two dollars and a half for
clerking at elections and carrying the tally sheets into Springfield. More valuable was an offer from John Calhoun, the
county surveyor, to make Lincoln his deputy in the New
Salem region. Sangamon County, as it then was, covered a
huge area which Calhoun found impossible to handle. Settlers
were pouring in, and speculators were plotting townships
everywhere. As a strong Jacksonian Democrat, Calhoun was
reluctant to give this position to a Whig, but he needed somebody who was capable of learning surveying and ready to take
odd jobs. Lincoln, given a copy of the surveyor's manual,
mastered it in about six weeks with the aid of the New Salem
schoolmaster, Mentor Graham. He then had to buy a horse
and surveying instruments on credit, which nearly led to
utter disaster. Suing for another debt, a creditor attached
Abe's personal possessions. Instruments and horse were put
up for auction, but friends came to the rescue and returned
them. He was managing to exist in New Salem because everybody liked him.

4

Vandalia

---◄◉►---

IN THE SPRING OF 1834, though his hand-to-mouth existence was unchanged, Lincoln determined to run for the legislature a second time. John T. Stuart, the Springfield lawyer with whom he had struck up a friendship during the Black Hawk War, was the recognized leader of the Sangamon Whig politicians. The organization of political parties was now becoming tighter, but Lincoln could hope for support from friends of Stuart. Meanwhile, the opposing party, the Jacksonian Democrats, was somewhat divided. Since this was not a presidential election, the Democratic moderates of New Salem felt disinclined to support their party extremists, especially against a neighbor whom they trusted. Elsewhere in the county, where Lincoln was less well known, there was a Democratic movement to squeeze out Stuart, the most dangerous man on the Whig ticket, by voting for Lincoln, an acknowledged outsider. As a result, Lincoln ran second while Stuart gained fourth and last place among the winners.

Carefully consulting with Stuart about how to handle these party maneuvers, Lincoln had conducted an unobtrusive campaign. Stuart, whose opinion of his friend was steadily rising, once more urged him to study law and offered to lend him the books that he needed from his own library, saying that it was not necessary to go to school. By this time Lincoln's own thoughts were turning in this direction. More than a year earlier he had bought a book of legal forms which had shown him how to draw up deeds and mortgages, and as a result he earned occasional sums. He had even been induced to oblige a few friends by arguing their cases on condition that he accept no fee, not being a qualified lawyer. Such experiences had given him confidence to accept Stuart's offer. Indeed he started so enthusiastically that some New Salem neighbors, who had hitherto been more tolerant of his studious habits than old friends in Indiana, began to comment on his laziness. On the other hand, Stuart's law partner in Springfield was becoming interested in the awkward, rather timid young man who walked or rode in from New Salem to borrow books. It was a little hard to get Lincoln talking, but "he surprised us more and more on every visit."

In preparation for the opening of the legislature in November, Lincoln borrowed another two hundred dollars to cover his living expenses and the cost of a suit. Never until he became President and was clothed by a really good tailor did his garments appear to fit him, partly because of his unusual shape and partly because of the awkward way in which he wore them. It may be assumed that his first suit bagged in all the wrong places, was short in the arm and leg and tight in the pants. It certainly must have been crumpled before he got to Vandalia, which was at that time the capital of the state. Lincoln had to go by stagecoach to Springfield, change there, and make a two-day journey by a second coach to reach his destination.

Vandalia was simply a spot which had been selected to build the state capitol, around which a town had grown up. When Lincoln first saw the place, it boasted about eight hundred inhabitants, which made it much smaller than Springfield. Like Washington, it was grandiosely planned but unfinished, its central square large, its streets wide, unpaved, and muddy, its buildings a mixture of frame houses and log cabins.

Vandalia contained not only the legislature, but the state supreme court, which was also in session. In other words the best brains of the state and its coming personalities were clustered together, many bringing ladies with them who were better dressed and educated than any whom Lincoln had previously known. The social season was also enlivened by ambitious men of various kinds appearing to lobby or to promote their own advancement. Among these was a young man of twenty-one named Stephen A. Douglas, lately come from Vermont and already a candidate for State's Attorney of the first judicial district. Physically Douglas presented a striking contrast with Abraham Lincoln, being five feet four inches high with short legs, massive body, and an impressive head, too large for his height. Democrat though he was, he represented a new type in Illinois. The southern part of the state had been largely settled by pioneer farmers from Indiana and Kentucky. The central and northern parts, where transport did not depend on the great river system of the central United States, were attracting northern adventurers like Douglas, interested in opening up the prairies by roads, canals, and railroads. Frankly ambitious and exceedingly able, Douglas knew how to compensate for his size by dressing smartly and taking the lead in every conversation or social group. If he were to develop a weakness, it would be for liquor.

There was not enough room in the lodging houses of Vandalia to accommodate all the people who came for the session in any degree of comfort. Lincoln put up in the same tavern with Stuart, who was already the leader of the Whig party in the House. It was to Stuart's room that people came for consultation on Whig strategy. Lincoln, introduced on familiar terms to the ablest members of his party, found his lack of education little drawback as long as his understanding of political issues was as keen as the next man's. The House of Representatives at this time had fifty-five members, about half of whom were farmers, while the rest contained more lawyers than men of any other one profession. Any awkwardness that Lincoln may have felt was quickly overcome by his natural liking for people. It took him only five days to get to his feet on the floor of the House, though merely to announce a bill he wished to introduce later.

In general Lincoln's work during the session was unobtrusive. Listening to a debate on President Jackson's attack on the United States Bank, he voted dutifully with the Whigs against upholding the President's action. He was chosen to introduce a resolution directing Illinois representatives in Congress to work for a law assigning the state a proportion of the revenues from sale of public lands within its borders. He voted to charter a state bank and to construct a canal connecting the Illinois River with Lake Michigan.

All these acts were routine Whig maneuvers, while Lincoln's committee assignments as a new member were unimportant. Stuart, however, wanted to go on to Congress and evidently had his eye on Lincoln to replace him as House floor leader in Vandalia. In consequence when Stuart was in conference during sessions, Lincoln was present to keep an eye on things. A number of bills introduced by other members are drafted in his clear, legible hand, indicating that he was making himself useful and might be playing a bigger role upon some future occasion. In sum, he took to Vandalia as easily as a fish to water, not making himself conspicuous, but finding that his natural method of getting about was perfectly fitted to the atmosphere in which he found himself.

Lincoln's published manifesto for his original, unsuccessful run for the legislature had been specific about the opening up of the Sangamon River, but vague on such wider subjects as education, cheap money, and further internal improvements. His second campaign had been distinguished by a careful avoidance of controversial topics, owing to the Democratic support which was coming his way. He arrived in Vandalia

to find the legislature concerned with a constitutional national issue—namely, Jackson's attack on the United States
Bank—as well as with the process of drafting local bills and
debating pressing state problems. He learned details of political manipulation during the election for state offices such as
Attorney General, State's Attorneys for various districts, and
United States Senator, all of which were at that time chosen
by the legislators. His fellow members were the best of those
who had possessed the enterprise to move into undeveloped
lands and make a new state. None of them had been born in
Illinois, few were experienced, but most were intelligent.
Lincoln found himself for the first time among his own kind.
He did not rise above them by virtue of superior character or
a loftier view of the political process. On the contrary, he was
a young man eager to learn the practical methods of making
political friends and striking bargains, how to hold his tongue
when required, how to vote with his party, and what to make
of intelligent debate on both local and national issues.

It was when returning early in 1835 to New Salem with
enough money from his salary to repay the two hundred
dollars and leave fifty-eight for personal expenses, that Lincoln learned that Bill Berry, who had been ill when he started
for Vandalia, was dead. Lincoln's creditors, who had previously had the signatures of two people as security for certain
debts, now depended on one. No matter how stimulating the
session at Vandalia had been or how deeply he was now
immersed in the study of law, his financial situation was
depressing. For this reason, it seems hardly a moment for
getting engaged or falling in love.

Ann Rutledge, daughter of the proprietor of the New
Salem tavern, where Lincoln had boarded when he first came
to the town, was a pretty red-haired girl, twenty-two years
old in 1835 and engaged to the partner of Samuel Hill, New
Salem's only successful storekeeper. John McNamar had

come from New York State, and after his engagement he had gone back to visit his family. A New Salem legend, supported or denied by various old residents thirty years after the event, says that McNamar neither returned nor wrote, leaving Ann Rutledge uncertain whether he had forgotten her or was detained by unexpected family problems. While she was in this awkward position, some say her affections were won by Abraham Lincoln. They desired to marry, but Ann was torn by her obligation to McNamar and worried herself into an illness aggravated by a fever, of which she died early that summer. Lincoln went nearly out of his mind with grief, they say, and his friends were seriously frightened that he might kill himself. He recovered, but never loved another and from then on was always subject to fits of melancholy.

We may dismiss a good deal of this tale as nonsense. There can be no question of Lincoln's later devotion to Mary Todd, the girl he married. Nor have we any reason to doubt that Mary's distress when the Ann Rutledge story was aired after Lincoln's death rested partly on the fact that he had assured her, not once but many times, that she was the only woman he had ever loved. Mary was not the most reliable of witnesses, but her protests ring true, precisely because she was horrified. What then is left of the Ann Rutledge story? Very little. Lincoln knew her and liked her. He was fond of her family and later took trouble to visit them often when they moved out of New Salem. He may possibly have been attracted to Ann, in which case he would take her death hard. It does seem unlikely that he felt more than a tenderness which had no chance to develop or that he would have proposed marriage at a juncture when his prospects of supporting a wife were so poor.

It is quite possible that, for whatever reason, Lincoln was visited in 1835 by an attack of depression, an illness with which later letters show he was familiar. He calls his condition "hypo," meaning "hypochondria," and is evidently used to its recurrence. We are, however, unable to tell how far these attacks were a consequence of physical illness and fatigue or of personal difficulties and sorrows. We do not even know how often he struggled with them. Friends found him reflective and serious-minded and sometimes commented on glimpses of utter sadness expressed by those features which fell so naturally into long lines. It was even said by one friend that he did not dare carry a knife lest he do himself harm, yet an unforgettable description of Lincoln on circuit portrays him holding up matters while he used his knife for whittling a stick to replace a trouser button essential to his suspenders.

Explanations which have been offered for Lincoln's melancholy moods are the merest guesses and vary from a permanent low-grade malarial infection to a habit of mind acquired in adolescence out of loneliness and lack of understanding, to too little sleep and too much study, or even to an inheritance from one of those ancestors about whom we know so little. At all events we may say that Lincoln's melancholy was modified by two outstanding characteristics. He had a genuine and unforced liking for people. Meeting them gave him pleasure, and in company he was usually able to throw off moodiness. Secondly, he was helped by laughter, enjoying his joke as a deliberate refreshment from sadness or fatigue. Without these qualities he could hardly have borne the tragic situation into which fate was to thrust this most peaceable of men.

Lincoln spent most of 1835 in New Salem, busy with his odd jobs and the study of law. Reduced to their essentials, the qualifications of a lawyer were an exhaustive knowledge of a few important textbooks, reinforced by plenty of practice. It was more usual for a young man to enter a lawyer's office as a pupil than for him to study law at college. Lincoln, it is true, was doing neither, but the bar examination was open to all who could get themselves certified by the local circuit court as of good character. In any case his thorough methods of study were perfectly suited to the job he had taken in hand. Lack of experience would be his weakness at first; but his acquaintance with Bowling Green, justice of the peace in New Salem, and with Stuart in Springfield gave him chances to see the law at work. Not having steady employment, he could manage to take days off when the circuit court came round to Springfield or when Bowling Green had an interesting case. Handled in this way, the study of law took him a little over two years of steady work. He had started around the middle of 1834 at Stuart's insistence; and he received his license on September 9, 1836. Two days later he appeared in three cases as substitute for Stuart, who was at that time a candidate for Congress and was busy canvassing.

In the meantime Lincoln's political position had been improved and his income increased by a special session of the legislature, which normally met only once in its two-year term. Its task was to pass a reapportionment law which would govern the next elections. Central and northern Illinois were filling up so fast that Sangamon County received three more representatives in the lower house, for a total of seven. Once assembled, the legislators did not confine themselves to their special business. They introduced a mass of bills calling for roads, railroads, canals, and bridges, indicative of the rapid growth of the state. Acting once more as Stuart's deputy, Lincoln consolidated his position as Whig floor leader for the next session. Always glad to meet or make a friend, well informed on political affairs, and a good party man, he was accepted without any serious question as Stuart's successor.

1836 was a presidential year in which elections were dominated by the desire of the Democrats to unite their dissident members behind Martin Van Buren, who was not a very popular choice. The cement which held political parties together in the days of Lincoln was the "spoils system." All administrative offices in what we nowadays call the civil service, ranging from the collector of the port of New York to the postmaster of New Salem, Illinois, were directly or indirectly under control of the President who, either personally or through his principal supporters, turned members of the opposition party out and put his own supporters in. Even those politicians who did not themselves want jobs depended on their power to bestow these favors at the local level.

Such considerations gave enormous importance to the choice of presidential candidates, and on this occasion the Democrats were determined to make all their followers support Van Buren. This was the more difficult to achieve because each state organization was independent from the next. Some were efficient while others were not. In particular, in rapidly growing states like Illinois, political parties found it difficult to keep their hold on a shifting population. In 1833, for instance, the postmastership of New Salem had gone to a Whig because it was not worth having. Yet its very lack of importance detracted from the power of local Democrats who had nothing of value with which to reward a faithful member.

The Democrats of Illinois, inspired to a large extent by Stephen A. Douglas, had decided to force Van Buren on their members by calling a party convention. This was a new procedure in Illinois and far from general in the more settled states of the Union. Local party groups were invited to send delegates to a Democratic convention which met, for convenience, in Vandalia on the first day of the special legislative session. Here a majority selected Van Buren as the Democratic candidate of Illinois. The minority were then told to conform or lose their affiliation with the party.

This device infuriated the Whigs, largely because it was effective. Much was said about the individual selling his conscience to the majority, and the Whigs passed a tremendous resolution denouncing such wicked ways. The convention system, however, had come to stay and was before long adopted by the Whigs in self-defense. For the moment it caused a great deal of heart-burning among those Democrats who did not like Van Buren. In the national election they voted for him because they needed their share of the spoils to stay alive politically. On the other hand, the election for the state legislature, which came about two months earlier, involved no national questions of patronage and gave the malcontents a vent for their ill-humor. In consequence the Whigs swept the board in Sangamon County, returning to the lower house seven members and to the Senate one. Since the hold-over senator was also a Whig, this gave Sangamon a united delegation of nine, known in Illinois history as the Long Nine because they were all tall men with an average height of over six feet.

The backing of this conspicuous group was all that Lincoln needed to consolidate his position as floor leader of the Whigs. The legislature which assembled at Vandalia in November, 1836, was a young and forceful body, conspicuous for the number of its members who were later to become distinguished people. It had two main tasks to perform, the most important of which was to make some practical plan for developing communications which would give direction to future settlement. The second, of particular interest to Sangamon County, was to order the removal of the state capital to a more central location in a town which showed more promise of growth than Vandalia. The Long Nine were naturally committed to making the capital Springfield, but there were several towns competing for the honor. Meanwhile the people of Vandalia, foreseeing ruin if the capital were moved elsewhere, had been building a new statehouse, which was still surrounded by rubble and damp with drying plaster when the session opened.

Lincoln's personal prospects were by this time transformed. Stuart, whose partner was moving to Beardstown, had offered Lincoln the partnership, ensuring that he would make a good start in the legal profession. Lincoln though personally sad at leaving old friends intended to move into Springfield after the session. By this time it was clear that the Sangamon was never going to be made navigable and that traffic to Springfield would go by a road through Petersburg, a few miles from New Salem. The little town was already dwindling and in four more years would cease to exist. Not only was Lincoln now ready to enter an established law partnership in what he hoped would become the capital of the state, but he had even become a matrimonial catch for a young lady with more than a local background.

Mrs. Bennet Abell, a cousin of the schoolmaster Mentor Graham, was a friend of Mrs. Bowling Green, whose husband was a distinguished man in the New Salem neighborhood. Mrs. Abell had been visited shortly before by her sister, Miss Mary Owens from Kentucky. In those days it was a recognized duty of married sisters to give the unmarried ones wider opportunities of meeting young men than they might get at home. As a friend of Graham and Bowling Green, Lincoln was one of those introduced to Mary Owens, with whom he soon became friendly. She was naturally intelligent and had been educated at a good Kentucky girls' school, which had given her plenty of social poise. She was in her middle twenties, about a year older than Lincoln, so that the problem of finding a suitable husband had been with her for some time. Notwithstanding, she returned to her home in Kentucky still unmarried.

Presently, Mrs. Abell mentioned to Lincoln that she was planning a visit to Kentucky herself. Lincoln, who never forgot an acquaintance, no doubt sent messages to Mary and even, perhaps, hoped she would return with her sister. This gave Mrs. Abell an opportunity, and the fact that she took it demonstrates as clearly as anything can how far Lincoln had advanced since he came to New Salem, or even since the fiasco of Lincoln and Berry. Mrs. Abell now told him in a joking manner that she would bring Mary back if he would undertake to marry her.

A proposition of this sort is already a little more than a joke when it is first made. Evidently Lincoln's social education had not yet equipped him to turn the matter off, for he replied, still speaking lightly, that nothing would suit him better. Inwardly, he seems to have felt the idea was a possible one. He had liked Mary Owens, was by now twenty-seven, and had domestic instincts. It was agreeable to him to think of marriage and flattering to find that Mrs. Abell thought him good enough for her sister.

Mary did return to New Salem, indicating clearly that a proposal from Lincoln would not be unwelcome to her. Unfortunately, though he now felt obliged to make her an offer, he did not like her as well as he had done on their first meeting. As far as we know he had nothing definite against her except that she had gained weight. She is said at this time to have been five feet five inches tall and to have weighed a hundred and fifty pounds, which would make her a solid armful. No doubt if Lincoln had ever cared about her, these extra pounds would not have mattered; but he soon discovered that he did not. She, for her part, though expecting a proposal, felt free to refuse him if she wished and was beginning to think that she might do so.

This tepid romance was still in progress when Lincoln went to Vandalia for the session of 1836–37. Evidently it worried him, while at the same time he was laid low by an illness which may have been only a bad cold contracted in the clammy atmosphere of Vandalia's new statehouse. He bestirred himself, however, to write Mary Owens a letter which

is very distinctly not a love letter, though it assumes a personal relationship which is not defined. Lincoln was struggling with his enemy "hypo," but it is not clear whether his
courtship of Mary or his illness or his approaching move to
Springfield had depressed him. Most of the letter describes
the political scene; a safe, impersonal subject. He apologizes
for feeling too unwell to fill out his page with anything else
and signs himself "your friend—Lincoln."

"I feel that I would rather be any place in the world than
here. I really cannot endure the thought of staying here ten
weeks," wrote Lincoln to Mary Owens at this time. It is
characteristic that the period which followed was one of intense political activity for Lincoln, who depended heavily on
his wit and his powers of persuasion to make political friends.
There is no evidence that his depression had the slightest
influence on his manner with other people or the persistence
with which he circulated among the members of the legislature, seeking their votes.

By the end of 1836, Illinois was expanding at what then
appeared a miraculous rate. In order to become great, the
state seemed to need nothing but capital to establish communications with the markets of the East. The assembly of
1836 was young, imaginative, and hopeful. Its optimism was
bolstered by an Internal Improvement Convention which
had been held at Vandalia just before the beginning of the
session and which had recommended that the state issue
bonds for about three million dollars to finance the construction of railroads. The project was turned over to a committee
on internal improvements, whose spirits soared when Lincoln, as chairman of the House Finance Committee, reported
a surplus of income over expenditures amounting to $2,739.24.
This modest sum, if applied to the annual interest on a big
loan, would multiply itself quite handsomely, while further
income would of course come in from tolls as projects were

completed and from booming industry which would spring up along new routes. Flushed with hope and inexperience, the legislators were in a mood to use their imaginations. The Committee on Internal Improvements reported a proposal for a seven-million-dollar loan, while every representative's home district put in its claim for a slice of pie, forwarding to Vandalia its pet projects for inclusion in the bill at public expense.

The situation grew completely out of control because few delegates had the hardihood to resist their own constituents. Most did not even wish to do so, since the legislature as a body had now lost all sense of proportion. Under pressure, the cost of the bill shot up to ten million, amid applause from speculators, optimists, newspapers, and representatives of local opinion. With enthusiasm it was agreed that all projects should be started at once, ensuring that the money should be spread out through the state from the very beginning.

No wiser than the rest, Lincoln was active in sorting out the amendments which were expanding the bill to suit everybody. It is usually said that he promised the support of the Sangamon delegation for this local project or that in return for votes for Springfield as the new state capital.

Unquestionably Lincoln already accepted the fact that the way to get a piece of political business done is by striking a bargain. It seems, however, that his tactics were hampered by the loose organization of political parties. The seven from Sangamon did not too frequently vote all the same way; and when they did so, they did not by any means always obtain votes for Springfield. In other words, people cast their votes as individuals more often than in groups; and any successes of Lincoln must have been largely due to his sociability and his persistence. His political strategy was, however, sound. Early in the session, he had helped put through a law declaring that the citizens of the town which should be selected for the permanent capital must give fifty thousand dollars and two acres of land to build a new statehouse. This disposed of the claims of less wealthy competitors such as Vandalia and Alton, leaving Springfield as the logical choice of the Assembly. The difficulty was to get the legislators to act at all, for Vandalia was happy to remain the capital by default.

This obstacle was finally overcome and Springfield was chosen. The victorious Sangamon delegation could congratulate itself on having obtained the only solid concession to local interests in the whole of that disastrous session. The internal improvements, planned in haste and commenced haphazardly in a spirit of reckless extravagance, soon perished, leaving the state treasury virtually bankrupt.

Lincoln was certainly no less to blame than his fellows, but it is impossible to prove that he was more so. The citizens of Springfield, honoring the triumph of the Long Nine by a banquet, did not suggest that their success was all due to Lincoln's "log-rolling." He did not even claim the honor for himself in later political speeches, which he surely might have done, had he deserved it. In backing the internal improvements bill he had apparently succumbed once more to the easy optimism which was the prevailing climate of the West. But though he was never to show any marked ability in dealing with financial affairs, at least he could learn from experience. The internal improvements scheme could help to teach him caution.

5

Early Days in Springfield

JOSHUA F. SPEED WAS THE proprietor of a general store in
Springfield, which in 1837 was a town of fifteen hundred inhabitants as well as a center for the farming districts which
surrounded it. It was possible in Springfield at that time to
buy silk and broadcloth, calfskin topboots, sets of china
dishes, and other household luxuries common in the East. All
the same, the general store, in the tradition of Berry and
Lincoln and others, would do most of its business in basic
necessities, ranging from kitchen pots through rough leather
shoes, bolts of calico, and cheap straw bonnets. It was at
Speed's that Lincoln stopped to ask the price of bedding when
he rode in from New Salem in April, 1837, with his worldly
possessions in a pair of saddlebags. Speed told him it would
amount to seventeen dollars.

"Cheap as it is, I have not the money to pay," Lincoln
answered. "But if you will credit me until Christmas, and my
experiment as a lawyer is a success, I will pay you then. If I
fail in that, I will probably never pay you at all." His tone was
gloomy, and Speed had the impression that he had never seen
anything so melancholy as that long face with its loose, leathery skin prematurely lined. On an impulse, he offered to share
his own double bed with the stranger. Lincoln accepted,
heaved his saddlebags upstairs into the bedroom, and came
back with his face lit up by a smile. "Well, Speed, I'm moved."

The experiment had started. William Butler, one of the Long Nine, had offered to feed Lincoln for as long as he cared to take pot-luck. John T. Stuart, who had not succeeded in his bid for Congress, was present to break his new partner in to the work. Stuart's practice naturally expanded as Springfield's growth began to shoot up in expectation of the legislature's move, now scheduled for 1839. Most of his cases centered around ownership of land or animals, collection of debts, probate, damages, or common assault. As a rule these presented no complex points of law, requiring Lincoln's talent for making issues clear rather than a knowledge of legal precedents. It would be natural for Stuart to take the difficult cases at first, leaving Lincoln a miscellaneous practice in Springfield and its environs which might send him out to see some rural justice of the peace for an informal session at his farm, or on one occasion in his cornfield. Fees for such services were usually five dollars and occasionally half that sum, often paid in kind. As a result, Lincoln soon collected a host of new friends and fresh stories.

His competence to do the work ought to have cheered him, but Lincoln felt like a country boy in a big city. He missed New Salem friends and found the society in which his partner moved beyond his means. "There is a great deal of flourishing about in carriages here," he wrote to Mary Owens, whom he had put off until the experiment of moving into Springfield should be successful. "This thing of living in Springfield," he tells her, "is rather a dull business, after all; at least it is to me. I am quite as lonesome here as I ever was anywhere in my life. I have been spoken to by but one woman since I have been here, and should not have been by her if she could have avoided it." He makes the worst of his situation, no doubt, because he wishes to persuade Mary that she would not like Springfield. He personally would be happy with her, he is careful to add, but only if she were contented with her lot. "You would have to be poor, without the means of hiding your poverty. Do you believe you could bear that patiently?" His desire to be rid of the entanglement is patent.

A girl who is nearing thirty and still unmarried may be excused for prolonging an understanding with an indifferent suitor if he has no rival in mind. Mary Owens had her doubts about Lincoln, but these were not connected, as far as we know, with his financial prospects. Accordingly, she neither advanced nor retreated, so that the situation dragged on uneasily until the summer, at which time she was planning to make another visit to her sister. In New Salem the pair tried to have a frank talk, but an understanding was not easy while the gentleman was over-anxious to "do right" and the lady had personal objections which she did not want to explain for fear of hurting his feelings.

The truth was, Mary Owens found Lincoln's manners to a lady lacking in the quick, protective courtesy which she expected from her menfolk. Lincoln's behavior toward women, conditioned by his early experience of hardworking settlers' wives, seemed perfect to Hannah Armstrong, wife of his old friend Jack, who used to patch the knees of his pants or let him rock the baby while she got a meal. Mary, more conscious of her petticoats, liked personal attendance. She noted that he did not offer to carry Mrs. Bowling Green's baby for her or to help Mary herself ride through a ford. These criticisms of Lincoln were sound. He was eventually to make a devoted but by no means easy husband with a habit of relying unduly on his wife to manage alone. Mary Owens was missing a great opportunity, but we cannot say that she was wrong to do so. The relationship was brought to a close by another letter from Lincoln, stressing his regard for Mary's happiness and leaving it up to her to decide if he could add to it. If not, he begged her not to send any answer. Mary was content to take this easy way out in August, 1837, after keeping her suitor in suspense for a whole year.

Though Lincoln had no desire to marry Mary, he was deeply chagrined when it dawned upon him that she had not liked him well enough to take him. He nursed his hurt feelings for half a year, unable to confide in New Salem friends who knew Mary Owens or to find anyone in Springfield with whom he wanted to discuss her. Eventually he vented his emotions in a letter to Mrs. Orville Browning, wife of a state senator from Quincy. Written on April Fool's Day, 1838, in a facetious strain which exaggerated Mary's physical drawbacks, the letter seems to have made Lincoln feel better without arousing Mrs. Browning's suspicions that the "romance" was anything but one of his humorous stories. Resurrected and connected with Miss Owens, it now seems in dubious taste, reminding readers of Lincoln's facetious poem on the Grigsby double wedding, which was also a salve for wounded feelings. Lincoln's habit of venting his emotions in writing persisted until the end of his life, though it became tempered with an admirable discretion. After bitter disappointments in the Civil War, Lincoln would write a reasoned, sometimes a moving letter—then lay it aside in his papers, not destroyed, but marked "unsent."

1838 was a year of financial panic. The state bank at Springfield suspended payment in specie, risking loss of its charter if it did not reopen for business as usual within sixty days. The Bank of Illinois at Shawneetown promptly followed suit. The governor called the legislature together for a short session in order to decide what ought to be done. He also took the opportunity to recommend that the internal-improvement plan should be abandoned before it consumed all the resources of the state. The legislators approved the action of the banks, but could not bring themselves to renounce a program of which they had spoken in such extravagant terms eighteen months earlier. The internal-improvement plan proceeded on its wasteful course, plunging the state so deeply in debt that eventually its entire annual revenue did not suffice to pay the interest on the sums which it had borrowed.

Meanwhile, the state elections were coming close again; and at the same time, Stuart was standing once more for Congress. His Democratic opponent was none other than Stephen A. Douglas, who had been elected to the state legislature for the last session and had immediately made his mark on it. It had indeed been Douglas who had originally brought the recommendation of the Internal Improvement Convention before the legislature, precipitating the avalanche which followed. Elections in which Douglas participated were always lively. The Whigs, who had tried to ignore the little man, soon found this policy impossible. Tempers grew so hot that the candidates flew at each other when they met in Speed's store, rolling over and over on the wet floor like a pair of fighting dogs. Later on, Stuart seized the little man by the collar and dragged him around the market house, while Douglas bit him so deeply in the thumb that he carried the mark for the rest of his life. Lincoln, whose seat in the legislature seemed fairly sure, spent most of his time stumping for Stuart. When Stuart fell ill, Lincoln stood in for him at a formal debate with Douglas in Bloomington. On election day, Stuart won over Douglas by thirty-six votes out of more than thirty-six thousand, while Lincoln kept his place in the state legislature.

This body met in Vandalia for the last time in December, 1838. Its most serious problem was the need to make decisions about internal improvements. Opinion was divided between those members who wished to abandon the whole program before more was wasted on it and others, like Lincoln, who did not want to give up a project which had already cost so much. Lincoln offered a resolution from the finance committee urging the federal government to let the state buy its government lands at twenty-five cents an acre, which the state could then sell to settlers at the government price of a dollar and a quarter. Since there were twenty million acres involved, the profit would pay not only the cost of acquisition, but the internal-improvement plan as well. The money, naturally, would take time to come in, but the state's ownership would give investors confidence, pushing up the price of the state bonds that might have to be issued. The chief drawback was that the Congress never had expressed any willingness to sell government lands for less than a dollar and a quarter and would sacrifice twenty million if it did so. As an interim measure the legislature adopted a property tax of twenty-five cents on the hundred dollars of assessed value. It was a measure members had not dared introduce before and which brought complaints from their constituents. It was necessary, however, to do something, lest the business of the state cease to be carried on for lack of money.

What made politics such an absorbing occupation was the way in which elections were staggered, preparations for the next seeming to follow almost immediately after one was over. In fact, there were nearly two years between the session at Vandalia and the presidential election of 1840, but this soon began to cast a long shadow on the scene. The Whigs, adopting the convention system, called their state convention in plenty of time, endorsed William H. Harrison, and selected a committee of five, including Lincoln, while also putting down his name as a Whig presidential elector. The Democrats, supporting Van Buren for a second term, were so ably headed by Stephen A. Douglas that some Whigs may well have wished him in Washington at this juncture. In response to Douglas's challenge, the Whigs agreed to a public discussion in Springfield with speeches every day for a week, during which various issues were taken up by different speakers. Lincoln, whose powers of argument had been steadily developed, not only by his political work but by his profession, won a resounding victory over Douglas, who was defending

Van Buren's administration from charges of extravagance. Quoting from government documents, Lincoln tore his opponent's arguments to shreds so successfully that he relied increasingly thereafter on written evidence.

Meanwhile, as one of the State Central Committee, Lincoln took a prominent part in organizing the Whig party for the election. For one thing, he emphasized the need for a thorough Whig speaking campaign throughout the state. In the central and northern parts of the state the Whigs were strong, but "Egypt," as southern Illinois was collectively called, remained a country of small farmers from the South. Conservative in outlook and strongly Democratic, they had been neglected in previous campaigns because Whig orators did not like to waste their time on hostile audiences. Leading the way in a new policy, Lincoln went down to Egypt and spent several weeks speaking on the banks of the Ohio and the Wabash. In the upshot, Harrison won the national election; but the Democrats, usually the majority party in Illinois, carried the local elections.

On July 4, 1839, the Illinois state archives were loaded on wagons in Vandalia for transference to Springfield. Here the new capitol, a handsome classical building, was rising on the central square in full sight of the office windows of Stuart and Lincoln.

Springfield, though more imposing than Vandalia, still looked unfinished. There were a few important buildings surrounding the square, of which the most imposing was the state bank. The county courthouse was on the second floor of a row of offices called Hoffman's Row, which was mostly given up to lawyers. Stuart and Lincoln, for instance, were directly above the courtroom in a small room heated by a wood stove and unpretentiously furnished by a table and chairs, a few shelves, a bench for waiting clients, and a small bed into which Lincoln folded himself on occasion. The shops in the square were mainly unimpressive, while the shanties which lined a part of it were frankly admitted to be a disgrace. None of the Springfield streets was paved, so that the clay, baked hard in summer and frozen in winter, dissolved between these seasons into bottomless mud. The wooden sidewalks which had been erected for passers-by increased the problem by providing free shelter and mud wallows for Springfield pigs. Enterprising storekeepers put out stones for street crossings which were soon squashed into the mud by passing wagons.

Despite these drawbacks, Springfield was a better capital than Vandalia, being not only more central, but bigger. The houses of its best citizens were spacious; there were more taverns and lodging-places; and the new statehouse was an architectural gem. Culturally Springfield was far from a dead town, since it boasted two papers, one Democrat and one Whig, a half-dozen churches, several schools of various sorts, a Temperance Society, a Young Men's Lyceum for cultural uplift, and a thespian group. In other words, those who came to Springfield for the session would not have to bring with them their entire social set. Springfield had its own hosts and hostesses, its theatrical performances, its concerts, even its unmarried girls come up to stay with sisters and eager for parties.

For all these reasons the first gathering of the General Assembly in Springfield, which took place in November, 1840, was a gala occasion, though the statehouse was unfinished and the lower house met in the Methodist Church. Another credit crisis had caused the governor to call a special session immediately before the regular one. Once more the state bank had suspended payment and had received permission to continue doing so until the Assembly should adjourn. The Democrats were therefore anxious to adjourn the special session formally, whereas the Whigs, in the interests of the bank, wished the session to stay open and simply merge into the regular one. To prevent all motions to adjourn, enough Whigs stayed out daily to stop the Speaker from declaring a quorum. Unfortunately, two days before the regular session, Lincoln and two friends were present and failed to perceive that the attendance was just sufficient for a quorum. A vote for adjournment was called, and the three Whigs, seeing that they would not be allowed to squeeze out of the door before they were counted, jumped out of the window.

This was Lincoln's last really noticeable act in the state legislature, for though the regular session immediately opened, he was ill and depressed in January, 1841. In any case, the legislature was strongly Democratic; and the power of Douglas had increased mightily. Despite Whig opposition, the Democrats managed to increase the state supreme court justices from four to nine, thus giving themselves a chance to appoint five Democratic nominees, of whom Douglas was one. The Internal Improvement Act, which no one dared to touch, went on sowing disaster until the state defaulted on its debts about a year later. In 1845, the investors in the Illinois and Michigan Canal were induced to put up enough money to finish this project. Thereafter tolls from the canal, a property levy, and the sale of all lands acquired for other improvements eventually rescued the state from the morass into which it had fallen.

Lincoln did not stand for the legislature again. Like Stuart, he was aiming at Congress. Furthermore, he and his partner were finding it a drawback to have both men in the office preoccupied with politics. Stuart, first elected to Congress in 1838, served four years, being reelected in 1840. In both these elections, Lincoln was also busy campaigning, substituting for Stuart in 1838 to debate with Douglas, and touring the state to speak for Harrison in 1840. Naturally this meant that during some months preceding the election it had been hard to keep the office manned. Worse still, Stuart had yearly departed for Congress, leaving Lincoln alone in Springfield. Triumphantly he had written across the office ledger, "Commencement of Lincoln's administration." Unfortunately the office really needed two people because a good deal of the partners' practice was in the local circuit courts, which moved from county to county over two three-month sessions in the year. At such times Lincoln must either sacrifice his Springfield practice or forego the circuit, which was essential to business. Old clients who found he was not in Springfield to draw up a will or argue a case before the justice of the peace would employ another firm and probably would never return to Stuart and Lincoln. It was a dilemma.

These drawbacks to a partnership with Stuart were accentuated by the fact that neither of the pair was a profound lawyer. Lincoln's law preparation had been sketchy, and despite his powers of concentration he was not by nature a systematic worker. It was easier to handle a great variety of simple cases than a few complex ones. The transference of the state supreme court to Springfield along with the General Assembly had meant opportunities of distinction for those Springfield lawyers who were capable of taking them. Springfield attracted, and was going increasingly to attract, such men. Stuart and Lincoln would lose clients unless they learned new habits.

The obvious solution for both men was a change in partners. In the middle of 1841, Lincoln was able to move into the office of Stephen T. Logan, who had no political ambitions at that time, but was a really good lawyer, renowned for his meticulous preparation of cases. The change involved some sacrifice in that Lincoln, who had split receipts equally with Stuart, was only to receive a third of the earnings of Logan and Lincoln. Wisely, he judged that the education he would receive in law was worth the price.

6
Mary Todd

———⟨●⟩———

IN 1839, WHEN THE CAPITAL of the state was moved to Springfield, Elizabeth Edwards, wife of a member of the famous Long Nine, could fairly claim to be Springfield's first lady. Unlike almost everybody else in that community, her husband, Ninian W. Edwards, was not a newcomer to Illinois. His father, whose memory was still green, had been the last governor of the Illinois territory and first senator from the new state. Ninian had less than his father's abilities, but had inherited from him enormous tracts of valuable land. Not needing to engage in any profession, he had entered the legislature, was prominent in the Whig party, and had built himself an imposing brick house a block or two from the square, where he and his wife entertained.

Elizabeth Edwards was the daughter of Robert S. Todd of Lexington, Kentucky, a man of wealth and culture with strong political interests. She was the eldest of a great many sisters, for Robert Todd had married twice. By his first wife, Eliza, who died in childbirth in 1825, he had four girls and two boys. He then remarried and had eight more children by his second wife, Betsy. Not unnaturally, Elizabeth Edwards felt it her duty to do something for her unmarried sisters. She had the position and the means, while Springfield attracted promising young men from all over the state. Betsy Todd, absorbed in childbearing and the upbringing of her own children, had little time to concern herself with the older brood. So well did Elizabeth do her duty that all three of her full sisters eventually married in Springfield.

In 1837, Fanny was already engaged to Dr. William Wallace; and it was the turn of Mary, third daughter and fourth child of Robert Todd, to visit Elizabeth Edwards. Mary was seventeen, had lost her mother at the age of six, and had been petted a little too much before that time and not enough after. For the last four years she had been a weekly boarder at an academy run by a French emigrè couple who had taught her to read and speak French with considerable fluency. Of course they had not neglected her dance-steps or dress and company manners. They had also given her a fair grounding in English literature and encouraged a habit of reading. Political education had been acquired at her father's dinner table. Robert Todd was a hospitable man who entertained the great Henry Clay and all other important Whigs in the state, encouraging his older daughters to listen to what these guests said about public affairs. On the whole Elizabeth Edwards must have felt that Mary did her upbringing credit. She was rather a pretty girl with blue eyes and reddish-brown hair, five feet two inches high, a little plump but with beautiful hands and graceful gestures. Impulsive, willful, always animated, she was a girl who wanted her own way and who, lost in the middle of an enormous family, had learned to assert herself by tears and tantrums.

There was no particular need for tantrums in Springfield; but when Mary went back home as a grown-up young lady, she did not get on with her stepmother. Since her grandmother Parker, who lived nearby, disliked poor Betsy also, Mary was encouraged in her spoiled ways and provided with an alternative home when she desired one. She remained in Lexington for a couple of years; but Elizabeth, who had now got Fanny married to her doctor, was anxious to have her next sister permanently. The prospect of an exciting social season when the General Assembly met in Springfield was alluring to Mary. In October, 1839, just a few months after the archives had been moved from Vandalia, Mary Todd came to make her home with her sister.

Elizabeth Edwards and Frances Wallace were not Mary's only relations in Illinois. She had an uncle in Springfield, Dr. John Todd, with a growing family; and three of her cousins were respectively John Stuart, Lincoln's first partner; Stephen Logan, his second; and John Hardin, who was soon to be his rival for the Whig nomination to succeed Stuart in Congress. It was therefore inevitable that Lincoln should be asked to some of the Edwards' parties. He had by this time lived two years in Springfield and was established as a lawyer and politician. He liked parties and joined in imploring Mrs. Orville Browning to come and enliven the social scene while the Assembly was sitting. His origin might have been humble, but Illinois was much less interested in where a man came from than where he was going. His awkward appearance was against him, but his costume though shabby was perfectly proper. There is mention in Mary's letters of a suit of "lincoln green" which had died and been replaced by some other color. He still shared a bed with Joshua Speed above his store, but nobody thought that undignified, especially as Speed himself was a presentable young man. Being unmarried, Lincoln had to lodge somewhere, while two in a bed was commonplace for lodgers.

It is not surprising to find that Lincoln was shortly invited to a cotillion at the Edwards'. He was thirty-one by this time, but still unattached. Devoted to children, he had paid a good deal of attention to teen-aged Sarah Rickard, a guest at William Butler's, at whose house he still took meals. Somehow the Biblical marriage between Abraham and Sarah had been the subject of a jest between them. Sarah, going on for sixteen, had become self-conscious about Lincoln, who was from her point of view both old and odd, by no means a romantic lover for a girl still looking forward to her debut. Lincoln felt a little uneasy about Sarah. If she proved to be pining for him, he might have an obligation. Luckily she did not, at least at the moment, seem unhappy. He was more or less free to take notice of Mary Todd, already established as the center of a group of lively unmarried girls who were all making long visits to relatives for similar reasons. Quick-witted, an excellent mimic, and yet well informed on serious subjects, Mary was fitted to shine in a social gathering of intelligent young men. Tradition says that Lincoln introduced himself to her, saying, "Miss Todd, I want to dance with you in the worst way."

"And he certainly did," jested Mary to a cousin, laughing over his big feet.

Lincoln was far from the only young man in attendance at balls, picnics, sleigh-rides, and whatever the time of year might offer for diversion. Despite the mark of his teeth on Stuart's thumb, Stephen A. Douglas was often at the Edwards' house. Joshua F. Speed, whose family had a plantation not far from Louisville, bought a new suit and paid attention to Matilda Edwards, a cousin of Ninian's who had been invited for the season.

It is hard to know why amid all these gay young people Mary Todd should have become attracted by Abraham Lincoln. Sparkling and witty herself, she may have enjoyed his humor. Unquestionably she liked his willingness to talk about politics more seriously than men generally did to young ladies. Mary was no snob, but Lincoln's awkwardness and provincial accent could not have escaped notice. Evidently his talk revealed his true quality, while perhaps his easy temper soothed taut nerves. It is much easier to see what Lincoln saw in Mary. Young, pretty, vivacious, the center of every social group and yet intelligent enough to talk about serious issues, she only needed to show him that she had an affectionate heart.

She took her time, playing her cards with an admirable discretion. As early as the middle of 1840, while she was paying a visit to an uncle in Columbia, Missouri, she wrote one of her Springfield girl friends a gossipy letter alluding to various acquaintances and their romances. Mary had received a Harrison campaign pamphlet which Lincoln had helped to edit, together with copies of the *Sangamo Journal,* to which he had long been a contributor. There had even been "some letters" which she *"must confess . . .* were entirely *unlooked for."* Admitting her love of gaiety, she adds: "I would such were not my nature, for mine I fancy is to be a quiet lot." All this Mary conveys to her friend Mercy Levering without once mentioning Lincoln by name. Nor does she speak of her situation in another letter to Mercy written in mid-December, 1840, when Mary was back in Springfield but Mercy was not. At that time Mary must either have been engaged or expecting to receive a proposal any minute, since on January the first the whole affair was over and an engagement between Mary and Lincoln was roughly broken off.

Everyone wants to know what happened to cause the breach, but it naturally was not a subject that either Lincoln or Mary cared to discuss. After Lincoln's death, William H. Herndon, who also publicized the Ann Rutledge story, maintained that the wedding was actually fixed but that the groom, who had tried in vain to break his engagement, failed to turn up. Herndon, who detested Mary, was attempting to show that Lincoln had never loved her. In fact, Lincoln did break the engagement and seems to have done so from a lack of confidence which is not surprising when we consider the difference between the ages and backgrounds of the couple. It is possible that he had learned that Elizabeth and Ninian

Edwards disliked the match. Lincoln was still a poor man—and though it seems probable that his New Salem debts were by now paid off, he could not offer Mary a carriage to flourish around in or even a house of her own to which she could invite friends. Mary was used to being feted and quick to show resentment. She might not be able to endure life with Abraham Lincoln in a town where she had led the social set.

To Lincoln himself more personal fears evidently occurred. Though instantly at ease with all sorts of men when he met them outside their own homes, he was diffident in social groups, as had been evident in his letters to Mary Owens. His habitual melancholy not only suggested he would not make Mary Todd happy, but caused him to wonder whether he was suited to enjoy the married state with anyone. He asked for release from the engagement, which she granted him. Far from giving him relief, this made him more miserable than ever. Whether wisely or not, Mary evidently loved him and suffered at their separation. Depression made him physically ill in the middle of the legislative session. To John Stuart in Washington he wrote, "I am now the most miserable man living. If what I feel were distributed equally to the whole human family, there would not be one cheerful face on the earth." Mary for her part behaved with great dignity, writing six months later that she had not seen him in the gay world for months and imagined that he was avoiding it altogether. If he would only be himself again, "much, much happiness would it afford me."

Lincoln was not himself, and it was unfortunate that Speed, his most intimate friend, had selected this moment for returning to Kentucky. Part of the bond between the two appears to have been that Speed's temperament resembled Lincoln's; it was surely no accident that a glimpse of Lincoln's melancholy mood had triggered the impulse which made Speed offer half his bed. In Kentucky, Speed fell in love with Fanny

Henning, whereupon he argued himself into the same despondency as Abraham Lincoln. Was he truly in love? Could he make this delightful girl happy? Did he really find her different from the girls he had flirted with in Springfield, or was he deluding himself? He covered pages with his self-doubts, while Lincoln put aside his own depression to cheer him up. Both of them had talked themselves into fear of marriage. Speed feared lest he wake to find his love a delusion, and Lincoln lest he fail to give happiness to one who loved him. Long letters went back and forth, Lincoln urging on Speed the married life he himself had renounced. In February, 1842, Speed did screw up his courage and found himself to his own surprise blissfully happy. His Fanny did not want to leave her native state, and Speed decided to sell out and depart from Springfield. He was going to establish himself on a plantation fairly near his family, whereas Lincoln, the son of a Coles County farmer, answered that he could not sympathize. He had not "studied" farming and knew nothing about it.

1841 had been a difficult year, perhaps Lincoln's worst. It had opened with the loss of Mary, which had affected him so badly that three weeks later he wrote to Stuart in Washington, asking for the appointment of his friend and doctor Anson G. Henry to the postmastership in Springfield, adding: "I have been making a most discreditable exhibition of myself in the way of hypochondriaism and thereby got the impression that Dr. Henry is necessary to my existence. Unless he gets that place, he leaves Springfield. You therefore see how much I am interested in the matter." These emotional problems had been increased by the parting from Speed, his subsequent letters, and the dissolution of Lincoln's partnership with Stuart. By early in 1842, he was working his way out of these troubles. Speed was then happily married. Lincoln, as he gradually recovered his own spirits, was learning a great deal about the practice of law from his new partner. Logan was ten years older than Lincoln, an irritable eccentric and deliberately shabby man, who never wore a tie and preferred a cheap summer straw or a fur cap to the formal silk "stove-pipe" affected by Lincoln. Logan was no orator and relied for his effect in court on devastating logic backed by meticulous preparation of his cases. Lincoln, with his natural talent for persuasion and his training through an enormous number of petty lawsuits, needed to acquire the habit of careful research into precedents which he could store in his capacious memory. Logan was a difficult but demanding partner at a time when Lincoln had to force himself to do his best. By now Lincoln was surmounting his troubles and ready to admit that he could be content, were it not for the unhappiness which he had brought on Mary.

Not everyone thought the Lincoln-Todd match would be unsuitable. Miss Julia Jayne, who was in Mary Todd's confidence, was more romantic. Mrs. Simeon Francis, wife of the editor of the *Sangamo Journal,* saw a great deal of Lincoln and thought that his future would be brilliant enough to satisfy any woman. Determining to re-unite the pair, Mrs. Francis asked both to a party, brought them together, and said, "Be friends again." Tentatively they began to meet in Mrs. Francis' parlor without taking anyone into their confidence but Julia Jayne. Presumably it was there that Lincoln showed the young ladies a series of letters which he had composed for the *Sangamo Journal* attacking James Shields, the Democratic auditor of accounts for Illinois. They were written in backwoods talk and signed "Rebecca," lampooning Shields's lady-killing ways as well as his political actions. Shields, a hot-tempered little Irishman, was furious enough to talk about a duel. Mary and Julia, who had giggled over the letters together, now composed another from "Aunt Becca," offering to pacify the little man by marrying him. In their hands the political satire gave way completely to the personal. Even more outrageously they followed it up by a poem celebrating Shields's acceptance of "Aunt Becca." The indignant Shields, who had extracted the name of Lincoln as the author of the letters, demanded a handsome apology—or else. Lincoln for his part did not wish to deny yet could not acknowledge his authorship of the most offensive of the letters and the poem. He accepted Shields's challenge with the intention of making it too ridiculous to go on with. As the challenged party he had the choice of weapons and decided on the longest possible cavalry broadswords, the combatants to be separated by a plank nine to twelve inches broad which they might not cross, which meant that the long-armed Lincoln could stand nicely out of range while he sparred with his smaller opponent.

He probably thought that Shields would refuse his terms, but the Irishman was in too much of a temper to consider the qualified apology which Lincoln offered. The combatants and their seconds therefore traveled to a sandbar in the Mississippi, situated in Missouri, which did not, like Illinois, have laws against dueling. Luckily, when they arrived on the ground, even Shields could see that a duel fought under the conditions prescribed would be absurd. He accepted a statement from Lincoln admitting authorship of the first letters from "Rebecca," and assuring him that they were written for political effect without the slightest intention of reflecting on his private character. The other letter, though far more personal, was by common consent left unmentioned.

Lincoln had been carried away once more by his talent for satire, while the girls had made it much worse by finding it funny and exaggerating it out of all reason. They had been, perhaps, a little frightened by Shields's reaction because it was definitely unladylike to write letters to the *Journal,* especially ones in dialect signed "Aunt Becca" and making fun of a prominent man. They were heartily grateful to Lincoln for keeping their names out of the affair. Gratitude made Mary frank, and the engagement which had been broken off nearly two years ago was now renewed. This time, however, the pair kept their own counsel, so that no one could interfere. On the fourth of November, Lincoln came into the room of his friend James Matheny and informed him while he was still lying in bed, "I am going to be married today." Presently, meeting Edwards on the street, he told him the same thing. The astonished Edwards replied that at least Mary must be married in his house, seeing that she was under the guardianship of himself and Elizabeth. He hurried home to find out from Mary if Lincoln's statement was true and learned that it was.

There was not much time to make objections. Elizabeth sensibly started to get the house ready and have a proper cake baked so that the ceremony might appear to go off in seemly fashion. Frances Wallace came in to help, a few close friends were invited, and nobody even remembered thirty-five years later what dress the bride had on. They only recollected that she had worn no veil or flowers in her hair. Lincoln's own preparations had been correspondingly simple. He booked a room at the Globe Tavern until further notice and ordered a plain gold ring for Mary's hand, inside which he had the jeweler engrave: "Love is eternal."

7

Family Adjustments

---◄●►---

MARY TODD, WHO HAD LATELY been the center of Springfield's gayest group of eligible girls, had married a man who could not even provide a home for her. The Lincolns took up their residence at the Globe Tavern, where they boarded for four dollars a week. To be sure, the Globe was a respectable tavern and a place where the stagecoach made regular stops. When the legislature was sitting, it was filled with assemblymen, some of whom brought their wives. At other times of year it was still a bustling spot though not well suited for female entertaining. Mary's marriage had produced a coolness between her and Elizabeth Edwards, who soon invited her youngest sister, Ann, to take Mary's place.

Mary bore with dignity the privations which she had foreseen. She did not expect to have a carriage and bought cheap materials to make her own dresses or retrim an old bonnet. For the present she was deeply in love with a man so different from herself that the normal adjustments of married life became all-absorbing. Even in appearance the pair presented a strange contrast. Lincoln was six feet four inches tall, lean, clumsy, and untidy, while Mary was five feet two inches, graceful, plump, and meticulously neat. Ambitious for her husband, she had determined to refine his manners and improve his appearance. She took pride in sewing him shirts of superior quality, encouraged because Lincoln was not, like his partner Stephen Logan, a deliberately casual dresser. He was perfectly willing to assume the long black coat and stove-pipe hat which marked him as a fairly well-to-do professional man. Mary could not, however, make these clothes fit, prevent his hat from bulging with papers or his suit from wrinkling up as he lounged on a chair. When he was away from her, she could not sponge the sweat-stains from his black linen summer coat, brush off the mud and horsehair from his trousers, and straighten his tie. She could not even prevent him from taking off his coat indoors and sitting in his shirt-sleeves or from lying on her hearthrug to read with his feet propped up on the wall. His country speech was less refined than hers, but he would not amend it because he preferred to talk like a man of the people.

Mary criticized and even nagged. How soon she lost her temper we do not know, but she was a creature of sudden rages with which her husband never learned to cope. A moody man himself, he did not resent her tantrums, seeming to regard her with special tenderness because she, too, had emotional problems. He did not, however, recognize these outbursts as demands for attention, preferring to go away or at least to make no answer. He had not the knack of helping her regain control.

Clashes about trivial things seemed unimportant to Mary because Lincoln shared his political aspirations with her. Encouraged since childhood to listen to conversations about politics and praised for expressing her opinion vehemently, Mary was passionately concerned with this side of her husband's life. She listened eagerly while he confided in her, not perhaps seeing that he talked openly precisely because women played no part in his political game. For this reason, if Mary tended to look on her husband's opponents as lifelong personal foes, her attitude did not matter to Lincoln, soon patiently seeking some new accord with them. He listened to her tirades, but did not take her advice.

By March, 1843, Mary knew she was with child and must
have felt some anxious moments in an age when many women
died in childbirth. Her situation did not prevent her husband
from leaving her for a few weeks that spring while he attended the Eighth Judicial Circuit. This circuit accounted for
a good deal of his business and kept him politically in touch
with people of statewide influence. Mary had three sisters in
Springfield, one married to a doctor, and at least in the tavern
she did not have heavy housework. Whether or not she asked
Lincoln to stay, she must have wished it, for Mary was a
feminine person who wanted and needed male protection.
There was a vein of iron in her husband which she lacked.

Perhaps even that first year Lincoln was glad to leave home.
He loved Mary, but on the circuit he felt like a boy out of
school. Twice a year the judge of the Eighth Judicial Circuit
made the round of an area of some twelve hundred square
miles, starting from Springfield and covering the Sangamon
valley as far as the Illinois eastern border. During the more
than twenty years Lincoln rode around with him, there were
various changes in the shape and size of this circuit, but basi-
cally it took about three months to cover and included twelve
or fourteen county seats. These varied in size, the largest
being Springfield and the smallest Postville. This, the county
seat of Logan County in 1837, consisted of three stores and
three or four families. Naturally so tiny a place would have
no regular lawyer, though it might just possibly have some
unqualified person who drew up documents, as Lincoln had
done in New Salem. Larger centers had part-time lawyers
who eked out a living by farming or keeping store and were
usually anxious for the help of a Springfield firm in difficult
cases. Lawyers who worked full-time in Springfield, Bloomington, or elsewhere, rode round with the circuit because
courts sat only a short time in any one place.

The result of these conditions was that after a session in Springfield the circuit judge set out on his trip accompanied by one of the partners from most of the law firms in town. In the early days of Lincoln's marriage everyone still went on horseback, since trails were rough and streams which had to be forded ran high in spring or after sudden rains. The circuit judge started out in early spring and late fall, avoiding the winter and the busiest times of the farming year. Rainstorms, early snowstorms, and bitter winds were frequent hazards of travel. In the days when men rode, they were protected by heavy underwear rather than by cloak or waterproof. Lincoln carried a wide muffler or shawl which he could tuck around his neck, draw across his face, or use to keep his hat on, but his horse went two to four miles an hour across rough country, and he might not find a single cabin for shelter in four or five hours.

Somewhat later in the forties, when roads began to improve, Lincoln acquired an unpretentious one-horse buggy and presumably at this time added to his equipment a black cotton umbrella, soon faded to green by sun and rain, tied up with a bit of twine, and displaying in Mary's careful stitchery the name "A. Lincoln." His luggage went into a pair of saddlebags while he rode. These were replaced by a cheap carpetbag which soon looked shabby when he moved into the horse-and-buggy era. Its contents consisted of a few law books and a change of linen, which was probably washed about once a week while court was sitting.

Some of the county seats were as much as sixty miles apart, so that it was necessary to spend a night on the way, not infrequently at a conveniently located cabin. Here judge and lawyers ate whatever the settler's wife could provide and bedded down in rows on the floor by the fire. Conditions were not much better in the county towns. Tavern beds were often verminous and crowded four or more to a room with no other furnishing than a cuspidor and perhaps a single chair. Lawyers all slept two in a bed and washed downstairs by the pump in a very small basin with the aid of liquid, homemade soap, and a single towel. Accommodation was at least cheap. Lincoln and a friend were charged seventy-five cents on one occasion for their supper, lodging, and breakfast, plus the stabling and feeding of their horses.

County courthouses in the earliest days were mere log cabins, sometimes a schoolhouse hastily cleared for the purpose. They were roughly furnished with benches for the jury, a chair or stool for the judge, a cuspidor or two, and a rail to keep back the spectators. Already in 1842 these primitive buildings were being replaced by clapboard or brick, ornamented with a cupola or tower and sometimes both. The fact was that the arrival of the circuit meant a great deal to a little town. It attracted not only litigants and lawyers, but country people coming to listen to arguments, to serve on juries, or even to gossip while they bought a plug of tobacco, a bolt of calico for the wife, or a pair of new boots. Horse races or shooting and wrestling matches were arranged. Itinerant preachers chose this moment to look for an audience, as did politicians, whether or not they were currently standing for office. Traveling troupes of entertainers appeared, invariably attracting Lincoln, who was laughed at by his friends for taking time out to visit a primitive "magic-lantern" show intended for children.

Indifferent to poor food and dirty lodgings, exceptionally strong in physique, Lincoln made little of the hardships of circuit travel. Since the majority of the lawyers attending the court rode round most of the circuit, we must not think of Lincoln as a lonely horseman, seizing the long hours as a chance to brood over great issues. It is true that the men could not chatter all day and that the trail was seldom suited for riding more than two abreast. However, even in his buggy,

Lincoln would usually have a passenger beside him. For a while he put Euclid in his bag along with his law books, studying late at night or at dawn when the others were snoring. Yet what he seems to have liked best was not the chance to be solitary, but the companionship of people who would not let him sit quietly in a corner, but expected him to make them laugh until they ached. Other lawyers were witty as well as he. In particular, Judge David Davis, appointed to the circuit in 1848, enjoyed his joke and made a favorite of Lincoln. Davis instituted a mock court which held comic trials in the evenings, condemning Lincoln on one occasion for letting down legal standards by accepting a scandalously low fee from a poor client.

Fees on the circuit were always small, running sometimes as low as fifty cents, but usually ranging from two-and-a-half to ten dollars. Sometimes preliminary work had been done by local "lawyers," while at other times the circuit riders were expected to handle complex cases on short notice. The circuit usually arrived in town on a Monday, and on Tuesday the visiting lawyers were to be found outside the court or tavern or crowded into a corner indoors on unpleasant days. Often they met old friends, since a man quite naturally tended to entrust his affairs to the lawyer who had handled his business before. Sometimes papers in connection with a case had been sent previously to the firm's headquarters in Springfield. More often Lincoln had perhaps half an hour to straighten out some tangled explanation and decide how to handle a case. Court opened on Wednesday, but at intervals more litigants appeared, seizing on a lawyer who was taking a moment's relief from the unwashed smells of the courtroom but must be back in ten minutes or so when a new case came on.

In these conditions wide experience was more important than legal knowledge, especially as country juries were not impressed by fine points of law. Lincoln's gift for lucid explanation made him one of the circuit's most persuasive men with juries, who liked his rural speech and use of anecdote. It was his habit to fix in his mind the crucial point on which he thought his case would hang and, keeping this in reserve, concede point after point until the jury began to feel that he was more concerned to bring out the truth than to win for his client. Judging his moment, he then produced his crucial argument and stuck to it so firmly that the jury, already disposed to trust him, was won over.

While Abraham Lincoln was embarking on a career so different from his father's, Thomas Lincoln had been trying to establish himself on a succession of farms in Illinois. It took him, in fact, until 1837, the year of Lincoln's move to Springfield, before he finally came to rest in a place called Goose Nest Prairie, about seven miles from the Coles County seat of Charleston. During the early thirties he either still had money from the sale of his own and Sarah's property, or he had made a lucky land speculation or was able to take out a mortgage. His actual movements seem to have been governed by those of his stepson, John Johnston, partly no doubt because Sarah wished it so, and partly because in his fifties he could not manage the hard work of clearing, fencing, and cultivating unaided. John Johnston, though personally liked by all his relatives including Lincoln, did not care for sustained hard work. He married young and had a large brood of children who shared the Lincoln cabin for a good many years. His tendency to run into debt quite often involved Thomas Lincoln.

Johnston could both read and write a letter, but Thomas Lincoln could not write, or even read with any ease. Consequently the letters that passed between Thomas and his son through the medium of Johnston were infrequent. It seems certain that Lincoln did visit his parents during those years in which he was at New Salem and the elder Lincolns were moving from one place to another, but records of these visits are not reliable. By the time that Thomas and Sarah were finally settled in Goose Nest Prairie, Lincoln was regularly riding the Eighth Circuit. This circuit never included Coles County, but surrounded it on three sides for some years; and, despite all changes, Charleston remained close to one of the towns in which Lincoln regularly practiced until 1853. It was therefore easy for him to spend a night or two with his parents when business took him in that direction; and the children of his step-brother, John Johnston, remembered the visits of "Uncle Abe" pretty well.

Until he acquired his own buggy Lincoln used to borrow a horse and wagon from Dennis Hanks, who lived in Charleston, in order to ride out to his father's farm, loaded up with useful presents—and maybe a little rock candy for the children. It was noted during these years that his pants, which suffered much wear from horse or buggy riding, showed patches on either seat and that his coat was too short to cover them. They were known in the family as Uncle Abe's "spectacle pants." It seems likely from what the Johnston children recalled that ten or fifteen dollars usually made their way from the pockets of the "spectacle pants" to those of Thomas Lincoln. It was not, however, until 1841, that unfortunate year of Lincoln's broken engagement, that Thomas Lincoln got into serious difficulty. He was living at this time on a farm of 120 acres adjoining forty belonging to John Johnston. As far as can be told, the two families were by now inhabiting a double cabin which shared a single chimney in the middle, the Lincoln part being sixteen by eighteen feet and the Johnston part sixteen by sixteen. This cabin was on the Lincoln land, possession of which was apparently endangered. Accordingly, in October, 1841, Abraham Lincoln purchased from his father the east forty acres for the sum of two hundred dollars on condition that Thomas and Sarah should have the use of it for life and that after their deaths John Johnston should have the option of purchasing it for the two hundred dollars Abe had given.

In this fashion Abraham secured a piece of property to his father which he could not mortgage or sell. This does not seem, however, to have solved Thomas' problems, since a few months later he mortgaged the eastern half of his remaining eighty acres for fifty dollars, which was to be paid back over two years in half-yearly installments. Another of Lincoln's cousins, John Hall, says that Uncle Abe "use to come down every six months and pay off the interest . . . He done that until he had money enough to pay the hull debt." If these sums seem small, it is well to remember that 1842 was the year of Lincoln's marriage, that he may still have been paying New Salem debts, and that he needed money to buy a house suitable for a woman who had been used to comfortable living.

In 1844, Abraham and Mary Lincoln moved into their permanent home on Eighth and Jackson streets. A few months later on his next round of the circuit Lincoln arranged to take into his home Harriet Hanks, daughter of his cousin Dennis and now eighteen years old. Harriet's purpose was to go to school in Springfield, but it was understood that she would also help Mary, whose eldest son was then about one year old. Harriet stayed a year and a half, leaving a couple of months after the birth of Eddie, the Lincoln's second son. It has been suggested that Mary Lincoln treated Harriet like a servant and that she left because she could not bear this any longer. We may note, however, that she did stay a considerable time and remained to help with Mary's second confinement.

Harriet benefited from her stay, as can be seen from her letters, which are far better spelled than those of her kindred. Her references to Mary Lincoln later were cool, but certainly showed no marked dislike. The experiment was successful enough to encourage John Johnston to suggest that his twelve-year old Abraham be given the same chance in 1851. Lincoln's reply seems unenthusiastic, but it was evidently Mary who most disliked the notion. Her oldest son, Robert, was by now eight years old, and Mary was determined that her boys should be gentlemen. The influence of a rough twelve-year-old brought up in a log cabin by almost illiterate parents was the last thing she wanted for Robert.

In 1847 Lincoln, having been elected to Congress, ceased for the time being to travel around the Eighth Circuit. It is significant that he had only been in Washington a couple of months when he received a letter from his father, written as usual by John Johnston. ". . . I was gratly in hopes that you would have come a past heer on your way to washington as I wished to see you, but as you faild to come a past, I am compeled to make a request by Letter to you for the Lone of Twenty Dollars, which sum I am compeled to razes, or my Land will be sold. . . ." The timing of this letter so shortly after Lincoln had ceased to come around on circuit strongly suggests that similar applications had been common in the past. Lincoln answered: "I very cheerfully send you the twenty dollars which you say is necessary to save your land from sale . . ." The "cheerfulness" makes the letter pleasant reading, but the phrase "you say" suggests a certain doubt of the emergency.

At the same time, and indeed on the same paper, John Johnston wrote an eloquent appeal for no less than eighty dollars, declaring: "I am dund and doged to death so I am all most tired of Living & I would all most swop my place in *Heaven* for that much money." In reply Lincoln reminded Johnston that he had helped him out several times before and had each time been told that all would now be well. He put Johnston's difficulties down to his habit of uselessly wasting time and suggested that he leave the cultivation of the farm to Thomas Lincoln and his own children and hire himself out to earn some cash. For every dollar he could earn by the first of the following May, Lincoln would add a dollar from his own resources. John Johnston preferred to be "dund and doged" rather than take this advice. This exchange of letters gives evidence that Thomas Lincoln and his stepson were reasonably used to receiving financial aid from Lincoln, who was getting tired of Johnston's applications.

The most peculiar thing about the relationship of Lincoln to his parents is that he never once took Mary out to see them. It is true that travel was not easy, so that Harriet Hanks is said to have taken two days to come from Charleston in a horse and buggy driven by her Uncle Abe. Thomas Lincoln died in 1851 when railroads in Illinois were still in their infancy. Mary liked to travel, however, and she did on occasion leave her children, though not often in the forties when she could not, perhaps, afford adequate help. There seems no explanation except that she would have had nothing to say to people who were living in what to her would have been the depth of squalor. Since Thomas and Sarah never traveled further than Charleston, the two halves of Lincoln's life remained quite separate. Though Lincoln himself was perfectly at home in either, he made no attempt to bring them together. After Lincoln's murder, Mary wrote to Sarah Lincoln affectionately, regretting that they had not met and dispatching a parcel of clothes which Sarah's relatives indignantly said were of no use. Prostrated by her loss, Mary could not bring herself to make the effort of going to see her husband's "Mama."

How far she had been encouraged in this attitude by Lincoln it is impossible to say. There may have been some soreness in Lincoln's mind because his background had been so different from Mary's. He may have wanted to protect her against the sort of appeals which were directed to himself. In 1851, when Thomas lay dying, Lincoln wrote to excuse himself from visiting his father because Mary was not sufficiently recovered from the birth of their third son a few weeks before. The letter offers the conventional consolations of the day, making reference to happy meetings with loved ones in the hereafter. It contains, however, one sentence which Lincoln's most fervid admirers have difficulty in making sound affectionate. "Say to him"—this was written of course to John Johnston—"that if we could meet now, it is doubtful whether it would not be more painful than pleasant." Lincoln was too busy with the supreme court session in Springfield to go to the funeral. Ten years later, when he was about to leave for Washington, he spoke of arranging for a gravestone, but never did.

If Lincoln's relationship with his father seems to have given him decreasing pleasure, he was not a man to forget a friend. He was not too busy to pronounce the eulogy at Bowling Green's funeral in 1840, where he broke down and could not finish what he was saying. New Salem itself was now deserted, but Mentor Graham, the schoolmaster who had helped him with grammar and surveying, was in Petersburg a few miles off, now county seat of Menard County. As long as Menard remained in the Eighth Circuit, court sessions there were times of joyous reunion. When boundaries were redrawn, Lincoln, unable to attend the court in person, sent his partner, Herndon. He did not, however, cease to visit his friends in Petersburg, sometimes on a political tour, occasionally to appear in court for a special friend, or even to talk over old times and political prospects with Graham.

When Mary married Lincoln in 1842, he was junior partner in the firm of Logan and Lincoln. Since Logan was a learned lawyer who did not care for the slipshod ways of the circuit, it was always Lincoln's job to make the tour. In 1844, when Logan wished to go into partnership with his son, Lincoln felt ready to establish a firm of his own, inviting William H. Herndon, who had just qualified, to be his partner. William was the son of Archer G. Herndon, a long-time political acquaintance of Lincoln's. Young Billy Herndon had clerked in

Speed's store and slept upstairs with Lincoln and Speed. Lincoln had encouraged him to study law and now offered him the chance which Stuart had given him. In some ways Herndon, who remained Lincoln's partner for the rest of his legal career, was an ideal choice. Not interested in a political career for himself, he was able to keep the practice going when Lincoln was absent. Casual in matters of detail, he did not resent the habitual disorder of the office, Lincoln's habit of storing papers in his hat or filing them in an envelope marked "when you can't find *it* anywhere else, look into this." In politics Herndon was a strong Whig, more radical than Lincoln and personally devoted to his partner. Socially he did not quite pass for a gentlemen, chiefly because, though in theory a temperance man, he occasionally got scandalously drunk. Whether for this reason or because of a tactless remark of Herndon's, Mary Lincoln took one of her strong dislikes to him. Never in all the years of the partnership was he invited to her house. Not unnaturally, Herndon collected the tales of Mary's exhibitions of temper, concluding that Lincoln was unhappily married.

In the firm of Lincoln and Herndon the senior partner was "Mr. Lincoln," while the junior, nine years younger, was always "Billy." It would have been natural for Billy to take over the circuit work, as Lincoln had done for Stuart and Logan. Unfortunately he detested the job and seldom went anywhere except as a substitute for Lincoln to Menard when it was cut off from the Eighth Circuit. It is clear, however, that the senior partner did not consent to travel for six months out of the year merely because Billy Herndon preferred to stay at home. Nor did he, as Herndon later implied, choose the circuit because it gave him six months away from his wife. Much evidence displays Lincoln's devotion to Mary and his children, but he liked the intimacy with his fellow lawyers and with the country folk whose problems he handled. In the fifties, when railroad travel came in, many lawyers found it possible to visit their homes on some weekends, but it was noticed that Lincoln never did so. Deliberately he chose to use the circuit for mending political fences, making fresh contacts, and finding out how public opinion was working. He would be more likely to take a weekend train to Chicago than to Springfield. In measuring Lincoln we always have to allow for his ambition as part of the secret of his continuous growth.

Mary Lincoln had to allow for it, too, and in 1843 while she awaited the birth of her first child in the Globe Tavern, she may already have seen that it meant sacrifices. Luckily she suffered no complications and was safely delivered of a son on the first of August. They named the baby Robert Todd after Mary's father, who had accepted his odd son-in-law with a good grace and soon made Mary an allowance of ten dollars a month, which must have helped with the problem of clothing. Lincoln's income was about twelve hundred dollars a year, but he had evidently learned caution from his unlucky borrowings in New Salem. He was waiting to buy a house until he had saved enough, though it was obvious that the Globe Tavern was no place for a baby. It was noisy, while diaper washing and drying must have been a problem.

As an interim measure Lincoln rented a three-room cottage in which Mary must have learned to cook and clean and carry water. There was no room for a maid, and there is no record that she had anyone to wait on her. Lincoln did the outside chores, splitting wood and bringing it in, or currying his horse. Presently the Lincolns were able to buy a frame building a story and a half high which was only a few blocks from Lincoln's office. Financially things were soon easier, too, although Lincoln still looked after his horse and milked his cow when he was at home. Mary began to have domestic help, which changed quite frequently because she could either find no fault or find no virtue in her servants. She had no halfway moods, but her critical acuteness tended to be stronger than her warm affections.

As a mother, Mary Lincoln idolized her children but was demanding of affection in return. Lincoln, though one of the world's most indulgent of fathers when his children began to walk and talk, was awkward with babies and not infrequently absent-minded. Since he did not accompany Mary to church, a neighbor once saw him, left at home in charge of the children, dragging two youngsters down the street in a little cart, his nose in a book. Presently a child fell out and lay yelling, while the father, his thoughts miles off, walked on, still reading. Mary, who returned in time to witness the scene, had an explosion of temper which was not restrained by the fact that neighbors were watching.

As time went on, Mary suffered increasingly from strange headaches. Her quarrels with tradesmen may have been rare, but were never forgotten and lost nothing in the telling. Her letters, often indiscreet about, for instance, the sharp tongue of her sister Ann, made enemies as often as sympathizers. Lincoln, who suffered most under the lash of her temper, was also aware of her unhappiness about the nervous explosions she could not control. Though her love for him did not prevent these outbursts, her temper did not affect her devotion. She cared for him deeply and had given up much for him. Lincoln went away on circuit and came back refreshed, leaving Mary to cope with the endless problems of running the house and tending the children. Owing her so much, Lincoln could not cease to love her even though she made him suffer. He grew in patience and self-control, while his Mary remained the impulsive, affectionate girl he had married, older but no wiser, every year a little more nervous as babies were born and family life increased in complication.

8

Lincoln in Congress

———⊶⟨◉⟩⊷———

AFTER FOUR TERMS in the Illinois legislature, Lincoln felt he was ready to go on to Congress. His interest in national politics had been developed by a series of excellent debates on issues ranging far wider than Jackson's dealings with the United States Bank. For instance, some of the southern states, horrified by the abolitionist propaganda which had been arriving in increasing quantities since the foundation of the *Liberator* by Garrison in Boston in 1831, had petitioned northern legislators to restrain abolition societies and cut off the rain of pamphlets which were merely making slave-masters more oppressive. The Illinois discussion of this subject in 1836–37 was intelligent and informed, resulting in resolutions that condemned abolitionist propaganda and stated that the Congress had no power to abolish slavery, even in the District of Columbia. Lincoln, listening with his usual care, formed opinions on the slavery question by which he was to abide for over twenty years. Slavery, he insisted, was founded on injustice and bad policy. It had, notwithstanding, the protection of the laws. Congress, he thought, did have power to abolish slavery in the District of Columbia, but nowhere else. He hoped it would not even do that without a demand from district residents.

These convictions were reinforced when not long after Elijah P. Lovejoy attempted to set up an abolitionist press in Alton, Illinois, and was killed defending it from a mob of wreckers. Though Lovejoy's conduct had been provocative in the extreme, Lincoln had the courage to speak out before the Young Men's Lyceum of Springfield on the danger and wickedness of mobs taking the law into their own hands. It is true that his examples were mainly culled from lynchings which had recently happened elsewhere, but the purpose of his argument was clear. Either abolitionists had a right to be protected by law, or else they should be restrained by it. In neither case was the intervention of a mob excusable. Lincoln's cautious mind did not allow his opinions to move too far ahead of the common men he knew so well, but he saw the rule of law as fundamental to democracy itself. For a basic principle of this kind he was ready to speak boldly.

Several other national issues had been lengthily debated by the legislature during Lincoln's term, but they had not formed the whole of his education. He had learned, for instance, what it meant to be a party man. For two sessions he had been Whig floor leader and had been put forward for Speaker of the House, only failing because the Whigs were the minority party. He had learned the secrets of making friends and putting men under the obligation of voting for something he wanted. He was master of the strategy needed to shepherd through a bill unpopular with many, such as the removal of the state capital to Springfield. He understood political techniques, but temperament and intelligence told him that more was to be gained by keeping bargains than by earning the reputation of being sly.

Outside the legislature he had established such friendly relations with the *Sangamo Journal* that the paper printed many of his unsigned contributions and generally reflected his views. He had been chosen a member of the Whig State Central Committee and had taken a large part in the reorganization of the Illinois Whig party from the grass-roots level up. He had spoken widely for President Harrison and was already counted an experienced and effective stump speaker. In fact, considering that he belonged to the minority party, he had gone about as far as Illinois would let him; it was time to move onto a larger stage. Meanwhile he was rising in his profession under the tutelage of Logan and had for some time been described as a coming lawyer.

Luckily for Lincoln, though the Whig party was in a minority in the state as a whole, this was not so in his own congressional district. If he could but get the nomination as congressional candidate, he was nearly certain to be elected. Accordingly early in 1843, shortly after his marriage, Lincoln began to write letters to influential Whigs in the various counties which made up his congressional district. He had two competitors in the field, both also in their thirties. Both were lawyers and veterans of the Black Hawk War. Edward D. Baker, like Lincoln a self-educated man, was a great orator of the rousing, emotional type. John J. Hardin, one of Mary Lincoln's cousins, was the son of a Kentucky senator and had received his law education under one of the justices of the Kentucky Supreme Court. He excelled in convincing logic and was considered, despite a speech defect, as a serious rival to Lincoln.

Reckoning up his chances, Lincoln thought they were fair, but to his distress Baker was preferred by Sangamon County, while Lincoln was chosen as one of the delegates pledged to support him in the district convention. The best he could do was to get his old New Salem friends in Menard County to put in his name and hope that his strength would pick up. He was especially chagrined because it appeared that his recent marriage had made many plain men reject him as the representative of aristocracy and wealth. The brother-in-law of Ninian W. Edwards was no longer thought of as the farm boy and flatboat hand who had risen by his own efforts.

When the district convention actually met, neither Lincoln

nor Baker had enough votes to defeat Hardin, who was nominated. Lincoln, however, put through a resolution naming Baker as the choice for two years hence, subject to the final decision of another convention. His intention was not merely to aid Baker, who besides being the nominee of his delegation was an intimate personal friend, but to establish a rotation system which would put Baker under the obligation to give Lincoln his turn after another two years. Hardin was duly elected, supported officially by Lincoln despite a coldness between the two men which caused him to cast no vote for any congressional candidate on the day of the election.

In 1844 the Whig candidate for President was Lincoln's political idol, Henry Clay. Chosen one of his presidential electors, Lincoln spoke continuously all over the Eighth Circuit to the neglect of his legal practice. In October he went down to Indiana to speak at Gentryville and other places which he remembered from his youth. Several Illinois counties went for Clay, including Sangamon, but James K. Polk, the Democratic candidate, carried the state and the nation. Lincoln's efforts had more practical effect on his own reputation than on that of Henry Clay.

In 1845 Baker duly succeeded to Hardin's place in Congress. When, however, he returned from Congress briefly between sessions, he was not sure that he wanted to give up his office at the end of his term. If he did so, he argued, Hardin might simply run again. It seems unlikely that Lincoln was still considered an aristocrat, since by this time his marriage was no longer news and it could be seen that the Lincolns lived simply. Possibly Baker and Hardin both thought that Lincoln's manner was too rustic for success in Washington. At all events, though Baker did yield to Lincoln's insistence, Hardin announced his intention of standing. Lincoln, however, had been cultivating the leading Whigs of the district to some purpose, and he received the nomination which he had been awaiting for two terms.

He was still under forty, but it could not be said that his rise had been meteoric. He presented, for instance, a great contrast to Stephen A. Douglas, who had entered the legislature two years later than Lincoln, become a member of the Illinois Supreme Court in 1841, and was elected to Congress in 1843, where he speedily made himself a great reputation. In 1847, when Lincoln at last entered Congress, Douglas moved up to the Senate, already a man of national importance. He owed his advancement to his talents, far showier than Lincoln's.

On October 23, 1847, Lincoln departed for Washington by way of Lexington, Kentucky, taking with him his wife and their two boys, Robert, now four years old, and Eddie, named after his friend and rival Edward D. Baker. After three weeks with the Todds, the Lincolns began an uncomfortable journey by stage and railroad to Washington, where they soon found cheap quarters in Mrs. Spriggs's boarding-house on the site of the present Library of Congress.

Washington was a sprawling, unfinished city in which shanties huddled beside great mansions, back yards contained privies, cowsheds, and pigsties, and garbage was thrown out into the streets, providing forage for pigs, geese, and chickens. Pennsylvania Avenue was paved with cobbles and during the session of Congress was lit by oil lamps. Other streets went unlighted and for the most part unpaved. The White House had spacious grounds which ended in marsh on the banks of the Potomac, which in summer was a breeding-ground for malarial mosquitoes. The Capitol, with a wooden dome and lacking its present side-wings, stood out as one of the few government buildings that had any appearance of being ready for use. Close by it was a slave warehouse where droves of Negroes for the southern market were temporarily collected.

Mrs. Spriggs's boarding-house was only one of a number of hostels for legislators, few of whom had brought their wives to share their uncomfortable quarters. Entertaining was largely in the hands of those who had houses in Washington, which included the President, the diplomatic corps, most of the cabinet, and a sprinkling of wealthy gentlemen or tradesmen who lived in the city. President Polk held public levees, but served no refreshments. Elsewhere balls, receptions, and dinners were generally occasions on which congressmen got drunk. Since the present administration was Democratic, the awkward countrified Whig from Illinois who did not drink received few invitations which he cared to accept. He could take Mary and the children to listen to the Marine Band, which played on the White House lawn on Wednesdays and Sundays. He could and did become a favorite with Mrs. Spriggs's other boarders, all Whigs like himself, since the small lodging-houses divided strictly by party. His fellow guests played whist, but he did not care for cards. They went bowling, at which he was unskillful but enthusiastic. They laughed at his jokes.

Mary Lincoln had little to do but look after Robert and Eddie, who were indulged by both parents and active enough to be a thorough nuisance. Socially she considered herself equal to the best that Washington could offer, but received few invitations and made no lasting friends. Among the boarders she had her likes and dislikes, was charming to some and rudely cutting to others. Not surprisingly, after a few months she decided to return to her father in Lexington, where she could have a girl to help with the children and plenty of social life. The couple were used to long separations, but the bond between them was still strong. "I hate to stay in this old room by myself," writes Lincoln to her. She answers: "How much I wish, instead of writing, *we* were together this evening." Presently Lincoln thinks it right to mention that Mary, who had told him she had paid all her bills, had left two debts behind her, amounting in all to about fourteen dollars. The sum was trivial, and he urged her in the same letter to spend money on a girl "to take charge of the dear codgers." No one would think twice about the incident, were it not that great things grow from little ones. Mary's secret debts were to mount later, and one wonders whether they had not already begun, perhaps as a protest against her husband's lengthy absences and the dullness of her domestic life.

A major issue during Lincoln's campaign for Congress had been the admission of the Republic of Texas to the Union. Lincoln spoke indifferently about the dangers of adding another slave state, but professed himself little concerned to extend present boundaries. The admission of Texas was being urged by Democrats like Stephen A. Douglas, an expansionist who was also anxious for a conflict with England over Oregon. The Texas situation was likely to produce a struggle with Mexico, which was not unwelcome to politicians who had perceived that other Mexican lands, California, for instance, were sparsely populated and might be easily seized from a country which had been in a state of continuous anarchy for years. Not long before Lincoln's actual election, the expected war broke out when Mexicans crossed the Rio Grande to establish their claim to a disputed area. President Polk proclaimed a state of war.

These were circumstances in which it was natural for men to support their country. Lincoln's rival, Hardin, volunteered and was killed at the battle of Buena Vista. Edward D. Baker, present holder of the seat in Congress to which Lincoln had just been elected, went to war also, leaving an undistinguished Whig to finish out his term. Lincoln, who had by the timing of Illinois elections somewhat over a year to wait between his election on August 3, 1846, and the opening of the Thirtieth Congress in December, 1847, was not disposed to forego his political career for the hope of military glory. He did his best to aid the cause by speaking eloquently at a war rally in May, 1846, to encourage volunteers. From this time on, however, until he left for Washington somewhat over a year later he was careful to avoid mentioning the war. Truth was that the Whigs as a party were against it, not only on its own merits, but because it was a Democratic war.

People who like to make an idol out of Abraham Lincoln may be disappointed to find that at this stage of his career he chose to follow the Whig party line, quite possibly because he did not have deep convictions about the Mexican War but was simply a man with his way to make who was ready to choose the course favored by his party. It is, however, fair to point out that he was a newcomer to the national scene and that he strongly believed that party discipline was needed to administer a country so large and so rapidly changing as the United States. His opinions were bound to be affected by the leaders of his party, especially by Henry Clay, who spoke against the war in Lexington while the Lincolns were visiting the Todds on their way to Washington.

The Mexican War had placed the Whigs in a difficult position. By the time that the Thirtieth Congress opened in December, 1847, the actual fighting was over. American armies had plunged deep into Mexico, winning splendid victories over difficulties of supply and terrain, as well as over a hopelessly ill-organized opposition. The only real problems which remained were how to set up a Mexican government with which the United States could make a peace treaty and how much territory the United States was going to acquire. The Whigs, who had neither made nor desired the war, were conscious that they faced political extinction if they failed to support it at this juncture. On the other hand, the presidential election of 1848 was likely to waft the Democrats back into office if Polk could successfully conclude the Mexican business. Whig strategy, therefore, was to attack Polk personally as the author of a thoroughly unjust war, while voting grants for supplies to American armies in the field.

This was not an easy line to maintain, nor was it likely to be popular in home districts still swept by war fever. Lincoln, an unknown congressman of little importance sitting in the back row on the Whig side of the House, might have voted quietly with his party without making himself conspicuous. He had not, however, come to Washington with the intention of remaining in the background. Owing to the system of rotation which he himself had established in Illinois, he could not look forward to a second term in Congress. It seems also clear that he was chiefly influenced in Washington by Whigs who really did speak for a portion of the people who disliked the war. Thus partly out of personal conviction and partly to distinguish himself among legislators who had a far stronger grip on their own constituencies, he put himself forward to introduce a series of resolutions intended to force the President to admit that Mexico had jurisdiction over the spot where the first clash had taken place. He reinforced these by a speech clarifying the issue and demanding an answer from Polk, who disdained to give it.

Lincoln's constituents in Illinois, whose contingent of "gallant heroes" had been led by the last two Whigs elected to Congress from Lincoln's district, were furious with their representative. The local Democratic paper seized on his resolution about the "spot" where blood was first shed to dub him "Spotty Lincoln" and to talk of him having an attack of "spotted fever" likely to prove fatal. Even a radical Whig like Billy Herndon wrote to Lincoln in a panic after a Whig vote condemning the President for his unjust war, but was answered: "Would you have voted what you knew to be a lie? I know you would not. Would you have gone out of the House—skulked the vote? I expect not."

Lincoln may have been right on principle, but as a matter of tactics his "spot" resolutions, his speech, and his vote were more likely to commend him to Whigs in Washington than to his constituents. He was diligent in his attendance and worked hard on his committees, besides voting for various Whig issues which were popular at home. Nevertheless his former partner, Stephen T. Logan, Whig candidate in his place, was defeated by his Democratic opponent. The Springfield Democrats attributed this to Lincoln's record rather than to Logan's fault, and both must have known that there was some justice in this.

The fact of the matter was that Lincoln was unlucky in his Congress. Not only was it dealing with war and expansion, two subjects on which Whigs frankly differed according to the section of the country from which they came, but it was chiefly concerned with the coming national election. It was customary for congressmen to make speeches which were neither interesting to the House nor listened to by its members, but which were printed and sent home to the congressman's district as election propaganda. Lincoln's next speech of any length in the House was on internal improvements, a subject on which the Whigs had long ago said all that it was possible to say, but one which remained perennially popular in Illinois. His greatest oratorical triumph was a speech delivered after the Democratic Convention had selected Lewis Cass for its 1848 candidate. This must have had the distinction of being one of the few of its kind that was actually listened to, not of course for its political merits, but because it was amusing. Both these speeches were sent back home in quantity and may have contributed to the success of the Whigs in the national election, though they could not save Lincoln's own seat for Judge Logan.

All in all the first session of the Thirtieth Congress, which lasted from the fourth of December, 1847, to August, 1848, was a do-nothing one. Polk had succeeded in making peace with Mexico on the basis of annexing not only Texas, but also

California and the Mexican territories later divided into New Mexico, Nevada, Utah, and Colorado. Gold had already been discovered in California, and the rush of prospectors thither made it very necessary to set up governments in the conquered areas. But the Thirtieth Congress, which had a Whig majority, did not propose to help a Democratic President solve the problems which his war had created. The Whigs had, they thought, an unbeatable candidate for President in 1848 and would prefer to have the kudos and also the jobs which belonged to the establishment of efficient government.

For all these reasons little was done in the pre-election session, and no opportunities arose for an obscure Whig to distinguish himself except in following the party line laid down by the leaders. Lincoln was, however, extremely active in promoting the candidacy of Zachery Taylor for the 1848 presidential election. It must have cost him a pang to realize that Henry Clay, leader and architect of the Whig party, had even less chance to win than in 1844. It was useless to run him. General Taylor, on the other hand, might be, and in fact was, swept into office as a popular war hero.

Unfortunately Taylor, "Old Rough and Ready," knew nothing to speak of about politics, was in favor of large annexations from Mexico, which the Whigs deplored, and was the owner of about a hundred slaves. The Whig party was not actually an anti-slave party and had the allegiance of southern slave-owners such as Robert Todd, Mary Lincoln's father. All the same its northern wing was pronouncedly against the spread of slavery, while its southern leaders, such as Clay, disliked the institution and had in several cases freed their own slaves. General Taylor had no personal qualifications for the office of President and actually opposed most of the "principles" on which Whig policy rested at the time. His only virtue was that he could be elected. Why then was Lincoln, whom we are accustomed to think of as a man of principle, active in Taylor's behalf from the beginning?

We can only guess at his motives, but several seem reasonable. Completely new to national politics, he was strongly influenced by the advice of leaders of his party. Moreover he had always been a party man rather than a man with a cause. He understood clearly that certain lines of policy are followed because groups of men with slightly different convictions can agree on general points of view. Once they refuse to do so, the party breaks up and the opposition has things entirely its own way. The success of the Whig party in electing Taylor, or indeed any other unsuitable candidate, must bring about a change not only in cabinet officers, but as we have seen, in administrators of every description throughout the land. This in itself was bound to affect policy.

A Whig President could cement the party together by the strong bond of patronage and power. He would attract hangers-on. He would possibly smooth the way for the election of a genuine Whig in 1852. Finally, the election of a President carries with it the election of many members of the same party both within individual states and to Congress. If all this might be accomplished by the election of a man like Taylor, it is understandable that the Whigs rallied behind him and that an ambitious man named "Honest Abe" could square it with his conscience to be very much in the forefront of the battle. We have to think of Lincoln, honest or not, as a man with a gift for politics, or in other words for getting done what he found possible.

Congress, as we have said, adjourned in August, and its members hastened to participate in the canvass for the coming election. Lincoln stayed in Washington for some weeks, sending out propaganda pamphlets on behalf of Taylor and followed this up by a speaking tour in Massachusetts, apparently at the invitation of a friend. He had already been appointed an "assistant elector" in Illinois, his duties being to make stump speeches throughout the state. He was not well received on his return to Illinois, and, as we have seen, his Whig constituency was lost to a Democrat. However, Edward D. Baker, returning as a war hero, was anxious to get a second term in Congress. Unable to contest the nomination of Logan for the district, he moved into a different area of the state and was successful. Thus the Illinois Whigs would, as before, have a single member in Congress.

The Thirtieth Congress reassembled on December 4 for the "lame-duck" session, which would last until the inauguration of President Taylor in March, 1849. For the second time the House was faced with the necessity of providing governments for the new territories, particularly for California, which was now ready to become a state. For the second time it was reluctant to act, not because the matter was not urgent, but because Congress preferred to have the work done by President Taylor and the initial appointments given to Whigs. The situation was further complicated by the attitude of the House toward slavery.

Already in the Twenty-ninth Congress David Wilmot, a Democrat from Pennsylvania, had proposed to add to the appropriation bill granting funds for the war a proviso prohibiting slavery in all territory to be acquired from Mexico. This immediately roused fierce debate, all Southerners opposing a measure which denied them equal rights in the exploitation of new lands, while northern opinion stiffened behind Wilmot on the grounds that the spread of slavery must be resisted.

In the first session of the Thirtieth Congress attention had been to some extent diverted from this issue by the imminence of the presidential election. With this question decided, however, the remaining months of Polk's administration were given up to the slavery controversy. Lincoln later claimed that he had voted for the Wilmot Proviso under one form or another "as good as forty times." Since House records only show that he did so on five occasions, it is clear that he must have been including petitions of various sorts in which he was active, caucus meetings, the matter of the slave trade in the District of Columbia which northern representatives thought a disgrace to the nation, and other peripheral affairs which immediately came up when slavery was in question. Militant Southerners under Calhoun organized a Southern party which warned that unless Northerners were prepared to grant them equal rights in the territories, to cease antislavery propaganda, and to pass an effective fugitive slave law, the South would have no recourse but to secede.

Among the legislators at Mrs. Spriggs's boarding-house was Joshua R. Giddings, one of the very few abolitionists in Congress. Giddings, though like most abolitionists a fanatic, was a man of attractive personal qualities who was respected by many people who did not share his opinions. Among them was Lincoln, who often used jokes and stories to calm the atmosphere when arguments between Giddings and fellow members of the boarding-house grew heated.

Lincoln's own opinion on slavery remained what it had been, but he soon saw that the feeling in Congress when slavery came up was far more intense than it was in the free state of Illinois. The rising fury of the controversy prevented the transaction of even routine business, so that a fist fight broke out on the floor of the House and essential bills were only passed on the last day of the session by stopping the House clock at fifteen minutes before midnight and prolonging the session until seven the next morning.

Thus Lincoln had two experiences on the subject of slavery which were novel to him. He was able to make a friend of an abolitionist fanatic who was a more attractive and convincing man than Billy Herndon, hitherto his closest associate with abolitionist opinions. He was also made aware of the dangerous pitch of feeling between the North and South upon this subject, especially in relationship to the new territories belonging to the nation. He did not say much in this session; and his intention of introducing a bill to abolish slavery in the District of Columbia was never carried out, despite discussion with Giddings and other members of his boarding-house. Lincoln was, however, exposed to experiences which seem to have deepened his original conviction that slavery must be kept from spreading further and must eventually die away if the Union was to be preserved. In other words, it is possible, though we have no proof, that Lincoln went to Congress as a party politician and emerged from it as a man with a settled conviction which might in time and irrespective of party feeling become a "cause."

Whether this was so or not, Lincoln had no further part in solving the slavery question in this session. The controversy was handed over to the Thirty-first Congress, which succeeded under the leadership of Henry Clay and Stephen A. Douglas in working out the Compromise of 1850, settling outstanding differences for the time being. Lincoln, both during the lame-duck session and thereafter, chiefly concerned himself with quite another problem which was purely partisan. The election of Taylor meant, as we have seen, a change in administration, not merely in Washington, but throughout the land. Lincoln, who was not by choice a constitutional reformer, accepted the patronage system as he found it, believing it, as indeed it was, the cement which bound a political party together. Lincoln was, as it happened, the only Illinois Whig in the present Congress. He had espoused the cause of Taylor from the beginning and had worked hard for him, while in Congress, during his Massachusetts trip, and in Illinois. No cabinet member from Illinois was contemplated by Taylor, but the preceding Commissioner of the Land Office, a very important civil servant, had been an Illinois Democrat, and it was understood that the post would be given to a Whig from Illinois.

Lincoln had a suitable candidate ready, since he considered it highly important to party morale that his services to Taylor should be recognized by the appointment of his man. Taylor tended to share this view, but his Secretary of the Interior, Ewing, who had received an angry letter from Springfield complaining that Lincoln's record had lost Logan the election, was less favorably disposed to him. This might not have mattered, had not Edward D. Baker, sole Illinois Whig in the Thirty-first Congress, demanded a say in the patronage and —not liking Lincoln's candidate for purely personal reasons —put forward one of his own. Naturally various others took this as a signal to advance candidates, some of them people who were not even from Illinois. By far the most diligent, however, was a man called Justin Butterfield, an Illinois Whig, to be sure, but one who had not even supported Taylor, having voted obstinately for Clay. To appoint such a man would be a slap in the face for every Illinois Whig who had reluctantly followed the party line. So many were the testimonials Butterfield collected that on Lincoln's return to Springfield, friends implored him to ask for the office himself. He at least could not be denied, while it was evident that his and Baker's candidates offset each other.

Conscientiously Lincoln asked for the withdrawal of the candidate to whom his word was pledged and prepared to return to Washington in a hurry in order to urge his claim in person. At this inconvenient moment, however, he received the following letter from his stepbrother John Johnston:

Dear Brother:
    I hast to inform you that father is yet a Live & that is all & he Craves to See you all the time & he wants you to Come if you ar able to git hure, for you are his only

Child that is of his own flush & blood & it is nothing
more than natere for him to crave to See you, he says he
has all most Despared of seeing you, & he wonts you to
prepare to meet him in the unknown world, or in heven,
for he thinks that ower Savour Savour has a crown of
glory, prepared for *him* I wright this with a bursting
hart. I Came to town for the Docctor, & I want you to
make an effort Come, if you are able to get hure, & he
wonts me to tell your wife that he Loves hure & wants
hur to prepare to meet him at ower Savours feet, we are
all well, your Brother in hast

J. D. Johnston

The letter was backed up by one from Augustus Chapman,
husband of Harriet Hanks, apparently written at the instance
of Johnston, rather than after visiting the old man, as it says:
"I am told that His Cries for you for the last few days are truly
Heart-Rendering. . . ."

Three days later Chapman, having talked with the doctor,
concluded that Thomas had not had a heart attack as had been
suspected, was a great deal better, and would doubtless be
well in a short time. By then, however, Lincoln was on his
way to see his father. How he felt when he found the old man
fairly well at a moment when his own presence was urgently
needed elsewhere we can only guess. Nor do we know
whether money for the doctor and other sums were demanded at a time when Lincoln had an expensive journey to
face. We can only wonder if the episode contributed to his
refusal to visit Thomas on his deathbed two years later.

Eventually Lincoln went off to Washington, but his errand
was unsuccessful. Whether he would have been named Commissioner of the Land Office had he arrived earlier we do not
know. The appointment went to the detested Butterfield to
the great discouragement of every important Whig in Illinois.

Someone seems to have drawn it to Taylor's attention that Lincoln had been badly treated. It was Taylor's practice to allow his cabinet ministers to make the appointments which went with their departments, and for this reason he had not insisted on Lincoln's being preferred to Butterfield. It seems, however, to have been at his suggestion that Lincoln was offered the position of governor of the Oregon Territory, a claim to which had been established by negotiations with England under Polk.

The governorship was not only in itself an important job, but it had political implications. Many a governor of a territory had, like the father of Ninian W. Edwards, become the first senator of a new state. Lincoln, however, was most unlikely to gain this distinction, since the territory was known to be strongly Democratic. It owed its existence to Polk, whose first governor had been popular. Unless Lincoln was ready to give up his political ambitions he would be wise to decline the post. It was also said that Mary Lincoln objected to bringing up her children in the wilderness and to undertaking a difficult journey with two small children, the youngest of whom was not strong. Though Lincoln refused the appointment, the offer gave a demonstration of his importance and that of the Illinois Whigs to the new government.

Having no discernible political future at the time, Lincoln devoted his energies once more to his profession, which was changing with the development of Illinois.

9
Lincoln, Lawyer in the Fifties

THE GROWTH OF ILLINOIS in the 1830s was remarkable; in the 1840s it was extraordinary; in the 1850s it was fantastic. Chicago, which in 1830 had a population of less than a hundred, numbered over six hundred thousand a generation later. The Irish potato famine of 1846–48 flooded the country with illiterate immigrants who, avoiding the South because of the competition of Negro labor, found employment on the railroads, bridges, and canals, whose construction was linking up the Midwest with eastern markets. Europe, seething like a boiling pot under the reaction which followed Napoleon's defeat, exploded in 1848 in a series of revolutions which, especially in Germany, proved abortive. Progressive Germans, some highly educated, followed the Irish to America. Foreign-speaking, but possessed of a rich cultural tradition, they tended to cluster in communities which rapidly spread over northern Illinois into Iowa and Wisconsin. Meanwhile the Gold Rush in California, the repeal of the Corn Laws in England, and the outbreak of the Crimean War in Europe sustained an increasing demand for American farm produce and aided the mechanization of agriculture in the prairies.

Politically speaking the early fifties were years in which Lincoln seemed to act as though his public career were closed. He refused renomination to the Illinois legislature and took little interest in a proposal that he run for governor. He made only perfunctory efforts on behalf of the Whig nominee for President in 1852, General Winfield Scott. He welcomed the settlement between North and South engineered by Douglas and Clay in 1850. This abolished the slave trade (though not slavery) in the District, accepted California as a free state, organized the territories of New Mexico and Utah without mention of slavery one way or the other, put through a tough fugitive slave law and gave federal courts jurisdiction over it to prevent states from passing personal-liberty laws to protect escapers. The slavery controversy sank, for a passing moment, into insignificance; but Henry Clay died in 1852, when an era in party alignments came to an end.

The death of the Whig party had already been foreshadowed by the election of Zachary Taylor in 1848, which had alienated many of Clay's followers. It was accelerated by the death of Taylor, which left the Presidency to Millard Fillmore, a man of no more Whiggish views than Taylor and much less strength of character. With the death of Henry Clay following hard on these events, the Whigs had no recourse but to nominate another war hero, General Winfield Scott, for 1852, hoping that the same trick would work again. It did not do so; and no one including Lincoln ever really expected that it would. The Whigs suffered an electoral defeat which was conclusive.

As one of the two great national parties split into fragments, a great change came over the American electorate, particularly in the North. Irish immigrants, finding southern attitudes more tolerant than those of Puritan New England, tended to vote Democratic and were cheerfully prepared to accept a fee for doing so and to cooperate in the art of voting several times. The Germans, on the other hand, had fled their fatherland in search of freedom. Revolutionary in outlook and with no tradition of allegiance to the American Constitution, they felt that the statement that all men are created equal embodied a more important principle than law. They were outraged by slavery and impatient of obstacles to abolition. Their convictions had considerable influence in the Northwest, while the publication of *Uncle Tom's Cabin* in 1852 swept the whole North with a wave of anti-slavery sentiment.

As a further complication, native Americans, most of them Whigs infuriated by the sight of gangs of Irish Democratic voters paid off in sight of the polling places, had formed a secret society vowed to restrict immigrants from voting. This surfaced briefly in the early fifties as the American party, also dubbed the Know-Nothings because initiates were taught to reply to queries about their association with "I know nothing." Northern Whigs were divided by abolitionists and Know-Nothings, while southern Whigs were alienated by the former and suspicious of the intolerance of the latter. With the loss of Henry Clay, the Whigs fell to pieces as a national party.

It is not perfectly fair to say that Lincoln's resolution to stay out of politics for the time being was merely a result of his unpopular record in Congress. He was doing after all no more than many a Whig who had no longer an effective party organization. He upheld the settlement of 1850, the last great work of Henry Clay, even to the extent of supporting the fugitive slave law, though hoping that its severities would be modified in time. He made no effort to hitch himself onto the rising American party and said nothing which could offend foreigners, especially Germans, whom he was learning to respect. Naturally he hoped that the Whigs would revive, but for the moment he was a politician without a party, condemned to be inactive because the conditions for a political career did not exist.

For the present Lincoln had plenty to do as a lawyer. He still rode the circuit, but no longer on horseback or even in a buggy. Railroads were coming to Illinois, and more were talked of. They were becoming faster than stagecoaches, had roofed over their passenger cars, improved their roadbeds, re-designed their tenders to prevent the sudden freeze-up of water pipes in winter, and were beginning to cope with snow over six inches deep. They were putting stagecoaches out of business, threatening river traffic, and building bridges to take the place of ferry boats. A railroad was a big corporation which could afford to engage local lawyers to protect its interests, seldom offering a retainer, but giving a free pass for travel and paying larger fees for important cases than lawyers had hitherto earned.

In 1853 the county of McLean voted to tax the property of the Illinois Central Railroad, whose charter from the legislature provided that it should be free from local taxes on condition that it pay 7% of its gross earnings to the state. Lincoln took the case for the railroad, argued it in the McLean circuit court before a local jury and, not surprisingly, lost. If the judgment had been allowed to stand, every county through which the railroad passed would have imposed taxes to the tune of millions of dollars. Naturally Lincoln appealed to the state supreme court, where he won a decision in favor of the railroad.

He presented a bill for two thousand dollars to the Chicago agent of the Illinois Central, who said that was as much as Daniel Webster himself would have charged, and paid him two hundred. Lincoln went home to consult his friends in Springfield, who told him to sue the railroad for five thousand dollars. Six of the highest priced lawyers in Illinois gave him a statement that five thousand dollars was not unreasonable considering the service he had rendered. He got his money, though the officers of the railroad said that paying a fee of that size to a mere western lawyer would embarrass the board of directors in New York. Perhaps it did, but the Illinois Central found Lincoln so useful that five months later they employed him again.

The Rock Island Railroad built a bridge over the Mississippi which was fifteen hundred feet long and was the target of abuse from every steamboat which carried freight on the river. In 1856 the *Effie Afton* rammed a pier, caught fire, and burned to the water's edge, setting alight part of the bridge, which fell into the river. The owners of the *Effie Afton* were delighted to sue the railroad for causing an obstruction to navigation. The case was a technical one, full of discussion of the angles of the piers, the current of the river, and the actions of the pilot of the *Effie Afton*. Lincoln, who acted as attorney for the Rock Island as well as the Illinois Central, confounded the opposition by the accuracy of his knowledge about technical details, in which he took an unfailing interest. He pointed out, moreover, that the railroad had hauled over twelve thousand freight cars and seventy-four thousand passengers across the river in eleven months, whereas the Mississippi was frozen at that point for four months of the year. This east-west traffic, which was opening up the farmlands of Iowa, had its rights just as much as the traffic north and south. The jury disagreed on a verdict, but the judgment was a victory for the railroad. The *Effie Afton* failed to get damages and did not try again.

Cases like these were giving Lincoln a reputation as a result of which he was hired in a very big case indeed which was tried in Cincinnati and which concerned two Illinois firms making reaping machines, that of Cyrus H. McCormick and that of John H. Manny. McCormick charged that Manny was infringing his patents and had demanded four hundred thousand dollars in damages as well as the closing of the Manny factory. A judgment for McCormick would soon have forced the closing of other businesses besides that of Manny. There were a couple of big eastern lawyers hired to defend Manny, but it was thought best to have an Illinois man as well. Testimony had already been taken, and Lincoln prepared his argument with care. One of the eastern lawyers was a man called

Edwin M. Stanton from Pittsburgh, who in the course of time would be Lincoln's Secretary of War.

Stanton was a hard man to get along with. When his eyes fell on Lincoln wearing, as he later said, a dirty linen duster for a coat, "on the back of which perspiration had splotched wide stains that resembled a map of the continent," he asked, "Where did that long-armed baboon come from?," adding that he would not associate with "such a damned, gawky, long-armed ape as that." Rudely he froze out Lincoln, denying him a chance to marshal the arguments over which he had taken such pains. In the circumstances most men would have left the courtroom. Lincoln remained for a week to learn what he could from the eastern lawyers and came to the conclusion that they were good. As he divided his two-thousand-dollar fee with Billy Herndon, he mildly complained that he had been roughly handled by "that man Stanton." No one had a better memory when he chose, but he did not nurse a grudge against "that man."

Another man with a future whom Lincoln met in the fifties was George B. McClellan, soon to be Lincoln's general-in-chief. McClellan was a West Pointer who became chief engineer of the Illinois Central Railroad in 1857. Since the job involved a good deal of traveling, McClellan and Lincoln met several times, waiting over in some country station at night or traveling together. The brisk young West Pointer, nearly twenty years younger than Lincoln, saw no genius in the clumsy, self-educated lawyer. Lincoln for his part seems to have noted merely that the young engineer was capable. Lincoln's railroad cases were less often technical than suits for unpaid subscriptions, which meant that he had little reason to work with McClellan in any way which would bring the two closer together.

His corporation work did not prevent him from suing a railroad on behalf of one of their brakemen who lost a leg on

the job. Many of his cases still involved unimportant persons
rather than great ones. Lincoln's stepbrother John Johnston
had a crippled son, Tom, who was jailed in Urbana for stealing. Lincoln told a friend that he was going to help the boy
out this once, but never again. He persuaded the complain-
ants not to press the case and got the boy released. His old
friend Jack Armstrong, formerly the leader of the rowdy
Clary's Grove boys, had twin sons who appear to have taken
after their father. One of them, Duff Armstrong, had a
drunken row with a man called Metzker, who died a few days
later from hemorrhage caused by a blow on the head. Duff
was arrested at the instance of a witness named Charles Allen,
who swore he had seen a fight between Duff and Metzker
between ten and eleven at night, but illuminated by the light
of the moon straight overhead. Duff had hit Metzker with a
slingshot and then thrown it away. Allen had picked it up.
Lincoln found a witness who had thrown away a slingshot the
day after the supposed fight. It had been one he had made
himself, and he identified it clearly as the one in Allen's
possession. Lincoln then brought out an almanac to show that
on the night in question the moon had set before midnight
and must have been too low in the sky to illuminate the scene
as Allen claimed. His appeal to the jury was an eloquent
account of his friendship with the Armstrongs, whom he
knew well as good people who worked hard, made their mis-
takes, but were the salt of the earth. As the jury filed out, he
assured Hannah Armstrong that her son would be free by
sundown, and he was right.

At times his common sense feelings of right and wrong got
the better of his instincts as a lawyer. A poor old farmer's
wife, Melissa Goings, had hit her husband on the head with
a billet of wood as he was trying to strangle her in a drunken
fury. Everybody who knew Goings sympathized with
Melissa, but the court seemed to have made up its mind to get

a conviction for murder. Lincoln, her attorney, got permission to have a private conference with her in the courthouse. How long that conference went on nobody quite knew, but Melissa Goings was never seen again. The court bailiff accused Lincoln of helping her escape, but he answered airily, "Oh no, Bob. I did not run her off. She wanted to know where she could get a good drink of water, and I told her there was mighty good water in Tennessee." On an earlier occasion, he had answered a possible client as follows: "Yes, we can doubtless gain your case for you; we can set a whole neighborhood at loggerheads; we can distress a widowed mother and her six fatherless children and thereby get for you six hundred dollars to which you seem to have a legal claim, but which rightfully belongs, it seems to me, as much to the woman and her children as it does to you. You must remember that things legally right are not morally right. We shall not take your case, but will give you a little advice for which we will charge you nothing. You seem to be a sprightly, energetic man; we would advise you to try your hand at making six hundred dollars in some other way."

Lincoln's attitude towards fees was fairly easygoing. He did not care to take much money from people who, he felt, could not afford it. A man arrested for stealing a horse asked for Lincoln to help in his defense. Lincoln went to the jail with the prisoner's attorney and found the man's pregnant wife was with him. The prisoner handed over ten dollars, saying that was all the money he had, whereupon Lincoln asked, "How about your wife? Won't she need this?"

"She'll get along somehow."

Lincoln handed the woman five dollars and divided the other five with his fellow lawyer.

There are many stories of this kind, illustrating Lincoln's good nature and unwillingness to take advantage of people in need. In addition he would not ask more than he thought his services were worth, estimating these not infrequently by the standards of his earlier days on the circuit. A Chicago firm for whom he had won a suit in Springfield netting them several thousand dollars got a bill for $25.00 and wrote to the banker who had enlisted Lincoln's services: "We asked you to get the best lawyer in Springfield, and it certainly looks as if you had secured one of the cheapest." To a man who mailed him a check for twenty-five dollars for handling a lease, Lincoln wrote: "You must think I am a high-priced man. You are too liberal with your money. Fifteen dollars is enough for this job. I send you a receipt for fifteen dollars and return to you a ten-dollar bill." It was not his habit to take his full fee in advance, though in large cases he accepted a retainer; but he made an exception for clients who lived far off, remarking that if he did not do so, he was apt to get nothing for his work. "We, therefore, are growing a little sensitive on that point."

It is fair to say that Lincoln thought himself entitled to what he did charge and that he brought suit on various occasions against clients who proved unwilling to pay. On the other hand, he often did not like asking a good friend for money until he really got short. He wrote an acquaintance to get him fifty dollars from Colonel Dunlap, who had asked how much he owed and had been put off. Lincoln was now in need of cash and did not think the colonel would consider this fee unreasonable. He told another friend he would not charge him at the time, but possibly some day he might ask him for something. Sure enough, he turned up late at night a good while later and wanted a hundred dollars at once. His partner, Herndon, on one of his periodical drunken sprees had landed in jail; and Lincoln needed a hundred dollars to bail him out.

When he did collect fees, he divided them with Herndon the moment he got back to the office. The partners did not keep books, and Lincoln explained that if he waited he might forget to give Herndon his share or forget who had paid it. Besides he might die any day, and Herndon would have no evidence that he was owed anything.

It was an important test of a good lawyer in those days that he should be ready for all emergencies. Lincoln's knowledge of law was never profound, but he knew when to use his common sense and when to put in long evenings of work in the Illinois Supreme Court library. To some extent also he relied on Billy Herndon, who did a good deal of the routine work of looking up precedents and complained sometimes that he did this drudgery while Lincoln got the credit. This may partly have been so, but there is no doubt that judged by the importance and the actual number of cases Lincoln handled as well as by the percentage he won, by the middle fifties he was the leading man of the Illinois bar. Surprisingly, considering the amount he got done, he remained a slow worker who needed time to make up his mind. Even in court his manner was leisurely. Herndon was always telling him to speak "with more vim," but Lincoln merely answered that when he did produce a thought, it had force enough to cut its own way and travel further.

Herndon remained devoted to Lincoln, but there is no doubt that in certain ways he found him trying. He did not think Lincoln's jokes funny and never could understand how his partner could tell the same story to four visitors in the course of a morning and laugh as heartily when he came to the climax the fourth time as he had the first. Instead of humor, Herndon had enthusiasms. He took up temperance, abolition, philosophy, or some other subject, and he wanted Lincoln to read all about them too. Lincoln did not read many books except for the purposes of study, but he read the local papers right through and a good many others. In fact he liked to spend the first hour of the working day stretched out on the shabby couch in the office reading the local paper aloud.

When Herndon protested, he said he could remember it better that way.

Neither partner ever considered cleaning the office, which got literally dirty enough to grow grass in a corner. An early letter from Lincoln apologizes for having lost a client's letter: "I put it in my old hat, and by buying a new one the next day, the old one was set aside, and so, the letter lost sight of for a time." Herndon was not much more systematic, but even Herndon got annoyed when on Sundays Lincoln brought two of his boys to the office with him and never reproved them when they spilled the ink or broke the pens, made darts out of documents, or wrestled together, upsetting furniture.

No boys ever were as spoiled as the Lincoln boys in Herndon's view. Mary herself said that neither she nor their father ever whipped them because they never needed it. The truth is that she did start out by correcting Robert and may have done so with Eddie, who died in February, 1850, after an illness of nearly eight weeks, apparently of diphtheria. Mary was inconsolable, collapsing into endless weeping and refusing food except when coaxed by her husband. Lincoln bore his loss better. Melancholy was a settled habit with him; but in a certain sense he had got the better of "hypo" in that he had learned how to work and talk and even laugh in spite of it. He started, however, attending church with Mary to support her in this time of mourning and found that the pastor of the First Presbyterian Church, James Smith, was a different kind of clergyman from the backwoods revivalists he had known in the past. He encouraged Dr. Smith to call and liked to talk over religious subjects with him. He even rented a pew and, though not a regular churchgoer, enjoyed mulling over the ideas which Smith presented to his congregation.

It had always been somewhat of a drawback to Lincoln, considered as a politician, that he was not a churchgoer in a period when a "good" man was conventional in these matters.

To some extent this remained true, yet Lincoln on almost
every page of his political writings stands out as a man whose
convictions have a moral and religious base. There is no
doubt, however, that the loss of Eddie and the necessity of
comforting Mary began to bring him more in tune with the
conventional attitudes of his day. The Civil War was to
deepen reflections which had begun at this time.

Less than two months after Eddie's death Mary was again
pregnant; and her third son, William Wallace (after her sister
Frances' husband), was born in December. Her fourth and
last in 1853 was christened Thomas, a little surprisingly, considering Lincoln's detached attitude towards his father. He
was immediately nicknamed "Tadpole" by Lincoln because
of his big head and little body. This was soon shortened to
Tad, by which name he was known for the rest of his life.
Willie and Tad, separated by seven years from Robert, pretty
soon formed a team which was not only inseparable but in the
eyes of many observers a terrible nuisance. The loss of Eddie
seems to have made both parents too tender-hearted to discipline the younger boys. Tad, who had a cleft palate, spoke
almost unintelligibly to strangers. Mary, protective of him,
liked to keep him a baby, unable to dress himself, unwilling
to learn reading, but an original mischief-maker who took the
lead from Willie when it came to thinking of something fresh
to do. Whether for Mary's sake or from his own choice Lincoln said that there was plenty of time for the boys to learn
when they really wanted to. He was always willing to be
climbed up or rolled over, indulgent with pennies, and never
too busy for little boys when he was at home. Robert, however, later complained that his father was either on circuit or
campaigning during practically all of his childhood.

Despite his moderate fees, by the fifties Lincoln was making a good income in Springfield terms; Mary was at last able
to buy herself silk for a gown. She had two servants in the

house, which had been raised to two stories and was furnished conventionally with patterned wallpaper, solid pieces, and looped draperies which trailed upon the floor. When the circuit court or the legislature sat in Springfield, the Lincolns repaid hospitality to people who had entertained Lincoln on his circuit travels. Mary still had her likes and dislikes, but she was an excellent hostess in her own house, setting a good table and conversing with intelligence and spirit. She read a good deal, kept up her French, and aired opinions which were usually vehement, but often clever. She was obviously devoted to her husband and concerned to show her pride in the man she had married. It was Mary who said he would be President some day, long before other people saw anything but folly in the notion. She and her husband took a normal part in the balls and dinner parties of Springfield's social season. All this had come gradually, restrained by Lincoln's desire for simple living. He was still economical, causing his wife to complain that he never gave her any money, so that she had to raid his wallet for what she needed. Perhaps he did not understand how much things cost; quite probably he did not see the need for a style of living which Mary thought important. Would he for instance have sent formal invitations to fifty little boys for a birthday party for Willie?

Lincoln was a man who preferred to save rather than to spend. Fundamentally he was right in this because he was getting on toward fifty and had old age to think of as well as three young sons to start in life. It is fair, however, to say that Judge David Davis of the Eighth Circuit, investing shrewdly in land and finding opportunity in Illinois's phenomenal growth, made himself a millionaire. Lincoln with equal opportunities preferred to lend his money out at ten percent, either on mortgage or to help small tradesmen whom he personally knew. In addition Lincoln's political activities had interfered in the past and were soon in the future to interfere again with his legal work. The result was that in 1860 he was worth about fifteen thousand dollars, most of which was invested in ways which did not make it readily available. He spoke after one campaign of having hardly enough for his domestic needs. What was Mary to do but run up debts if a raid on her husband's wallet found it empty? Tradesmen thought her anxious to beat their charges down and called her stingy. The truth was that she fought to keep up her position and was determined that her sons should be brought up as gentlemen.

By his middle forties a man's character is at least in outline developed, but no one yet realized Lincoln's possibilities. Even the microscopic examination which has by the present time been given to every known action of his life cannot fairly point to him at that particular stage as a man capable of, or even likely to achieve, the Presidency in a time of great national crisis. He was, however, in a certain sense a lucky man because the enormous development of Illinois, the transition from log cabins to industrial towns, from wooden spades to mechanical reapers took place at a time in his life when many people settle back. It faced him as a lawyer with situations which were increasingly complex, bringing him into contact with men of large capacities. He might have proved unequal to the challenge and sunk into the position of a reliable, second-class lawyer. But Lincoln rose to an opportunity which was, even in the context of his own time, unusual. It happened that he was the kind of man to make the most of it. In the Manny-McCormick reaper case, Ralph Emerson, one of Manny's partners, knew Lincoln well and watched him listening to the court proceedings from which he had been rudely ejected. When the hearing ended, Emerson and Lincoln walked down toward the river together. "I am going home to study law!" exclaimed Lincoln repeatedly. That, replied Emerson, was what he had been previously doing. "No, not as these college bred men study it," Lincoln answered. "I have learned my lesson. These college bred fellows have reached Ohio; they will soon be in Illinois, and when they come, Emerson, I will be ready for them." In other words, he continued to develop his powers of comprehension, logic, and expression with the same concentration that he had used since his boyhood. He was interested in the power of words as well as logic. Instead of Euclid and algebra, he took Shakespeare around on the circuit, and it is notable that when he returned to politics in the middle fifties, his oratorical powers had greatly matured.

Some of Lincoln's growth was visible to his contemporaries, but rarely did he talk of his purposes as freely as he had done to Emerson. Having learned in boyhood to keep his own counsel among men who did not sympathize with his ambitions, he had brought to perfection the politician's trick of fending people off. An awkward question or a casual meeting reminded him equally of a little story which had to be told whether his companion liked it or not. Once he had the conversation on his own ground, Lincoln was a master at keeping it there as long as he wished. Even to Billy Herndon, with whom he spent so much of his time, he very seldom broke into reminiscence or talked freely about personal feelings and ambition. Even his learning was carefully disguised. He knew, for instance, many more classical tales than those of Aesop, but wove them into what he said under the pretext that "somebody had once told him about a man who. . . ."

For all of these reasons, though most of Lincoln's friends of the fifties survived him, few knew him well enough to sum him up. Rather they fixed upon some part of his character and tried to explain it. "O Lord wasn't he funny!" exclaimed one of his fellow circuit riders. "Melancholy dripped from him as he walked," said his partner Herndon. Others at various times saw him lapse for half an hour or more into abstraction so profound that he noticed nothing of what was going on before his eyes. Young law students stressed his willingness to take time to give them advice. His honesty continued to make an indelible impression, even among men equally high-minded. It was not that he refused a case which might turn out a bad one, or that he was not ready to give his client the benefit of the doubt like any other lawyer. It was, as it had always been, the quality of his manners which drew attention to this characteristic. Once, for instance, he brought suit for a client to recover a debt, only to find that at the trial the defendant could produce a receipt in full. He withdrew from the courtroom. The judge sent to the tavern after him, and he answered: "Tell the Judge I can't come—my hands are dirty and I came over to clean them."

An intensely popular man, he was no back-slapper. His friends called him Lincoln and only the country folk he met on the circuit addressed him as "Abe."

Throughout his life Lincoln had shown strength of character and moral courage in learning to live with and master his melancholy moods, in standing up for principles of law and order, in refusing to conform to religious conventions which did not mirror his private opinions. None of these, except perhaps the first, are unusual accomplishments. They were simply Lincoln's response to varied situations which other men have faced without achieving greatness. Compared with contemporary great men like Stephen A. Douglas he seemed singularly lacking in enterprise and dash. It is impossible to know how far he was conscious that life had not yet demanded of him all that he could give, since he refrained from discussing what he aimed for. Herndon says his ambition was unsleeping—but what is ambition? Is it desire for high place? Is it a drive for self-improvement? Is it desire for a job which a man may feel within his capacity? Ambition varies with the man, and Herndon was very often at fault in his judgment of others. As far as we can tell, in the early fifties Lincoln realized that the break-up of the Whig party had destroyed his chance of political advancement. He could certainly become a successful lawyer, but it was not likely that a legal reputation would take him beyond Illinois. People who set out to carve a niche for themselves must very often be content with a smaller one than they once expected. If Lincoln's melancholy moods were ever caused by the knowledge that he was not fulfilled by his profession, he would have been the last man to admit it, even to Herndon.

10

The Founding of
the Republican Party, 1854-56

────────⋘◉⋙────────

LINCOLN'S RETURN TO POLITICAL LIFE and his swift rise to fame
were both brought about by Stephen A. Douglas, though
much against Douglas's wishes and intentions. By 1854 the
"Little Giant" was one of the most distinguished men in the
Senate, where he was regarded as a fixture until he found an
opportunity for moving on to the Presidency. Franklin
Pierce, who occupied the White House at that moment, was
one of the weakest of a series of undistinguished Presidents
and had been nominated because during a period of political
controversy he had been inactive enough to make few enemies. Pierce was southern-dominated but Douglas stood out
as the ablest leader of the northern wing of the Democratic
party. The Democrats were now almost unchallenged by organized opposition, yet they needed to beware lest the growing North-South rift which had destroyed the Whigs endan-
ger their own existence as a national party.

It was in these circumstances that Douglas headed the important Senate Committee on Territories, which handled the
future of the undeveloped regions of the country. In 1852–53
a bill was introduced in Congress for the organization of the
Nebraska Territory, in other words, of the future states of
Kansas and Nebraska. The bill was referred to the Committee
on Territories, which knew that decision was urgent because
an east-west railroad linking California to the rest of the

United States was being planned. If the Nebraska Territory could be organized in time, the railroad would go that way to the benefit of the northern section of the country. Otherwise it would take a longer, southerly route, which would of course bring profit to the South. Douglas, as a representative of Illinois, favored the northern route but as a politician he understood that he could not expect to get it without making concessions to the South.

Up to this point, northern thinking on the subject of Kansas and Nebraska had been governed by the Missouri Compromise of 1820 which during over thirty years of controversy had been regarded as a fixed and definite North-South settlement. It had provided that Missouri be admitted as a slave state, but that slavery should not be legal in any other territory to be developed above the 36° 30′ parallel. Unfortunately southern support of the Compromise had declined, since the future of Missouri as a slave state was no longer in question. The continued development of cotton plantations in the deep South had emphasized the shortage of slaves which resulted from the banning of the African slave trade. It is true that some slaves continued to be smuggled from Africa as late as 1860, but prices had gone up steeply, making the breeding and selling of slaves an important part of the cash income of farmers in Virginia, Maryland, Kentucky, and even Missouri. For this reason, it was not convincing to argue that the Nebraska area was more suitable for corn than cotton and, therefore, unfit for slavery. It was just across the Missouri River from the state of that name and might easily develop a mixed economy of farming and slave breeding.

Douglas was aware that the Missouri Compromise had been considered sacred in his home state since 1820, but he was also determined to get the northern transcontinental railroad. He came, moreover, to the conclusion that a stroke of policy was needed to lift the nation above the controversy of slave

state versus free. He wished to pave the way for further expansion through the acquisition of Cuba, American efforts to
spread south to Panama, or the conquest of Canada right up
to the Arctic Circle.

As a patriot Douglas saw the American experiment in
democracy as a government founded by white men for the
benefit of themselves. The prospect of acquiring Cuban slaves
or Mexican Indians in a state of peonage did not disturb him.
Outraged, however, by the conservatism of the current em-
pires of Spain, France, Prussia, and Austria, he was eager to
drive European oppressors of free, white people out of the
New World. Of Britain he thought little better, never having
appreciated the slow progress of that country toward democracy which was to culminate in the Reform Bill of 1867. Essentially Douglas saw plenty for America to spend her energies
on. Warned, however, by the controversies which had arisen
from the gains of the Mexican War, he wished first to put
forward some principle which rose above bargaining in Congress about whether new lands should be slave or free. The
important thing to Douglas was that they should be American.

The Nebraska Bill as originally reported out of committee
contained the provision that the people of the territory should
decide the question of slavery for themselves. This might just
possibly have been accepted as a basis for discussion on the
grounds that Utah and New Mexico (the latter including
Nevada which, like Utah, was above the 36° 30′ parallel) had
been organized on these terms by Henry Clay's Compromise
of 1850. These conquests of the Mexican War, however, had
not belonged to the United States at the time of the Missouri
Compromise—made nearly thirty years earlier. Nebraska, on
the other hand, was covered by the Missouri Compromise.
Besides, it was far more likely that Missouri farmers would
take their slaves into Kansas and Nebraska than that the

South, which had Texas to spread into, would combine to make slave states out of Utah and Nevada. The Nebraska proposal was thus in a real sense a new policy. That the South accepted it as such became clear when southern radicals insisted on a clause explicitly repealing the Missouri Compromise. Without this, they maintained, no slaveholder would dare to take his slaves into the Nebraska Territory.

Douglas was reluctant to agree, correctly predicting that open repeal would raise a "Hell of a storm." Not many years earlier he himself had assured his Illinois constituents that the Compromise was sacred to the American people and that no one would ever disturb it. He realized, however, that his present plan implied repeal whether or not any statement was made on the subject.

Douglas was a man of great personal magnetism, a natural fighter, and a lover of bold action. Though he understood that he would raise a tumult, he thought that he was strong enough to dominate it. If he could assert himself as the man who had solved the question of slavery within the territories, he could make himself the leader of a united America ready to expand. The Kansas-Nebraska Bill went back into committee and was brought before the Senate in January, 1854, with a clause expressly repealing the anti-slavery provision of the Missouri Compromise.

A battle began to rage immediately, not only in Congress, but throughout the country. Democratic senators like Salmon P. Chase of Ohio accused Douglas of selling out to the South in order to further his ambition of becoming President. Northern "free-soilers" consisted of far more than abolitionists and clergy in whom the anti-slavery propaganda of the last few years had developed scruples. Every Northern man who wanted to go West feared the competition of Negro labor. Immigrants still pouring in, sons of the large families of New England farmers, adventurers, petty tradesmen, all understood that slaves in Kansas would give economic advantage to the man who could afford them. Editors of all northern papers, Whig, Democrat, Know-Nothing, or abolitionist, were for once unanimous in denouncing the bill.

Somewhat surprisingly, the South was not so deeply stirred by the concession which had been intended to purchase its support. The fact was that Southerners feared that northern hordes pouring into the territory would make the repeal of the Compromise a dead letter. In the Senate, however, southern representatives did rally behind the Pierce administration, which had determined to push the bill through as a matter of party discipline. But those who voted with Douglas left the fighting to the Little Giant, who proved equal to it all. Almost single-handed, Douglas pushed the Kansas-Nebraska Bill through the Senate by matchless oratory, masterly tactics, even by the sheer force of his fury as he trampled down the hesitations of northern Democrats frightened by rising opposition at home. After six weeks of struggle, culminating in seventeen continuous hours of session during which Douglas was almost constantly on his feet, the bill passed the Senate in the early morning hours of March 4. Eleven weeks later with Douglas as unofficial manager of administration forces it passed the House also.

Northern editors, clergyman, and even congressmen had hurried to denounce the bill while Douglas was engaged in his tremendous battle. Abraham Lincoln had not done so. Indeed he had spoken little on the subject even to close friends. He was turning it over in that slow-moving mind of his, examining from every angle the principle of self-determination as applied to the territories. When for instance would the decision about slavery take place? Would a thousand settlers, ten thousand, thirty thousand be sufficient to vote on whether slavery should exist in the area or not? What would become of the slaves already there if Kansas should reject the

Sarah Lincoln, stepmother of Abraham Lincoln. Sarah outlived her stepson, whom she described as the best boy in the world. Before Lincoln left for Washington, he made a special trip to say goodbye to his beloved "Mama."

The log cabin of Thomas and Sarah Lincoln in Goose Nest Prairie, Illinois. It is a double cabin with the chimney in the middle. The second half housed Lincoln's stepbrother, John D. Johnston, with his wife and eight children. The cabin was probably built in 1840, and the lack of windows implies real poverty since glass was generally available by that date.

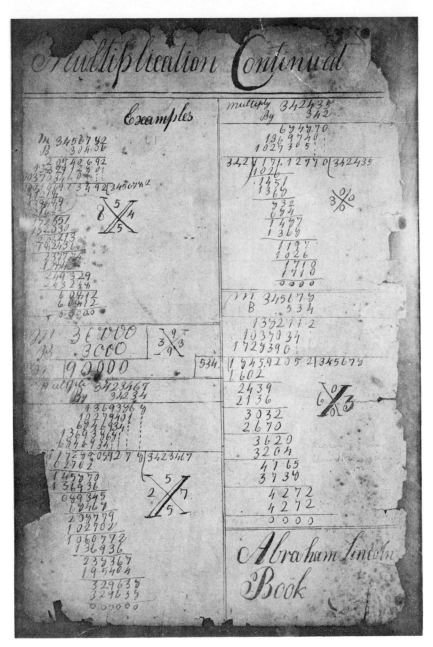

*A page from Lincoln's arithmetic book, showing
the earliest examples of his handwriting.*

*The Globe Tavern, Springfield, where Abraham and
Mary Lincoln started their married life.*

The earliest known portraits of Lincoln and his wife, Mary Todd, made about 1846. The portraits are daguerrotypes, an early type of photograph produced on a silver or silver-covered copper plate. Because of this method of reproduction only one copy of each picture could be made. The portraits hung in the Lincoln home. (Photographs of daguerrotypes courtesy of The Library of Congress.)

This shows the Lincoln house much as it looks today. The Lincolns added the second story some years after they had moved in.

A good example of a newspaper illustration of the Lincoln-Douglas debates.

The Old State House, Springfield, Illinois. This fine building was erected to house the state legislature when the capital was transferred from Vandalia. Lincoln's law office faced onto the square in which it stands.

The poster above, issued in September of 1860 and obviously pro-Lincoln, shows him easily outsprinting (from left) *Bell, Breckinridge, and Douglas.*

A facsimile of the first letter carried over the plains by pony express, bearing the news of the election of Lincoln.

institution and eventually enter the Union as a free state? Was it fair in any case that a few settlers should decide a question about which the whole nation felt the deepest concern? Above all, if the Missouri Compromise could be brushed aside after thirty-four years, what permanent settlement of the slavery question could ever be made? With these thoughts, Lincoln went out on the circuit as usual and was in Urbana when the news arrived that the act had passed the Senate. He was aroused, he later said, as never before.

Lincoln had always been a party politician. He had canvassed for candidates who had been selected by a convention and were not his own personal choice. He had voted for Whig measures and had studied to make himself master of the arguments in their favor. He had done this out of no lack of conviction; his Whig principles were perfectly genuine. He had, however, accepted the fact that no individual can expect to shape the entire policy of the party he belongs to. He understood that politics is a form of bargaining. In return for one concession, you obtain another. But the Kansas-Nebraska Act found him in an entirely new situation. There was no longer an effective Whig party. There were only Democrats, ex-Whigs, free-soilers, abolitionists, Know-Nothings, and in a word just neighbors—all of whom had to make up their individual minds about an issue which was equally new to all. Abraham Lincoln was not a party representative, but a person who had to decide where he personally stood.

In some ways this was not difficult. Lincoln stood just where he did in 1837 when he had said that slavery was founded on injustice and bad policy, but that he did not believe the federal government had power to interfere with state property laws. He still supported the fugitive slave law, though he did not like its provisions. He foresaw no future time when the more populous North could force abolition on an unwilling South. He was, however, a man who had

steadily voted to uphold the Wilmot Proviso during the life
of the Thirtieth Congress and had not moved from this position. Slavery could not be interfered with where it existed,
but it must be prevented from spreading further. The more
Lincoln thought about the question, the more important he
found this particular principle. He could see no possible end
to slavery but a gradual withering away, which he admitted
might take a hundred years. The life of the institution would
be prolonged if it was allowed to spread into future states.
The Missouri Compromise had marked out a segment of the
country as permanently free. To repeal it meant a change of
direction which Lincoln must definitely oppose, whatever the
actual result in the states of Nebraska and Kansas. Nevada
and Utah had not been explicitly protected by the Compromise and might legally be left to become free states as a mere
matter of geography. The repeal of the Compromise, however, raised more than a particular point with regard to a
limited area of land. It embodied a principle. Had slave-
owners a right to move into any new territory? Since slavery
was wrong and must be encouraged in every lawful way to
die out, Lincoln's answer was, "No."

Lincoln's decision was not in the least unusual, and was
shared by many people who had tried to think the issue
through. In Lincoln's case, however, it was founded on two
important and to him immovable principles. Slavery was
wrong, but in no circumstances must the United States Constitution be sacrificed to right this wrong or any other. He
was impervious to the frantic emotions which caused other
people to say and do things which they would later regret.

Stephen A. Douglas had proved equal to riding the storm
in Congress, but he could not restrain guerilla warfare from
breaking out in Kansas almost as soon as it was opened to
settlers. Gangs of slavery men from Missouri, who soon
earned the title of "border ruffians," crossed the river, not to

settle the new land, but to stuff ballot boxes on election days and to harass the free-soilers who were coming in from the North. Northerners in their turn subscribed to societies dedicated to financing whole trains of indigent settlers for Kansas and, as the border ruffians grew more openly insolent, to arming them with rifles.

Soon the two parties set up rival governments, each complaining that the other side had refused to hold a fair election. Border ruffians thinly disguised as the posse of a pro-slavery U. S. Marshal invaded the town of Lawrence, center of the free-soil movement. They broke up printing presses, burned the hotel, and looted houses. John Brown retaliated by butchering five innocent pro-slavery settlers on Pottawatomie Creek. Horse stealing, cabin burning, tarring and cottoning (since the territory lacked chicken feathers) went on unchecked by the government, while southern adventurers came up to join the border ruffians against free-soilers subsidized by Yankee money. These events reverberated through the country painted in lurid colors, not only through prejudice, but because the combatants were too generally illiterate to send accurate reports. Furious emotions shook North and South alike, reflected and exaggerated by confrontations in Congress.

In 1854, Lincoln's convictions urged him to re-enter politics but did not clearly show him what to do. He spoke widely in Illinois for Richard Yates, who had voted against the Nebraska Bill in Congress and was standing for re-election. He himself and his ex-partner Logan agreed to rally Whig forces by standing for the legislature in the next election. These were, however, only stopgap measures. The real question was how the Whigs of Illinois were to proceed. They had three choices: to join the American or Know-Nothing party, to work for a revival of Whiggism, or to form part of an anti-Nebraska coalition which would be frankly sectional and northern. None of these was easy or at the moment attractive. The Whig party was perhaps not dead in Illinois, but in the South and border states the American party had badly eroded its strength. Illinois Whig leaders, perceiving that they needed the help of the German immigrants at the polls, could see no future in combining with an anti-foreign group like the Know-Nothings. On the other hand the Whigs, who had always gained the bulk of their support from well-to-do professional groups, were by nature conservative and strongly unwilling to join abolitionists and radical fanatics in a new party which did not represent the whole country.

In 1854 Lincoln's cautious temperament and his almost infallible political instinct inspired him to play a waiting game. He still called himself a Whig, making use of the party machinery which he had helped to build, but speaking boldly against the Nebraska bill and distinguishing himself mainly from his more radical allies by the moderation of his language. With his usual skill he found plenty to say without treading heavily on the toes of the Know-Nothings, without alienating the Germans, and without slamming a door in the face of northern Democrats whose anti-Nebraska feelings were inspiring them to question administration policy in Kansas. If a coalition was to be formed, the time to do it would be in 1856 when the chance of electing a presidential candidate might force cooperation between those who were at the moment too far apart to reason together. To change one's political allegiance too soon would be a disaster, resulting merely in loss of influence when decisions were made. If Lincoln went so far as to seek a new party, he wanted to form it along conservative lines. It was accordingly as a Whig that Lincoln took up the challenge when Douglas returned to Illinois to defend the repeal of the Compromise.

All the way home, the Little Giant had seen his effigy burned publicly in the streets of northern towns. His reception in Chicago was so threatening that his friends feared for his safety. A situation which would have frightened most men merely aroused him to announce well beforehand that he would speak in the North Market Hall in the middle of the Irish district on the first of September.

He had chosen his ground well. Douglas had spoken with his usual indignant force against the Know-Nothings, and the Irish were with him to a man. They let it be known through their political leaders that blood would flow if Douglas were roughly heckled. Rumor said that the Know-Nothings were arming themselves for a demonstration against Douglas, but more peaceful anti-Nebraskans felt too strongly to be frightened away by the prospect of a pitched battle. So many people attended that the Market Hall had to be given up, and Douglas spoke in the open air to a crowd jammed in the square and also into the windows, balconies, or on the rooftops of the buildings which overlooked it. The situation was favorable for hecklers, many of whom had entrenched themselves in places where Douglas's self-appointed bodyguard of Irish could not reach them. In consequence he was soon drowned out by groans, catcalls, and hisses. Douglas lost his temper and tried to shout the crowd down, but it was too big to be controlled. Eventually he shook his fist at the audience and retired, his speech undelivered.

Undaunted, Douglas went out on tour of the state, followed everywhere by opposition speakers. When he got to Bloomington, it was Lincoln's turn, and a joint debate was suggested. Douglas refused it. "I come to Chicago," he said. "I am met by an Abolitionist; I come to the center of the state and am met by an old-line Whig; I come to the South and am met by a Democrat. I can't hold the Whig responsible for what the Abolitionist says: I can't hold either responsible for what the Democrat says . . . This is my meeting." He had put his finger on the nub of his problem. He had to face opposition not from an organized party, but literally from everywhere. Lincoln, waiting until he had finished, announced that he would speak the very same evening.

Lincoln pursued the same tactics at the State Fair in Springfield and twelve days later in Peoria. Since Douglas was making essentially the same speech everywhere, Lincoln also advanced with the same series of arguments, delivered in substantially the same language. It was hot that fall, and Lincoln spoke in Springfield in shirtsleeves and without collar or tie. He presented the usual strange contrast to his well-dressed opponent, whose oratorical manner tended to violent gestures and deep bellowing tones as he threw back his mane of springing hair and brandished his clenched fists. The thesis of Douglas was that the Compromise of 1850 had substituted the principle of popular sovereignty for the concept of a geographical line marking off slave territory from free. This principle he had in good faith applied to Kansas and Nebraska, which were climatically as unfitted for the growth of slavery as Utah and New Mexico.

Lincoln began his answer haltingly. His voice, though excellently clear, was shrill whenever he raised it to address an audience and usually made a poor first impression. This was reinforced by his ungainly height and huge extremities, emphasized by his slack pose with hands clasped or hanging loosely. But he was not too nervous to raise a laugh in Peoria, where matters had been so arranged that Douglas, who had already spoken, should have an hour afterwards to rebut his arguments. Lincoln had consented, he said, "for I suspected if it were understood, that the Judge was entirely done, you Democrats would leave, and not hear me; but by giving him the close, I felt confident you would stay for the fun of hearing him skin me."

Quietly he began a lucid explanation of agreements controlling the spread of slavery from 1787 through the Louisiana

Purchase of 1803 and up to the time of the Missouri Compromise. Equally seriously he went through the troubles caused by the Mexican War and their settlement in the Compromise of 1850. This led him to the destruction of the Missouri Compromise. Having got his audience with him, he began to demonstrate the emotional powers which he possessed. As he warmed up, the animation of his features increased. He started to emphasize points by gestures which might seem clumsy at first but were soon discovered to be appropriate and even inspiring. It was an age when oratory tended to be grandiloquent, and Lincoln to emphasize an important statement would bend his knees and then slowly rise up to his full height with his arms lifted, demanding and receiving his applause.

His appeal was pitched to men's innate sense of fairness. The Kansas-Nebraska Act was wrong, not only in its repeal of a solemn compact, but in the principle on which it rested. This was, as Douglas himself freely admitted, that slavery did not matter one way or the other. If the people decided that it was to their advantage, they might have it. This was as much as to say that self-interest was the only right principle of free action.

Carefully distinguishing his own position from that of the abolitionist, Lincoln refrained from criticism of Southerners who had grown up with slavery. He personally in their place would act as they were doing. What was more, if all earthly power were given him at that moment, he would not know what to do with slavery in the states where it existed. This did not mean, however, that slaves ought to be admitted into places where the institution did not already flourish. Either the Negro was a man or he was not. If he was, then he was born with the right to self-government like other men.

No government, Lincoln insisted, could be anything but a despotism if it attempted to govern others without representation. Slavery had been born out of the selfishness of man's nature, and opposition to it out of his love of justice. "Repeal the Missouri Compromise—repeal all compromises—repeal the declaration of independence—repeal all past history, you still cannot repeal human nature. It still will be the abundance of man's heart, that slavery extension is wrong; and out of the abundance of his heart, his mouth will continue to speak."

He had roused their emotions, but he would not leave it so. The time to hammer is when the iron is hot. Lincoln the politician well aware that people's actions are governed by prejudice or cupidity, as well as by ideals, had something to say about the threats posed by the Nebraska Act to the Union and to the Illinois voter. He wanted to explain why even moderate people should act in concert with abolitionists on this particular matter. Finally he wanted to head off Stephen Douglas from skinning him in the last hour. Now was the time to do these things, while he held the people in the hollow of his hand. Moving down from his peaks of high emotion, Lincoln descended over minor peaks to that clear tone of argument and sense with which he had begun.

Lincoln's oratory as a matter of course received elaborate praise from opposition papers and showers of scorn from Democratic ones. Nobody, however, who reads this speech, or indeed any of the great ones soon to follow can have any doubt that here was an orator who spoke with power. This was no discovery to those who had known Lincoln long, but in the crisis of the Kansas-Nebraska Act he had risen to a new stature. As he had first comprehended during his session in Congress, the Union was literally endangered by controversy over slavery. The Union had found in Lincoln a defender who was concerned not only for its existence, but for what kind of Union it was going to be. Upon these subjects he felt passionately. All his apprenticeship in law or politics was brought into service to explain, convince, inspire, coax, lead those ordinary people with whom he had lived on familiar terms so long. Within himself Lincoln had discovered the difference between a master politician and a statesman.

He did not lose the one gift while gaining another. The very day after he had spoken in Springfield, urging all men of goodwill, whether Whigs, ex-Democrats, abolitionists or free-soilers, to unite on the one point on which they agreed, the anti-slavery radicals, who had already assumed the name of Republicans, gathered in Springfield to form a state organization. Lincoln, however, perceiving that the radicals were by no means the only group prepared to fight on his side, was not yet ready to be labeled. He decided he had business out of town and left in a hurry. The Republicans elected him a member of their State Central Committee, on which he immediately refused to serve.

Douglas departed for the next session of Congress, but excitement did not die down in Illinois. Lincoln was duly elected to the legislature, but resigned his seat in favor of a more important chance. His old dueling foe, James Shields, colleague of Douglas in the Senate, was coming up for re-election in the state legislature. Local disapproval of the Kansas-Nebraska Act had given this body a majority of thirteen against it. The group, however, was made up confusingly of Whigs, anti-slavery Democrats, and a few Republicans. Lincoln saw a chance to win the seat as champion of the Whigs, and he therefore proceeded to write a series of confidential letters, both to members of the legislature and also to prominent Whigs of his acquaintance. To read these letters is to understand something of the patient, careful, untiring work which had made Lincoln a power in the politics of his state. Where he suspects a rival, he is tactful. Where he fears a rebuff, he gets a friend to make approaches. Where objections are made to him, he is quick with an answer. If he receives no reply, he turns to someone else to make inquiries. "That man who thinks," his partner Herndon said, "Lincoln calmly sat down and gathered his robes about him, waiting for the people to call him, has a very erroneous knowledge of Lincoln. He was always calculating, and always planning ahead."

Lincoln became the candidate of the Whigs, but the anti-Nebraska Democrats, though few in number, preferred to put up Lyman Trumbull, one of their own group who had married Mary Lincoln's girlhood friend Julia Jayne. When the legislature finally met to make its choice, Lincoln was only five votes short of a majority, but the supporters of Trumbull, who had mustered just five votes for him, would not give way. Those voting for Shields, who perfectly understood that he could not be elected, had chosen a secret candidate of their own—namely, Joel A. Matteson, governor of the state and possessor of a great personal following. Matteson had privately assured anti-Nebraska friends that given some small proviso which would not be difficult to grant, he would later join them. When therefore the Democrats, having demonstrated their loyalty to Shields on six ballots, shifted abruptly to Matteson, enough anti-Nebraskans followed to put him within three votes of election. Trumbull's men still held firm, and Lincoln hastily threw him his remaining votes which proved just sufficient to give him a majority.

It is interesting to see that despite his hard work Lincoln took this disappointment as a possible gain for the cause, whereas Mary Lincoln was furious that Trumbull had not swung over his five votes in the early ballots when Lincoln was running ahead. She carried her feeling far enough to quarrel with Julia Trumbull, who had been one of her two confidants in the matter of her secret re-engagement to Lincoln. Even when she went to Washington as the President's lady, Mary kept up her feud with Mrs. Senator Trumbull.

Lincoln went back to the practice of law, where the McCormick case and that of the *Effie Afton*, the Duff Armstrong murder case, and many others took up his time. His failure against Trumbull had shown that Whigs in Illinois were not strong enough to defeat a Democratic candidate unless they would combine with anti-Nebraskans in general. If anything of real importance was to be achieved in the presidential election of 1856, there must be a coalition. This necessity was reinforced by continued political turmoil in Congress and also in Kansas, where Governor Reeder had called for elections to a territorial legislature, only to discover that 4,908 out of 6,130 votes were fraudulent. Despite his efforts to prevent it, a pro-slavery legislature assembled, chose Lecompton as the capital, and adopted a civil and criminal code which made it a felony to deny the right to hold slaves and prescribed the death penalty for aiding slaves to escape. Free-state men set up a government of their own and sought recognition.

While Lincoln thought over what he should do, his old friend Joshua F. Speed, now a plantation-owner in Kentucky, wrote to find out where he stood. Speed admitted in the abstract that slavery was wrong, but as a Southerner he would rather see the Union dissolved than yield his legal right to own a slave if he wished to in accordance with the provisions of the Constitution. Speed, who had shared a bed with Lincoln and understood his melancholy, having suffered from an attack of it himself, was one of the few people with whom Lincoln talked about his deepest personal feelings. Now established in slave-owning Kentucky, Speed was on the other side of the fence. Substantially he saw the problem as Lincoln did, yet just in reverse. It was not possible for Lincoln to discuss the slavery issue even with him in terms satisfying to Southern opinions.

"I acknowledge *your* rights and *my* obligations under the constitution," Lincoln wrote, "in regard to your slaves. . . . In 1841, you and I had together a tedious low-water trip, on a

Steam Boat from Louisville to St. Louis. You may remember, as I well do, that from Louisville to the mouth of the Ohio there were, on board, ten or a dozen slaves, shackled together with irons. That sight was a continual torment to me; and I see something like it every time I touch the Ohio, or any other slave-border. It is hardly fair for you to assume, that I have no interest in a thing which has, and continually exercises, the power of making me miserable. You ought rather to appreciate how much the great body of Northern people do crucify their feelings, in order to maintain their loyalty to the constitution and the Union." The appeal was hopeless. Mary Todd Lincoln was split from her Kentucky family and Lincoln from his own best friend by the slavery issue.

1856, as we have seen, was the year of decision and the Know-Nothings were the first to demonstrate that they could not hold together in face of the rising feelings generated by troubles in Kansas. Meeting at Philadelphia, they nominated Millard Fillmore and Andrew J. Donelson of Tennessee, but only at the expense of a split with their northern members who insisted that a statement opposing slavery extension be inserted in the platform. Failing to obtain this, they withdrew and nominated candidates of their own. The latter had no chance of success without some coalition with other anti-Nebraska forces.

It so happened that on the day of the Know-Nothing meeting, a Republican National party with no present program save opposition to slavery extension was organized and issued an invitation to a convention in Philadelphia in order to select a presidential candidate. Naturally the dissident Know-Nothings were ready to amalgamate, particularly if their candidate for President, John C. Frémont, a colorful explorer, should be selected.

Again on the same day, which was Washington's birthday and a convenient holiday for meetings, a group of anti-

Nebraska newspaper editors assembled at Decatur, Illinois, to consider the formation of a coalition in that state. With them was the cautious, moderate Abraham Lincoln, making his first tentative step in the direction of a new party at the exact moment when it was beginning to take shape on a national scale. His purpose apparently was to keep extremist sentiments out of the platform on which the coalition was to rest. So successful was he that the newly formed Illinois party did not even call itself Republican. It opposed the extension of slavery, introduced a mild anti-Know-Nothing plank to pull in the German vote without offending too many native Americans, and elected a committee consisting of an abolitionist Whig, a Know-Nothing Whig, and a German Democrat to issue a call to an anti-Nebraska state convention.

Shortly after this meeting a Sangamon County convention was summoned to select delegates to the proposed state-wide gathering. Lincoln was away on the circuit, but Herndon put his partner's name at the head of a list of a hundred and twenty-nine persons who signed the call. Stuart, an old-line Whig, came rushing to Herndon to find out if he had been authorized to do so. Lincoln had been ruined politically by the gesture, Stuart insisted. Lincoln, on the other hand, sent back the message: "All right, go ahead. Will meet you, radicals and all." Actually by moving from a moribund party into this new coalition, Lincoln was to gain the political backing of an organization which would only be a minority for a short time. Careers which were ruined by the shift proved to be those of men like Stuart, too inflexible a Whig to change with the times. It was to these old party friends that Lincoln chiefly addressed his appeal in the presidential campaign of 1856.

Just before the state convention came news of pillaging and burnings in Lawrence, the free-state capital of Kansas. As if that were not enough, the outrage was almost immediately followed by an attack on Charles Sumner of Massachusetts as he sat at his desk in the Senate. He was beaten nearly to death by Preston S. Brooks of South Carolina in retaliation for an anti-slavery speech. Partly as a result every shade of anti-Nebraska opinion turned up in Bloomington. The convention contained people who had not been on speaking terms for years, but now had to choose a slate for an election in which they must work together to win. They were hardly a party, and many still avoided the name of Republican. Somehow they had to be welded together if they were to make themselves felt. Abraham Lincoln undertook to do this in a speech which apparently so enthralled his audience that even reporters forgot to take notes. Amid the tumultuous applause which followed, the Republican party of Illinois was born.

11

The Dilemma of Douglas

---◁◉▷---

LESS THAN A WEEK AFTER the Illinois Republican Convention, the Democrats met nationally to select their presidential candidate. True to their policy of offending no one, they passed over Douglas to nominate James Buchanan, an old party wheelhorse from Pennsylvania with a distinguished career which had culminated with an appointment as Minister to England. He had been out of the country during the Kansas-Nebraska controversy and had not acquired determined enemies. The Republican party also met nationally, but was hard put to it to satisfy the different views of the ex-Democrats, ex-Whigs, abolitionists, and other groups of which it was composed. Finally the Republicans agreed on the anti-Nebraska and Know-Nothing favorite, John C. Frémont of California, who was nationally known as "The Pathfinder" for his daring explorations in the West. The Illinois delegation put forward Lincoln for Vice President, and he actually received 110 votes in a preliminary ballot, proving that he was beginning to be heard of outside his own state. Too many, however, were still inquiring: "Who is this Lincoln?," and William L. Dayton of New Jersey was chosen by the convention.

The main body of Know-Nothings remained a distinct third party and had made as good a showing as possible by their nomination of Millard Fillmore, a Whig and one who had been President already without bringing actual disaster to the Union. Not unnaturally, he drew a good many Whig votes from North and South.

The presidential campaign of 1856 in view of the heated state of the country was more frantic than usual. Bands and fireworks were noisier, parades and banners bigger, rallies more numerous. Orators spread out all over the nation. Lincoln made over fifty addresses, once more paying some attention to southern Illinois, a conservative, Democratic stronghold usually avoided by opposition candidates. His general task was to persuade old-line Whigs that a vote given to Fillmore would not elect him, but merely result in one less for Frémont. Some Southerners, however, were already predicting secession if the Republican candidate were chosen, thus frightening many into voting for Fillmore. In the event Buchanan won the election, but with a popular vote of 400,000 less than the combined opposition. The Know-Nothings, who had been badly beaten, subsided as a party; but it was by no means clear whether the votes that they had garnered would have gone mainly to Buchanan or to Frémont.

The election made Buchanan the last President with a chance to avert civil war because he represented the only party which had found support in every section of the country. Though himself a Pennsylvanian, the new President was southern in sentiment, and he was not above jealousy of Douglas, the ablest Democratic politician. It was no surprise to find that the cabinet was to be dominated by Southerners. This did not, however, dispose of northern influence in the Democratic party. Under the previous administration, also southern-dominated, the Kansas-Nebraska Act had been put through by Douglas, establishing the principle that the inhabitants of a territory should have the power of choosing whether slavery was to be admitted or not. Since this had led to a state of warfare in Kansas and a deep political division between North and South, the public was naturally eager to know if changes in policy would follow the change of President. Buchanan's inaugural speech, setting the tone for the next four years, was anxiously awaited.

It was sheer coincidence that Dred Scott, a Negro, was currently suing for his freedom on the grounds that he had accompanied his master for several years, both to Minnesota, where slavery was forbidden by the Missouri Compromise, and also to Illinois, where slavery had been excluded ever since the Ordinance of 1787. Dred Scott had returned to Missouri with his master, but was now too old to work and had been encouraged to claim his freedom and back pay, partly because none of his master's heirs wanted him in the household. The Missouri Supreme Court had held that his residence out of state, since it had always been intended to be temporary, had made no change in his status according to the laws of Missouri. Dred Scott had appealed to the United States Supreme Court, whose Chief Justice, Roger Taney, a jurist of great age and distinction, was a Marylander with southern views on slavery. Since the majority of the court was southern also, it did not seem likely that Dred Scott would win his freedom. The distinction of the lawyers arguing the case had, however, given rise to a rumor that larger issues were involved. The Court might make a general pronouncement on the status of Negroes, or it might give a decision on the legality of banning slavery from the territories.

Nothing could have suited Buchanan better. Perhaps it was his absence from the country during the last years which had made him naive enough to imagine that a verdict from the Supreme Court would fall like a bucket of cold water on a pair of fighting dogs. Associate Justice Catron was indiscreet enough to inform the President-elect that the Court had been unable to agree to confine its opinion to the actual status of Dred Scott. Buchanan unwisely put personal pressure on one of the justices to support a wide interpretation of the law. In consequence in his inaugural address, amid much talk of peaceful satisfaction for the southern point of view, he reminded the nation that the questions in dispute were at that moment being considered by the highest court in the land, which would settle the controversy once and for all.

Two days later the Chief Justice delivered a majority opinion which stated that the signers of the Constitution had placed the Negro in the inferior position of a non-citizen. This meant that were he slave or free, Dred Scott had no right of appeal to the federal courts. Since the supreme court of his native state of Missouri had pronounced him a slave, a slave he was. Whether or not Dred Scott could have asserted his freedom when he was in Illinois, Taney pointed out that he had not done so. His residence in Minnesota had made no difference in his status because the Missouri Compromise, under which Congress had banned slavery there, had been an unconstitutional exercise of congressional power and was therefore void. The Congress had never been given the right to ban slavery in the national territories. It was over fifty years since the Supreme Court had thus ventured to annul an act of Congress.

There are some things even a Supreme Court cannot do. Buchanan's inaugural had paid lip-service to the Douglas doctrine of self-determination within the territories because it was the official point of view of the Democratic party. In other words he had said to his Republican opponents, "You stand for exclusion of slavery from the territories and we for self-determination." Taney, on the other hand, had in effect said: "The end and object of your party is to keep slavery out of the territories, which is unconstitutional. You will have to disband your party altogether."

With a howl of rage, Republicans accused the Court of entering into a conspiracy with Buchanan. The President's negotiations with some of the justices had remained secret, but his words in the inaugural had been followed with most suspicious speed by Taney's decision. Far from disbanding, the Republicans were determined to gain control of the government and to keep it long enough to change the personnel of the Court. For the time being they refused to accept the decision as a permanent one or as affecting anything more than the future of Dred Scott. The abolitionist wing of the party and even such moderates as Lincoln were outraged not only by the denial of the Missouri Compromise, but by the declaration that the Negro was and always must be an inferior person. Lincoln appealed to the Declaration of Independence, which asserted that all men were created equal. New England legislatures passed votes condemning the Supreme Court decision—and several more states passed personal-liberty laws, asserting the freedom of all within their borders in flagrant defiance of the Fugitive Slave Law.

While the Republicans thus defied the Court, Stephen A. Douglas and his northern Democratic followers were indignant to discover that their great principle of self-determination within the territories had been destroyed by Taney along with the Missouri Compromise. If Congress had no power to exclude slavery from the territories, territorial governments, which derived all their powers from Congress, could not do so either. Their freedom of choice on the subject was consequently lost. Since party loyalties are a strong bond, the Douglasites still called themselves Democrats, but they hated the Dred Scott decision almost as much as the Republicans did. The relationship between Douglas and Buchanan, which had never pretended to be close, was further strained.

It was not improbably at the very moment when Lincoln swung his senatorial votes to Trumbull that he faced the necessity of running against Douglas when the latter came up for re-election in 1858. It was a task of almost impossible magnitude. Illinois was largely Democratic, and the hold of the Little Giant on his followers was immense. Yet it was necessary to topple Douglas if the Kansas-Nebraska Law and now the Dred Scott decision were to be reversed. Lincoln, however, was not without his own advantages. Within the area of the Eighth Circuit he literally knew everybody, while elsewhere in the state his connections were legion. Douglas, spending a large part of his year in Washington and only returning at intervals for a round of speech-making, was comparatively out of touch. Lincoln was ambitious for the Senate, not merely because he believed that Douglas must be beaten, but because it was, and very likely always had been, his ultimate aim. He was ready and knew himself ready for the job. Thus he felt his way through the maze of politics in Illinois with the intention of becoming the obvious choice of whatever party should emerge. So carefully did he play his cards that the Republicans accepted him as their strongest man and the most likely to have a chance in what was bound to be a desperate struggle.

While Lincoln was strengthening his position in Illinois, Douglas was looking for an answer to the Dred Scott decision which would enable him to retain his Democratic leadership in Congress without losing his hold on the electorate at home. He found one based on a rough expediency which suited his dilemma and was as characteristic of the man as Lincoln's clear perception of basic principles had been of him. The Dred Scott decision was correct, argued Douglas, standing by the administration and in general by the southern wing of the Democratic party. On the other hand, no slave-owner would dare bring his slaves into a territory where his property was not protected by curfews, provisions for pursuing runaways, and other such laws. The Dred Scott decision could not force a territory to pass these regulations, and for this reason slavery could be effectively banned even where it could legally enter.

It was perfectly possible for the Buchanan administration to accept this position, little though southern members may have liked its barely concealed opposition to the verdict of the Supreme Court. 1857 was not an election year, so that there was no need for hurry to keep party members exactly in line. Unfortunately, though in principle the question of slavery in the territories was now settled, in practice it was still being fought out in Kansas. The only real solution for the Kansas problem was to make the territory into a state with all convenient speed. Even the Supreme Court conceded that a state constitution might be drawn up for or against slavery as the inhabitants should choose. Buchanan accordingly sent out a Mississippian, Robert J. Walker, as governor, charging him to hold an election for delegates to frame a state constitution. Unluckily the anti-slavery men, who had a clear majority, were suffering under a pro-slavery territorial legislature which had been elected by flagrant illegalities and falsifications of the ballot. Deciding that a new election run by such a group would be equally unrepresentative, the anti-slavery men boycotted it.

Governor Walker, who arrived to take up his duties only a few weeks before the scheduled election, made a visit to Lawrence. Here in the capital of the anti-slavery interests, an unofficially elected anti-slavery legislature gave him facts and figures tending to prove that their supporters had been debarred from voting in the coming election by various devices. Walker went on to Lecompton, capital of the official, pro-slavery legislature, where he was met by cynical threats of violence, drunken boasting, and an open determination to bring slavery in by force.

Governor Walker, though a Southerner, was a fair-minded man. He very soon saw that if numbers were to prevail, Kansas must become a free state. On the other hand, there was no reason why it should become a Republican state unless it felt unfairly treated. He thought it important to keep it in the

roster of states which supported the only national party. As
it happened, however, he was unable in the short time at his
disposal to control the election, which duly chose pro-slavery
delegates. These met at Lecompton, but before they had completed their work of drawing up a pro-slavery constitution,
elections for a new legislature and a congressional delegate
were held. Walker could not avoid the conclusion that exten-
sive frauds had been practiced. Investigation enabled him, for
instance, to produce the election returns of Oxford, Kansas,
a hamlet on the borders of Missouri which contained six
buildings. Oxford had sent in sixteen hundred and one pro-
slavery votes, fifteen hundred of which had been copied, in
the handwriting of one industrious person, from William's
Cincinnati Directory, without even bothering to change the
order of the names.

Southern leaders in Washington and throughout the South
were furious with Walker. All they saw was that at the present moment there were sixteen free and fifteen slave states.
Minnesota and Oregon were on the verge of statehood, both
bound to become free. Missouri had a strong free-state
minority which might yet succeed in overturning its pro-
slavery constitution. The crux of the matter really was that
the flood of immigrants pouring in from Europe was manifestly destroying the balance between North and South. In
these circumstances Southerners were not disposed to argue
the rights and wrongs of majorities in Kansas. They saw it as
a possible slave state and claimed it as a matter of survival.

Buchanan, dominated by his southern cabinet, wavered.
He was frightened by the talk of secession reported ever more
ominously from the South. He was threatened by his own
personal friends on whom, being a bachelor, he depended not
only as colleagues, but as cronies. On the other hand Walker,
whom he himself had selected to settle the problems of Kansas, was appealing for his support. What was he to do?

One member of the Democratic party had no doubt. Stephen A. Douglas was the man who had substituted the principle of self-determination for the Missouri Compromise. He had intended the country to rise above the slavery problem, but it had conspicuously failed to do so. Nevertheless there was something left to Douglas. If Kansas were allowed to choose its own solution by free majority vote, his policy could be put forward to solve other potential conflicts. He had nailed his colors to the mast, and his political future depended on the popular will being expressed in Kansas.

Since the Kansas Constitutional Convention assembled at Lecompton was composed of pro-slavery men, it drew up a constitution deliberately difficult to amend. Nor did its members propose to submit its provisions to a referendum, except for the pro- or anti-slavery one. If slavery was rejected, slaves already in the state and by implication all who could be smuggled across the line would be ferociously protected.

Uproar arose in Kansas from the anti-slavery men, freely echoed by the northern press, all agreeing that the Lecompton constitution by no means represented the wishes of a majority of Kansans. In the South, however, it was hailed as a signal victory over the intrigues of Governor Walker. In Washington where the decision lay, Buchanan's southern associates brought every pressure to bear on him to dismiss Walker and uphold the Lecompton constitution. Predictably Buchanan, whom even his supporters were beginning to despise, did as they told him. Equally obviously Douglas faced the crisis of his life. If he upheld the admission of Kansas under Lecompton, he would be admitting to his own constituents that self-determination was nothing but a sham. On the other hand, if he fought to overthrow Lecompton, he must attack the administration of his own party, accepting the charges of disloyalty that this would bring.

Perhaps the dominant thing about Douglas was that he was

a fighter. For the last three years he had been defending his policy on the grounds that it would prove itself right in the end. He was too great a man to back down. Politically a fair decision in Kansas meant life or death to him even more surely than an open split with the leader of his party. He had won fights before and grown greater. He went into this one with the clear consciousness that he was a better man than Buchanan and that opportunity as well as danger lay ahead.

Buchanan, though generally an indecisive man, was not without his own standards. All his life he had followed the Democratic line because it had given him a definite policy to hold fast to. In other words experience had taught him that party discipline was the basis of political life. Thus the moment Douglas threw his tremendous force against Lecompton, President Buchanan was ready to declare war to the knife. The personal strength of Douglas in the Senate and his support among northern Democrats were difficulties for which Buchanan had no direct answer. As President, however, he had a great deal of power which could be exercised not only in Washington, but in the constituencies of offending members. Almost every postmaster, customs official, or other civil servant in Illinois owed his appointment directly or indirectly to Douglas. These could all be dismissed and replaced by men prepared to oppose him. The Illinois State Central Committee could be made to understand that they might expect no favors as long as they supported Douglas. Even in Washington there were Douglasites who could be dismissed and congressmen who could be threatened with loss of patronage in their own states.

Despite these tactics Douglas battled mightily for a fair decision in Kansas, supported not only by a few northern Democrats, but by the opposition. Rumors soon began to run that Douglas would turn Republican. There were already a number of ex-Democrats in the Republican party who saw advantages in such a change. William H. Seward, potential Republican candidate for President in 1860, seemed not unwilling to offer Douglas a cabinet position if he would cross over. Simon Cameron of Pennsylvania, an inveterate intriguer for his own advancement, saw advantages in being the man to bring Douglas into the Republican party.

There was one place in which these negotiations, given publicity by the New York *Tribune* and other newspapers, found no favor. The ex-Whigs who formed the backbone of the Republicans of Illinois had battled Douglas too often to be reconciled. His toothmarks were still visible on Stuart's thumb. Besides, having sent Trumbull, an ex-Democrat, to the Senate, Republicans felt that in fairness their next candidate must be an ex-Whig. In this case the obvious choice was Abraham Lincoln, whose 1856 contests with Douglas and over fifty speeches for Frémont had established him as a speaker of ever-increasing power. Nobody had been longer in politics, had known the members of the State Central Committee more intimately, had a more devoted band of friends among leading lawyers, took a more moderate position, and was less tainted in the eyes of immigrants by association with Know-Nothing policies. Lincoln's own political wisdom understood the problem of interference in favor of Douglas. He went up to Chicago to talk it over with Norman B. Judd, old acquaintance and Illinois chairman of the State Central Committee. Since Billy Herndon had certain contacts in the East who might come in useful, he was sent on a trip to sound out Republican leaders there.

Illinois local conventions met during the early summer, all but five of them selecting Lincoln as their candidate for United States Senator. The state convention, which met at Springfield on June 16, not only adopted Lincoln, but made its feelings plain to any Easterners who had shown signs of wanting to interfere. "Abraham Lincoln is the first and only choice," they said, "of the Republicans of Illinois for the United States Senate as the successor of Stephen A. Douglas." The significance of this statement at the time that it was made is often forgotten. It was a period when the members of the legislature chose the senator and in making this declaration the Republicans were treating their legislature more or less as an electoral college. They were commanding all Republican candidates to vote for Lincoln as a matter of party loyalty, avoiding the sort of split which had in 1855 produced the election of Trumbull.

Lincoln's startling victory was intended as a lesson to eastern newspapers like the New York *Tribune*, which had been urging reconciliation with Douglas. Its effect was to arouse the interest of the whole nation as a new departure in the method of choosing Senators. What made it incomprehensible outside the state was that Lincoln, who had hardly left Illinois for the last nine years and whose record in Congress had not been outstanding, should have been put forward in this fashion. The inactivity of the Whig party in decline had concealed the fact that Lincoln's position within it was growing steadily and that his shrewdness in stepping forward at the exact moment when a Republican federation was needed had established him as the leading man of a party with far more political possibilities than Illinois Whiggery had ever offered. One man in Washington was not surprised. "I shall have my hands full," said Stephen Douglas. "He is the strong man of his party—full of wit, facts, dates—and the best stump speaker, with his droll ways and dry jokes, in the West."

Douglas also knew that Democratic money was pouring into Illinois to support other candidates than himself, to buy anti-Douglas editorials, and to subsidize Democratic conventions which were likely to nominate some other candidate. He was beset on both sides but his strength lay in battle.

12

Dead Lion vs. Living Dog

———◆———

LINCOLN HAD SET THE TONE for the coming struggle in his acceptance speech at the Republican Convention, which was widely reported. " 'A house divided against itself cannot stand,' " he had quoted. "I believe this government cannot endure permanently half *slave* and half *free*. I do not expect the Union to be dissolved—I do not expect the house to *fall* —but I do expect it will cease to be divided. It will become *all* one thing, or *all* the other. Either the *opponents* of slavery will arrest the further spread of it, and place it where the public mind shall rest in the belief that it is in the course of ultimate extinction; or its *advocates* will push it forward till it shall become alike lawful in *all* the States, *old* as well as *new*, *North* as well as *South*."

These strong words marked Lincoln as radical, when in actual fact he was conservative about the slavery issue. He was, however, aware that he had undertaken to fight not only for a cause, but against a definite and dangerous opponent. Lincoln had, as the convention proved, the support of Republican leaders. It was harder to be certain of the rank and file of a party so recently and hastily assembled. How would ordinary people vote when Douglas came before them with his fiery oratory, insisting that he had fought for a free constitution for Kansas by opposing Lecompton? Would they be confused when they saw him attacked by Buchanan's pro-

Southern cohorts? Would they be overwhelmed by the Little Giant's national fame and persuaded that he could express their point of view in the Senate with more force than Abraham Lincoln, whom no one had ever called "giant" except in stature? It was necessary for Lincoln to outline his difference from Douglas in terms that would make Republicans feel they had to elect him. He therefore proceeded to trace the alarming advance of the slavery cause, starting with the repeal of the Missouri Compromise by Douglas, leading through the administrations of Pierce and Buchanan to Lecompton, and through the Dred Scott decision in the direction of another Supreme Court pronouncement which might in due time be delivered to the effect that a *state* could not exclude slavery from its borders. Lincoln insisted that Douglas, Pierce, Buchanan, and Taney had formed a conspiracy to produce this result, pointing out that when we see the framework of a house has been put together, we have the right to suspect that the joiners actually intend to build one.

This theory of a conspiracy was not invented by Lincoln, but some historians dismiss it as mere froth on the raging waters of the slavery controversy. A sagacious man like Lincoln, they claim, could not have believed it, but was using it to stampede the common herd. Pierce and Buchanan, neither one strong or farsighted, had simply yielded to continuing southern pressure. Roger Taney, whatever we may think of his decision in the Dred Scott case, was a man of rigid uprightness. As for Douglas, his fault was that he did not care about an issue which his fellows insisted was vital. Douglas had many times stated that he did not mind whether slavery was voted up or down, adding that he was all for the black man—against the crocodile, but for the white man every time against them both. If it suited white men to make black men slaves, let them do so. If not, he had no objection to their freedom. If he now fought against Lecompton, it was not to make Kansas free, but to ensure that its constitution represented the wishes of its inhabitants. As for the suggestion that the Court might some day prevent even states from banning slavery, some critics dismiss it, as Douglas did, calling it a ridiculous notion.

It was certainly expedient for Lincoln to associate Douglas with Pierce, Buchanan, and Taney, in order to prevent people from forgetting that the Little Giant's attack on Lecompton was incidental to his repeal of the Missouri Compromise. The "conspiracy" did help Lincoln draw a hard line between himself and Douglas, showing clearly that his opponent, though on the Republican side in the matter of Lecompton, was not and never could be an anti-slavery champion. Douglas was a great man, Lincoln admitted, nailing down his subject in phrases which would re-echo throughout the campaign. He was a lion, but a caged and toothless lion when it came to opposing slavery in the territories. "A *living dog*," as the Bible says, "is better than a *dead lion*."

It is perfectly true that Lincoln was a politician in the fullest sense of the word, and that his basic honesty had not prevented him from succeeding. He kept his own counsel marvelously well, so that we have on occasion to note what he said without precisely knowing what went on in his mind. In fairness, however, we must admit that there had been some collusion between Buchanan and members of the Supreme Court, which Pierce and even Taney may have been privy to. Douglas saw his repeal of the Missouri Compromise as a concession to Southerners which would raise "the hell of a storm" in the North. Impossible though it may be to imagine the four sitting together to plan the stages of pro-slavery advance, it is not difficult to see that they had approached their problems with something common in mind. Exchange of opinion was possible and at times inevitable among men in their positions. Lincoln does exaggerate their collusion, but whether because political rhetoric paints in bright, contrasting colors or because the times were hysterical, it is hard to say. There is not enough evidence to conclude that Lincoln described a "conspiracy" in which he did not believe and continued to uphold it throughout his campaign simply because it was useful to do so.

The most we can concede is that Lincoln's attitude was perhaps not too far different from that of Douglas in accusing Lincoln of being an abolitionist. Douglas knew perfectly well that in the literal sense he was not one. On the other hand, Lincoln aspired to lead a party containing these extremists and might easily be forced in the course of time to support their position.

There has been a tendency to judge one or the other of these great contestants by a rigorous standard without applying it to his opponent. Either Douglas is described as more unscrupulous than Lincoln, or Lincoln's famous honesty is dismissed as at least partly show. It is easier to criticize Lincoln than to work out in terms of his day precisely what was meant by honesty in politics.

The man whom Lincoln had described as a dead lion was in fact more alive and formidable than ever. When his wife, whom he had sincerely loved, died in the early fifties, Douglas had turned to alcohol for consolation to an extent which seriously alarmed his friends. The habit had sustained him through the hectic days of the Kansas-Nebraska Bill. His dress, hitherto conspicuously neat, had grown careless; his health had been visibly affected. All that was now past history. Douglas was remarried to an imposingly beautiful girl many years younger than himself. Adele Cutts Douglas, a grandniece of Dolly Madison, had made herself virtual leader of the Washington social set. Her husband, transformed in appearance and improved in health, was eager to present her to his constituents in the coming campaign.

In April, the Kansas controversy had been settled in Congress by the "English Compromise," which pleased neither half of the Democratic party. Kansas was offered a chance to accept or reject the Lecompton Constitution, but acceptance was encouraged by the bribe of immediate statehood and a large government land grant. Rejecting Lecompton, the territory must wait till its population rose to about a hundred thousand, which would probably take several years. There was no doubt in anyone's mind that Lecompton would be rejected and that though slavery could not then be forbidden in the territory because of the Dred Scott decision, it would not flourish there for lack of protection. Kansas was bound to become a free state, and the English Compromise was a shabby, hopeless attempt to bribe it into accepting Lecompton. The measure was nothing but a face-saver for the administration, deeply humiliated because it had been powerless to enforce its policy.

All the same the bill was in fact a solution to the Kansas question and left nothing to be decided save whether Douglas and Buchanan could be reconciled. Great pressure was brought on Douglas to vote for the bill on the grounds that it would eventually give him what he had been fighting for. Douglas wavered. To agree to such a scandalous piece of legislation was difficult for him. On the other hand, the reunification of the Democratic party was vital both to the nation and to his own chances of becoming President. He half consented, but the violent reproaches of those Democrats who had stood by him in Congress together with the instant reaction of his constituents in Illinois made clear to him that he could not do it. He voted against the bill and in a sense sealed the fate of the nation. Buchanan with the enraged South behind him was ready to tear the party in shreds rather than accept the domination of the man who had not only lost Kansas as a slave state, but who would not even pretend to fall back in line behind the party leaders. Douglas therefore went home to fight his own battle in the way the Kansans were to fight theirs. The administration would use bribes and promises against him, actually preferring that his Republican opponent win.

If Douglas was dismayed by the breach, he did not show it. Illinois was a long way from Washington, and most Democrats there saw the possible victory of Abraham Lincoln in an entirely different light from that visible to Buchanan. The personal following of the Little Giant was tremendous. Under his leadership Illinois Democrats had embraced the principle of self-determination within the territories. The unfortunate results of this policy were overshadowed by the fact that Douglas had fought unflinchingly for it against the whole power of the South and had, in effect, won. Immigrants pouring into the West had ensured majorities in territories there for anti-slavery, while the fate of Kansas had shown that the country would not stand interference with the people's wishes. In fact some writers on the period claim that the slavery question was actually settled. Slavery was confined to the states which already had it, and the object of the Republican party had been achieved by the Little Giant. If this was really so, the immense power of Douglas in Illinois is easily explained. We must even raise the question: What was the issue that Lincoln was fighting about?

The Little Giant planned his campaign in heroic style. Though he had lived extravagantly in Washington and was in debt, he mortgaged his lands in Illinois, sold his Washington house, borrowed money which he was prepared to spend for the sake of making a public appearance. Not to be outdone, Illinois Democrats hired a special train to transport a brass band and a delegation from nearly every county in the state to meet him in Indiana and escort him over the border to Chicago. As the Douglas train ran through the streets of

Chicago into the station, it was greeted by immense crowds of cheering men and announced all over the city by the crash of artillery salutes. In an open barouche drawn by six horses and escorted by guards who could hardly make way for it, Douglas drove to the Tremont House, in front of which a vast crowd, estimated by enthusiasts at thirty thousand, was gathered in the square. Darkness was already falling, and their numbers were illuminated here or there by blazing torches and occasional rockets.

In one of the seats on the balcony behind the speaker sat a long, lean, leathery man whose sleeves and trousers were still too short, whose turndown collar emphasized his stringy neck, and whose stovepipe hat made his height almost grotesque. Lincoln had not altered his apparel for the campaign and was later seen to travel with a worn black satchel, his shawl, and an old umbrella which had long ago lost the knob at the end of its handle. The opponents shook hands, and Lincoln folded his length back into his chair to listen with the intention of announcing at the end of Douglas's speech that he would answer the next night.

Douglas had had two sleepless nights, not surprisingly considering the conditions of railroad travel and the company of a brass band and four hundred supporters. His Chicago speech, however, had been carefully prepared. He managed to take credit for the defeat of Lecompton without ever once mentioning President Buchanan by name and always referring to his opponents in the vaguest terms as "they." He would not do anything to widen the rift in the party, fully conscious that in two years' time he would want it to rally behind him in a presidential campaign. It was simpler for him to attack Lincoln in answer to the "House Divided" speech. The United States had always been divided he pointed out, not only into slave states and free. It had always presented a rich diversity emphasized by climatic conditions, economic life, and differing constitutions. Was there any reason why it should not continue to be so? Lincoln's position was simply that of an abolitionist. His real reason for hating the Dred Scott decision was not its refusal to allow Congress to exclude slavery from the territories, but its statement that Scott as a Negro was not and never could be a citizen, even if he were free. Lincoln stood for Negro equality with white men, while he, Douglas, was only prepared to give the Negro such protection as was proper for a dependent and inferior. We may note that Douglas, too, was drawing a line to mark his position.

On July 16, the Little Giant left Chicago with his wife and attendants in a gaily decorated private car hitched onto the regular train and accompanied by a flat-car mounting a twelve-pounder cannon which was fired off at every stop to let the neighborhood know that the candidate was passing by. Young George McClellan, by now promoted to be Vice President of the Illinois Central, was seen from time to time to join the parade, and it was commented that all this Douglas splendor was the merest favoritism on the part of the railroad. In fact Douglas probably paid heavily for the convenience, but it was also noticeable that Lincoln, one of the railroad's own lawyers, was left to travel on his free pass in the ordinary day-coach. Indeed on occasions when the times of trains did not suit his engagements, he was forced to go by freight-train, which was officially forbidden and was only grudgingly made possible for him. In Bloomington Lincoln once more sat on the platform behind Douglas, but made no answer to his speech. In Springfield, on the other hand, he answered within a few hours.

Douglas's managers presently issued a list of dates and places where he would speak, wishing naturally to give his supporters time to collect their audience, tune up their band, make their posters, erect a stage from which their hero could be heard, buy yards of bunting, and plan the biggest demonstration ever. Lincoln's advisors felt it expedient to have their candidate visit many places at the same time in order to profit from the capacity of the Little Giant to draw crowds. On the other hand, it would look undignified if Lincoln merely trailed around in the wake of his opponent. For this reason Lincoln publicly challenged Douglas to a series of formal debates. Let one speak for an hour, followed by the other for an hour and a half. Finally let the first man have an additional half hour more to answer his opponent's arguments.

From the point of view of the canvass this was an obviously convenient arrangement. Everybody regardless of his politics would take his holiday on the same day. Both candidates would speak to their supporters and their opponents. It was, however, clearly less to the advantage of Douglas, whose campaign was more flamboyant and who was far more famous than Lincoln. For this reason, his agreement was grudging. He saw it would not do to refuse an open challenge, but was anxious not to concede too many public meetings. He consented to one joint debate in each of seven of the nine congressional districts in the state, expressly excluding both Chicago and Springfield, where Lincoln and he had spoken already. The first of these meetings was fixed for August 21 at Ottawa. The intervening three weeks were spent by Douglas following his charted path through the towns of the state. Lincoln, perhaps not wishing to be too obvious in pursuit, spent half the time at home, working on his speeches and writing letters, but the second half following Douglas and speaking as far as he could to the same audiences.

Each contestant, reading daily what the other one had said, knew well that personal exchanges were better entertainment than a mere statement of principles. The tone of the debates was already outlined before the first formal meeting at Ottawa. Douglas, excelling in ability to dominate by fury, called

his opponent "liar," "coward," and "sneak," and threatened
to have a fight with him. Lincoln, equally determined to en-
tertain the crowd, but not by any means as melodramatic,
raised roars of laughter by accusing his "distinguished
friend" of being "a little excited." He refused the challenge,
not only because a fist fight would prove nothing, but because
"I don't believe he wants it himself. He and I are about the
best friends in the world, and when we get together, he would
no more think of fighting me than of fighting his wife." In
fact, Douglas was trying "to excite—well *enthusiasm* against
me . . . And as I find he was tolerably successful, we will call
it quits." To read these words a hundred years later is to
conclude that Lincoln had much the better of this kind of
exchange. It is notable that Douglas generally refrained from
personal threats thereafter. It must be remembered, however,
that the excitement of the moment and the vehemence of
Douglas were not less formidable at the time even if they no
longer impress us now. Every witness agrees that the impact
of the Little Giant was terrific.

Ottawa was a town of six thousand people which played
host on August 21 to an audience of over ten thousand, according to various reporters. Special trains, displaying banners,
puffed in from Chicago. Special boats ran up the Illinois and
Michigan Canal. Roads choked with clouds of dust brought
a continuous train of farm wagons, carriages, and men on
horseback. Slogans, flags, bunting flapped everywhere. Douglas entered Ottawa in a four-horse carriage accompanied by
men on horseback carrying banners and signs. Lincoln, arriving modestly by train from Chicago, was escorted to a decorated carriage and taken to the home of the mayor. Rival
processions then carried their candidates to the public square,
where the crowd was packed so tightly that it took half an
hour to get everyone on the platform. People had climbed on
top of the wooden awning which had been put up to protect

the speaking platform from the glare of the midday sun. No sooner was everyone more or less in place than a section of this collapsed under the weight, bodies falling on top of the members of the Douglas committee. One way and another it was fairly late before the debate got properly started.

What the candidates said, though vigorous and timely, does not after the lapse of years seem remarkable. Douglas, speaking first, was at pains to describe both Lincoln and the Republicans as abolitionists. Lincoln, when it came to his turn, denied this. "I have no purpose, either directly or indirectly, to interfere with the institution of slavery where it exists ... I have no purpose to introduce political and social equality between the white and black races." Nevertheless he upheld the truth of the Declaration of Independence. In many ways the black man might not be equal to the white, "but in the right to eat the bread, without the leave of anyone else, which his own hand earns, he is my equal, and the equal of Judge Douglas, and the equal of every living man." Lincoln was ready to agree with Douglas's general proposition that diversity within the Union of states was not only possible but desirable. Slavery, he maintained, had been a different sort of division and its influence had always been pernicious. Hitherto its existence had been possible within the Union because the founding fathers had cut off its source in the slave trade and excluded it from new territories, so that the public had looked on it as a dying institution. Douglas, by deciding that expediency rather than right or wrong should govern the actions of a territory about slavery, had raised it to a dangerous national problem which had to be settled as a matter of survival.

Lincoln's eloquence aroused his partisans to such a pitch of enthusiasm that they seized him and carried him away from the platform on their shoulders. It is hard for anyone to look dignified when hustled around in this fashion, let alone a long, awkward fellow like Abraham Lincoln. The *Chicago Times*, a Douglas paper, announced in headline type: "Lincoln's Heart Fails Him! Lincoln's Legs Fail Him! Lincoln's Tongue Fails Him! Lincoln Fails All Over! The People Refuse to Support Him! The People Laugh at Him! . . . Douglas Skins the Living Dog! The 'Dead Lion' Frightens the Canine!" Meanwhile, the New York *Evening Post* reporter, though admitting that in repose "Long Abe's appearance is *not* comely," comments on the animation and fire he expressed when warmed up until he showed himself "a man of rare power and strong magnetic personality. He *takes* the people every time, and there is no getting away from his sturdy good sense, his unaffected sincerity, and the unceasing play of his good humor, which accompanies his close logic and smooths the way to conviction . . . He is altogether a more fluent speaker than Douglas, and in all the arts of debate fully his equal."

From such extracts it is clear that anyone's impression must depend upon what paper he preferred to read. The interesting thing about the debates is not the attitude of the national papers, but the extent of their coverage. This was actually the first political campaign in which major speeches were stenographically reported. The publicity was in large part owing to the Little Giant's stature, but it is fair to say that the novel tactics of the Republican Convention in refusing to accept any other candidate than Lincoln had brought about an interesting situation. Three years before when Lincoln had stood against Trumbull within his own party, he had waited till after the election before canvassing the members of the legislature. Now by carrying his appeal directly to the people he focused the eyes of other states upon his novel tactics. In spite of the prejudice of partisan papers the nation was having a chance to find out that this obscure local politician was holding his own against the unbeatable "Giant."

Illinois in a curiously exact way presented a political rep-
lica of the nation. In the north lay Chicago, urban, industrial,
Republican, with a booming immigrant population, among
whom the Irish were Democratic and the Germans frankly
abolitionist. In the middle lay a border district dominated by
Springfield, the section of the Eighth Circuit where Lincoln
had personal friends. In this area strengths were nearly equal
and positions not far apart. "Down Egypt" the south was
populated by rustic farmers, mostly of Kentucky extraction,
Democrats, though by no means always pro-Douglas. They
detested abolition and the burgeoning North. Both candidates found it hard to adapt themselves to these divisions and
were quick to accuse each other of saying things in one part
of the state which they dared not repeat in another. Neither
Lincoln nor Douglas brought up any issue but slavery. There
were plenty of problems to raise about a tariff, better communications, free homesteads, or national expansion. The
preceding winter had been one of financial panic, particularly
acute in the industrial North, where the immigrant worker
without savings was rapidly brought to the point of starva-
tion. Nobody, however, seemed to feel that anything had
been omitted in the Ottawa debate, since the attendance at
Freeport for the second debate rose to over twelve thousand
despite cold drizzling weather.

By this time each candidate was ready for the other with
a series of questions designed to trap him into making an
unpopular answer. The difference was that those which
Douglas addressed to a local man seemed less important to the
outside world than those asked him by Lincoln. Among these
latter were two of historic importance. First, how did he
reconcile the Dred Scott decision with popular sovereignty?
The point was not how Douglas would answer, but whether
he would answer at all. Before he left Washington, Douglas
had said that though the Dred Scott decision forbade legisla-

tion against slavery in the territories, it by no means forced the legislatures there to pass laws without which slavery could not survive. The effective power still lay with the people and their representatives. Would Douglas be willing in a public campaign so extensively reported to repeat a doctrine offensive to the South? Lincoln had written to one of his friends a few months earlier predicting that Douglas would answer and adding, "If this offends the South, he will let it offend them, as at all events he means to hold onto his chances in Illinois." He was perfectly right in his guess. If Douglas had not answered, Lincoln would have quoted his earlier words and hammered them home, with the addition that he said in one place what he dared not say in another.

The Little Giant, fairly cornered, was explicit. Southern papers exploded in fury, and it has often been said that it was this Freeport answer which cost Douglas southern support in 1860 and ruined his chances for the Presidency. Indeed it has been suggested that Lincoln had this precise effect in mind. Both statements can at most be only partially true. The breach with Buchanan over Lecompton was just as destructive to Douglas as the Freeport answer, especially as North and South already knew what he would say. It is true, however, that the publicity of the occasion gave his answer special force, as Lincoln had perceived that it would. Lincoln was not at the moment looking forward to the Presidency for himself, and he knew that the best way to keep Douglas out of it was to defeat him for the Senate. In other words, this was less an astute move to discredit Douglas in 1860 than an attempt to increase his disfavor with the Buchanan Democrats in Illinois at the moment.

Lincoln's success was partly evident in the next debate in Jonesboro, at the tip of southern Illinois. The audience in this poor area was small, about fifteen hundred. Such as they were, however, most were unfriendly to Douglas as well as to Lincoln, being southern in outlook and loyal to Buchanan. It was hot, and by this time both candidates had been touring the state for nearly two months, speaking almost daily in the smaller towns. Even with the aid of a private car, railroad travel was by modern standards abominable. Adele Douglas later complained that she had bought her husband four dozen shirts and that he came out of the campaign with three, one of which did not belong to him. Lincoln hashed over details of strategy with politicians on the Jonesboro station platform, while waiting for the midnight train for Charleston. He was to meet Douglas there on the following day after riding nearly all the way in a crowded coach without a chance to sleep or even alter his speech in the light of what Douglas had said a few hours earlier. He had, however, if he perceived it, one consolation. Despite his private car and attendant wife, Douglas was showing signs of exhaustion. He was drinking too much again, partly to show good fellowship, but partly to keep himself going. His voice, a loud and rather monotonous bellow, did not carry well and was growing hoarse. Lincoln's physique was still as hard as iron, and his high, shrill tone, though disagreeable to many, was clearly audible.

Charleston, in Coles County, was Lincoln country. Dennis Hanks was living there, as was his daughter Harriet, who had profited by the eighteen months she spent in Springfield and had made a fairly good match. It even seems likely that Sally Bush Lincoln was staying for the time with one or the other. It was only recently that the press of business had forced Lincoln to give up attending court at Charleston, so that he knew the local lawyers and many old clients. The debate dealt once more with the issues raised at Freeport, Lincoln's supposed abolitionist views and Douglas's answer to the Freeport questions. There was plenty to say on both subjects. Lincoln hammered away on the Dred Scott decision, pointing out that Douglas's answer was really untenable, amounting, as he finally summed it up, to saying that "a thing may lawfully be driven away from where it has a lawful right to be." He also discussed what Douglas had said in answer to his other important question. If the Supreme Court were to declare it unconstitutional for a state to outlaw slavery, would Douglas support its verdict? Douglas replied that the suggestion was preposterous, for he dared neither admit in Illinois that he would uphold such a doctrine, nor declare in the hearing of the South that he would not. Lincoln was quick to point out that the Dred Scott decision itself would have been called preposterous before Douglas repealed the Missouri Compromise. If "Dred Scott" followed that act in so short a time, how long would it be before the doctrine that expediency rather than right should prevail had so eroded the public sentiment about slavery as to make another decision of the Court possible?

On a cold, damp 7th of October, the two men drew some twenty thousand at Galesburg despite a nasty wind that tore their banners down. Douglas shared with Lincoln the politician's gift of never forgetting a face or the circumstances under which he had met it. Mrs. Lanphere, with whom Douglas took dinner the night before, was famous for her mince pies. He did not omit to say to her, "Matilda, have you got a mince pie such as you used to have in those old times." She had baked one specially for him, and he would eat nothing else, remarking: "That pie and that coffee were worth taking a long trip to enjoy." Meanwhile Lincoln halted a five-mile parade escorting him from Knoxville to drink a dipper of water with an old friend.

In the debate Douglas shook his clenched fist under Lincoln's nose, and the Quincy *Daily Whig* said that he "foamed at the mouth." Lincoln, who spoke in second place, was shivering from the cold when he got up, and the *Chicago Times* said that the chattering of his teeth could be heard all over the stand. A train from Peoria carrying two thousand extra people broke down on the way because the load was too heavy, bringing its disappointed passengers into Galesburg just as the debate was over.

Six days later the candidates were at Quincy on the Mississippi, speaking to twelve thousand who had come by boat from Iowa and from Missouri as well as from Illinois. It was dawning on an astonished country that this unknown Lincoln, who had hardly been seen out of Illinois for the last nine years, was a match for the best-known leader in the nation. Reading these speeches long after the event, it is possible to conclude that he was more convincing than Douglas, but this was not apparent at the time.

Both rose to eloquence. Douglas swore he would never abandon the sacred principle of popular sovereignty. "I have defended it against the North and the South, and I will defend it against whoever assails it, and I will follow it wherever its logical conclusion leads me." Lincoln, who had in the Galesburg debate succeeded in defining in the clearest terms his differences with Douglas, developed this theme still further at Quincy and finally drove it home in the last debate at Alton. "The real issue of this controversy—the one pressing on every mind, is the sentiment on the part of one class that looks upon the institution of slavery *as a wrong,* and of another class that *does not* look on it as wrong . . . That is the issue which will continue in this country when the poor tongues of Judge Douglas and myself shall be silent. It is the eternal struggle between these two principles—right and wrong— throughout the world . . . Wherever the issue can be distinctly made, and all extraneous matter thrown out, so that men can fairly see the real difference between the parties, this difference will soon be settled."

Lincoln truly had the last word. This *was* the issue. It is Lincoln's answer to the accusation that he deliberately stirred up the country to a frantic pitch of excitement over a problem which had been virtually settled by the rejection of Lecompton. Why, it is sometimes asked, did he do so? Was it simply and solely because he wanted to be a United States Senator? To achieve this position was he prepared to do his best to foment a quarrel which was going to lead the country into war? If he had used his influence on the Republicans to accept the Little Giant, as they had accepted Trumbull and other Democrats earlier, could not Douglas have run for President in 1860 as a moderate candidate representing the mass of people North and South? In other words is not Lincoln responsible as anyone for an unnecessary war waged to settle a predetermined question?

This is a very serious indictment, but there is a good deal to be said against it. First of all, who are we to decide that the slavery issue was settled by 1858? It did not look settled then. Southerners had expansionist ambitions which might have added Cuba and lands south of the Rio Grande to their slave empire. It has been said that southern slavery depended on cotton, whose cultivation had very nearly reached its natural limits. This, however, has only a momentary truth. Already in the South slaves were beginning to be used in factories and mines. The cotton empire had been casually founded in a week or so by the ingenuity of Eli Whitney in inventing a simple device to comb out cotton. There was no telling what other slave empire might be founded in as short a time by another invention. In fact, the South was determined to expand and might have done so in a number of ways.

In the second place, if Douglas had crossed over to the Republican party, it is more likely that he would have split it to pieces than have swelled its ranks with a substantial number of Democrats. It is true that the mass of the people, both North and South, still felt loyalty to the concept of the Union. It is fair to wonder, however, whether they could have coalesced around Douglas. After all Douglas was returned to the Senate in 1858. Lincoln beat him by about four thousand in the popular vote, but owing to an outmoded apportionment law which gave extra strength to the southern part of the state, Douglas commanded a majority in the legislature. In Washington his victory was seen as a striking triumph over the administration, particularly as nearly all northern Democrats who had upheld the party line on Lecompton lost their seats. But though Douglas returned to the Senate more powerful than ever, he proved unable to close the breach in his party or in the nation. Men's minds were excited by John Brown's raid and other events both small and large over which he had no control. In any case he was unacceptable to Southern leaders and had been so ever since his split with Buchanan. How then could he have created a nationwide party in alliance with moderate Republicans when he could not do so with northern and southern Democrats?

Finally, Lincoln's ethical point has validity. He saw America as the only spot on the globe where the high ideals of liberty and equality had been established as the basic principles of a government which had endured. Despotism in the form of slaveholding had unfortunately been embedded in the structure. Lincoln saw it as a corrupting influence which might well destroy the American ideal. It was not good enough to say that slavery would wither in the present territories because it was unsuited to their climates or was not expedient. He saw it had to be recognized as wrong. Otherwise why not enslave the Irish in a factory system in the North? On what principle could states exclude the institution if some of their people found it profitable? Once the conviction that all men were created equal was eroded, it would be difficult to draw a hard-and-fast line between those to whom it applied and to whom it did not.

After the Quincy debate, second-last in the series, a news

reporter went to see Lincoln and found him "surrounded by admirers, who had made the discovery that one who had previously been considered merely a curious compound of genius and simplicity was really a great man . . . He sat in the room with his boots off, to relieve his very large feet from the pain occasioned by continuous standing; or, to put it in his own words, I like to give my feet a chance to breathe. He had removed his coat and vest, dropped one suspender from his shoulder, taken off his necktie and collar, and he sat tilted back in one chair with his feet upon another in perfect ease. . . . I never saw a more thoughtful face. I never saw a more dignified face. I never saw so sad a face."

Later, in his last speech before the election, delivered in Springfield, Lincoln himself summed up his attitude in words which it is hard not to believe. "The legal right of the southern people to reclaim their fugitives I have constantly admitted. The legal right of Congress to interfere with their institution in the states, I have constantly denied. In resisting the spread of slavery to new territory and with that, what appears to me to be a tendency to subvert the first principles of free government itself, my whole effort has consisted. To the best of my judgment I have labored *for*, and not *against* the Union." He further added: "Ambition has been ascribed to me. . . . I claim no insensibility to political honors; but . . . could the Missouri restriction be restored, and the whole slavery question replaced on the old ground of 'toleration' by *necessity* where it exists, with unyielding hostility to the spread of it, on principle, I would, in consideration, gladly agree, that Judge Douglas should never be *out*, and I never *in*, an office, so long as we both or either live." While it is not necessary to believe Lincoln automatically, it must at least be admitted that no position could have been more clearly or forcibly stated.

13

Lincoln Moves
onto the National Stage

———◆———

THE ELECTION OF NOVEMBER 2, 1858, gave Lincoln a popular majority, but Douglas retained control of the legislature by which the senator would be chosen. The fight had been so close that Lincoln had hoped at times to win. Now he knew that he had lost and could reckon up what lay ahead. He was only a few months short of his fiftieth birthday and would have to wait for another six years for a chance at the Senate, since it would not be fair to oppose Trumbull when he came up for re-election. "I shall fight in the ranks," he wrote to Norman B. Judd, Republican chairman of the Illinois State Central Committee. This meant that he would campaign for the presidential candidate and do his best to help Trumbull in 1860, but that his personal future in politics did not look rosy. He must have often remembered that Douglas had entered the Senate at thirty-four.

Matters were not helped by a letter from Judd, asking what he could contribute to the Republican treasury, which was in debt—largely on his account. Lincoln himself had made over sixty speeches, but had merely been the hardest-worked of many. German-speaking orators had been drafted, some from out of state. The actual legislators running on the Republican ticket, Senator Trumbull back from Washington, and all other available persons had been drawn in. Republican news editors had worked themselves almost to death, only to see the great prize lost by a hairsbreadth. There was a general feeling, which some well-meaning people passed on to Lincoln, that nobody liked to follow a leader who had been beaten.

Lincoln made the best of the hard facts before him, writing to Judd: "I am willing to pay according to my ability; but I am the poorest hand living to get others to pay. I have been on expenses so long without earning anything that I am absolutely without money now, for even domestic expenses." He had campaigned extensively for four months, during which time he had paid his own modest expenses for travel and accommodation as well as contributing $250 to the campaign. He now promised $250 more. He was not destitute, but his savings were tied up in long-term investments, very often loans to friends. Mary Lincoln was going to have to make do until his earnings from legal practice began to bring in income. It seems probable that home was at this time a depressing place.

Lincoln had not taken Mary with him as he toured the state, but was heard with rare malice to remark that his wife did not have to trail around with him to make sure he did not get drunk. Mary liked to travel, but no woman subject to sick headaches could have endured the discomforts of this campaign. Adele Douglas had contributed nothing but her looks and her care of her husband, not venturing anything so unladylike as speaking. Mary Lincoln was now forty and had preserved her figure, her smooth white arms, and her small hands very well; but her face had developed lines which betrayed her years. She had nothing to put in competition with Adele Douglas. In any case she was needed at home. No one seems to have got more fun out of "Paw's" campaign than Willie and Tad, and "Mother" must keep these irrepressibles in line.

Mary had traveled to hear the final debate at Alton, but apart from this she had been little seen. Her role was a hard one for a woman of her ardent temperament, and she had buoyed herself up by an irrational optimism based chiefly on strong Whig principles and a belief in her husband. She had told him he was not only going to be senator, but President of the United States, as Lincoln confided to the correspondent of a German newspaper, laughing heartily. "Just think of such a sucker as me for President," he said. Disappointment and lack of ready cash must have been hard on Mary. No evidence suggests that she reproached Lincoln, but the nature of her tensions disclosed itself later.

Lincoln himself was concerned to cheer up his supporters, maintaining that Douglas was due for a great fall, since he could not forever play the opponent of slavery in the North and its advocate in the South. The difficulties of Douglas's position were underlined by the fact that he had left Illinois immediately after the election for a tour of the South, his object manifestly being to undo any damage his words in Illinois had produced.

Still more encouragingly, the Illinois Republicans had gained greatly in strength since 1856, so that they actually might have won had not conservative eastern leaders remained lukewarm or even endorsed Douglas. Their hope had been that a coalition of anti-Lecompton Democrats and moderate Republicans might rally behind him to form a party which was not entirely northern. In particular, Horace Greeley, editor of the New York *Tribune*, which published a weekly widely read in Illinois, had throughout the campaign either refused to mention Lincoln or damned him with faint praise, deploring the blindness of Illinois Republicans in failing to see that Douglas was their natural leader.

For himself personally, Lincoln drew what consolation he could from reflecting: "Though I sink out of view and be forgotten, I believe I have made some marks which will tell for the cause of civil liberty long after I am gone." Despite his habitual melancholy, he had great powers of resilience. As he started home on the night of the election, one foot slipped on the path and knocked the other from under him. He felt himself falling, made a quick twist, and regained his footing. "It's a slip and not a fall," he said to himself, finding comfort in the vague, superstitious idea that it was an omen.

Hardly was the campaign over before small Illinois newspapers, echoed by one or two out of state, began to capitalize on the debates by suggesting that Lincoln would make a good candidate for the Presidency in 1860. When Lincoln next went to Bloomington, his old friend Jesse Fell introduced him to his brother, who had just returned from the East with the news that everyone was asking, "Who is this man Lincoln?" The Fells agreed that he was a presidential possibility and wanted him to supply facts for a biographical sketch. Lincoln was unimpressed. What was the use, he demanded, of talking about him for President when among Republican statesmen who desired the place were several who had long been nationally known? All such men had made enemies, Fell pointed out. The Republicans had been so lately put together out of widely differing groups that a public man of any stature almost inevitably had powerful sections of it against him. Lincoln was suitable precisely because he took a moderate position and had not so far been in the limelight.

Lincoln disagreed, refused the biography for the present, and did his best to discourage this sort of talk. As far as can be known, he thought the idea preposterous, but it may be that his infallible political sense told him merely that it was premature. If his nomination were ever to be seriously canvassed, it must not be too early lest it give time for an opposition to form.

By early in 1859 it was clear that Lincoln's reputation had profited far more from the debates than had that of Douglas. Indeed, their effect in Washington had been adverse to Douglas. Southern leaders had been stirred up by his attitude on the Dred Scott case to demand special protective laws for slavery in the territories, while a cabal encouraged by the administration had during his absence deprived him of the chairmanship of the Committee on Territories. Douglas was finding it difficult to retain any following among the Democrats of the South, whose support was essential if the party was to win in 1860.

On the other hand Lincoln, preparing to publish the great debates in book form, had everything to gain from them and nothing to lose. His political stature had grown enormously. Some states held elections in 1859: many of these were anxious to have Lincoln as a speaker. Furthermore the Republican party, aware of its own divisions, was trying hard to pull together abolitionists, immigrants, anti-immigrants, ex-Whigs, and ex-Democrats into a harmonious whole. Some political leaders were disposed to ask advice from Lincoln, whose campaign had shown how much could be done in this fashion. They soon noted that his judgment was sound.

Lincoln spoke in Kansas and also in Iowa. Douglas was asked to help Democrats in Ohio, and Republicans there immediately wanted Lincoln to come and answer. Taking Mary for the sake of the trip, he spoke in Columbus, Cincinnati, and smaller towns, urging Republican moderates to stick by their party and not make common cause with Douglas. A little later he was off again to speak at the State Fair in Wisconsin. His oratorical style was by now fully developed, and all of these speeches were important ones. The debates had hammered out his message, helping him to define clearly how a moderate Republican like himself must differ from Douglas and would betray his cause and his conscience if he did not. This was exactly what northern audiences wanted to hear, since the vast majority were anti-slavery moderates. Their leaders were asking men to make a stand and then blurring the issues, so that they did not know which party to stand by. Lincoln was perfectly clear, eloquent, and convincing. His fame spread over the bounds of his state, but his need to earn a living prevented him from traveling far.

In Washington the tension grew ever greater between North and South, giving Douglas little chance to improve the atmosphere. More and more he was being pushed into the position of a purely northern politician, hated by the administration and the South. Events over which he had no control raised feelings to white-hot heat. Lincoln was speaking in Kansas at the time that old John Brown was hanged in Virginia for trying to engineer a slave uprising by his seizure of Harper's Ferry. Brown's financial backing came from New England, from wealthy abolitionists who would probably vote Republican. Lincoln was at pains to tell Kansas clearly that lawless deeds and muddled enthusiasms were no answer to the national problem. Douglas of course agreed, but all knew that Brown had served his apprenticeship in violence in Kansas, where the struggle had resulted from Douglas's own plan for the territories. It was in any case hard for Douglas to appeal to moderates because there were fewer in Washington than in the Northwest. The Little Giant had too many enemies to be able to control events.

Lincoln had the advantage that he was not trying to control events because no one expected him to. He was working to build the party by putting forward the basic principles on which all must unite. He by no means entirely relied on his own eloquence to do this. Secretly, for instance, he bought a German-American newspaper published in Springfield on the understanding that it should express Republican sentiments in the 1860 campaign. In the wake of the debates Illinois was busy organizing in a practical, political way. The size of the vote for Lincoln had shown that further effort ought to be worthwhile. New lodges were being founded, headquarters established, letters written. A series of political speeches enlivened the dullness of rural or commercial life. Norman B. Judd, still chairman of the Illinois State Central Committee, was aided in this work by Jesse W. Fell, the man who had had the notion of publicizing Lincoln's background in the hope of making him a presidential candidate.

Late in the fall of 1859 Judd represented Illinois in a New York meeting of the Republican National Committee, which was charged with selecting a site for the Republican Convention of 1860. Friends of the three most prominent candidates put forward various places where they thought their own man would have an advantage. A wrangle followed during which Judd suggested with seeming casualness that since Illinois had no special candidate of her own, Chicago would be a neutral choice. The idea suited everyone. All eastern politicians would be at equal disadvantage. The influence of the Northwest in the Republican party was great and growing, and no national convention had hitherto been held west of Cincinnati. Moreover analysis of the 1856 elections had shown there were four states which Republicans had then failed to carry whose support was essential if they were to win in 1860. Illinois was one of these. Chicago itself was now a city of 110,000, a place of many transients, raw, bustling, full of hotels and boarding-houses, not to mention saloons and brothels. There was room in it for a big convention to spread out.

The selection of Chicago had an important effect on Abraham Lincoln. All year there had been increasing mention of him as worthy of a place on the national ticket. Cameron of Pennsylvania and Chase of Ohio, both hot in pursuit of the prize, had spoken of Lincoln as a possible running mate. Things had gone far enough for Lincoln to send Jesse Fell the autobiographical sketch which he had refused a year earlier, commenting: "There is not much of it, for the reason, I suppose, that there is not much of me. If any thing be made of it, I wish it to be modest, and not to go beyond the material." He was not taking seriously his chances of nomination, but he had by now to consider that they existed.

Now that the convention was to meet in Chicago, Lincoln immediately saw that his political future depended on getting his name put forward by the Illinois delegation. If these men would not vote unanimously for him during one or two ballots as their favorite son, it must damage his chances against Douglas four years later for the Senate. For this reason and not because he seriously expected a nomination, Lincoln began to ask for commitments. "I am not in a position where it would hurt much for me not to be nominated on the national ticket," he wrote to Judd, "but I am where it would hurt some for me not to get the Illinois delegates." This change in attitude on Lincoln's part excited people who would like to be king-makers. Joseph Medill, editor of the *Chicago Tribune*, was a rather late convert, but early in 1860 he began to keep Lincoln before the public eye, publishing extracts from his speeches, keeping in touch with his movements, and reprinting a Milwaukee article which had argued that Lincoln of Illinois would be easier to elect than Seward of New York or Chase of Ohio, the latter of whom had been till now the *Tribune*'s choice. Medill went to Washington to persuade Republican congressmen that Lincoln could carry the doubtful states whereas others could not. In February the *Chicago Tribune* came out openly for Abraham Lincoln of Illinois.

In October, 1859, before the drive for Lincoln as President had gathered momentum, he had received an invitation to lecture at the Reverend Henry Ward Beecher's Plymouth Church in Brooklyn, New York. Henry Beecher, brother of the authoress of *Uncle Tom's Cabin*, was a man whose gift for dramatic sermons had made his church so famous that two thousand applicants for pews were turned away each year, while its income, derived solely from pew-rents, was prodigious. Plymouth was by all odds the most prestigious church in the East, and it could afford to pay two hundred dollars for a lecture in front of the most sophisticated audience in New York.

The offer was especially attractive to Lincoln, because his family concerns gave him a motive for visiting the East. Robert Lincoln, his eldest son, exposed to indifferent schooling in Springfield and never much encouraged by his father on the grounds that when he wanted something he would start to work, had wanted to go to Harvard. After he failed fifteen of the sixteen entrance examinations, it had been decided that he should have a year at Phillips Exeter Academy to prepare him. Here he now was, and his doting parents, unused to the absence of one of their sons from the family circle, were glad of a chance to find out how he was getting on. It would be possible for Lincoln to return via New England, while the two-hundred-dollar fee would pay for the trip. For several reasons therefore Lincoln inclined to favor the notion. Though he still probably had not the least idea of becoming President, it was evident that his increasing reputation might send him to the United States Senate in 1864. There was, however, one problem. Lincoln had never been a success as a lecturer on general subjects. He had tried on various occasions, but either conviction or education had seemed lacking. Aware of his own deficiency, he inquired whether a political lecture was acceptable. He was told it would be.

Lincoln realized that this occasion called for more than a good campaign speech. Since Beecher was strongly anti-slavery, his congregation would tend towards abolitionism rather than to making common cause with Douglas. Lincoln needed a subject and thought he had one which would give substance to what he had to say. In his recent debates with Douglas the two had differed sharply about the attitude of the founding fathers of the country toward congressional power to control slavery in the territories. Neither of them had been well enough versed in the minute details of constitutional history to refute the other. Now, after a great deal of painstaking research, Lincoln proved to his satisfaction that a clear majority of the signers of the Constitution and also of the members of Congress who passed the first ten amendments had acted on the belief that Congress did have this power. With this as basic material for his speech, Lincoln bought himself new boots and a better suit to face New York in. These Mary packed in a trunk belonging to herself, since it was, she said, less shabby than his own. Fortified by a basket of food, he boarded the train for a slow, uncomfortable, sitting-up ride to Philadelphia, whence another train took him to New Jersey and then a ferry boat to New York.

On Saturday afternoon, February 25, 1860, Henry C. Bowen, the editor of a nationally known religious weekly, was still in his New York office trying to catch up with his work. He was interrupted by the appearance of Abraham Lincoln, who said he was just in from Illinois and very tired. Could he lie down on the couch and listen while Bowen explained the arrangements for Monday night's lecture?

Bowen, who was suffering from the usual shock that Lincoln's appearance inflicted on people who had not met him before, hardly knew what to say to this rawboned prairie lawyer who, as he could see at a glance, would be a comic figure to the best society of New York. What made the matter worse was that Plymouth Church had had last-minute doubts about the "political lecture" and had adroitly transferred it to the Young Men's Republican Union of New York City, an anti-Seward organization which was interested in any possible rival to the New York senator for the Presidency. Lincoln had been informed of this fact when directed to seek out Bowen, but not that the place of the lecture had been moved to the Cooper Union Hall, the largest in Manhattan, seating about two thousand. Horace Greeley of the New York *Tribune*, who had a deadly political feud with Seward, had given the coming occasion wide publicity; and a large audience from the elite of New York was expected. Introducing Lincoln would be William Cullen Bryant, editor of the New York *Evening Post* and a literary figure of international fame. Bowen, who had been largely responsible for the new arrangement, concluded with a sinking heart that Lincoln would not impress this sort of audience.

Since it was impossible to cancel the lecture, Bowen talked and gradually began to feel a little better. Noticing Lincoln's gentle dignity and absence of self-consciousness, he hoped these qualities would make up for his defects. Meantime he asked Lincoln whether he would like to share his pew in Plymouth Church on Sunday in order to listen to the great preacher. Lincoln agreed that this would indeed be a treat and departed for the Astor House, where Judd had stayed during the momentous meeting of the Republican National Committee.

Even for New York the Astor House was large. It accommodated six hundred guests at about two dollars a night and was known for the excellence of its restaurant and bar. Lincoln's sponsors, who had promised him that he would meet "in this great Commercial Metropolis a right cordial welcome," did not appear with a reception committee until late on Monday morning. Bowen, content with having invited Lincoln to church, where he could introduce him to a number of men who would be sitting on his platform, had turned back to his interrupted work, stifling his misgivings. A politician, however, is never really a lonely figure even in a small room in a large hotel in a city strange to him. During his short stopover in Philadelphia Lincoln had received a card from Simon Cameron, senator and presidential aspirant, and one from David Wilmot, author of the famous proviso which Lincoln had voted for "as good as forty times" during his term in Congress. He had paid a call in return and, finding no one, had time to write a polite note before taking the train.

Similarly in New York, Elihu B. Washburne, congressman from Illinois, came up from Washington to see Lincoln on Sunday. On Monday an old acquaintance who had been solicitor for the Illinois Central Railroad paid a call and was followed by a delegation from New Jersey, which had read Greeley's announcement and wanted a speech. Only after these did the Young Men's Republican Union wait on Lincoln, inquiring somewhat late in the day what arrangements he had made to have the text of his speech printed in the papers the following morning. Finding that he did not know how to go about this and had only brought one copy, they took him over to the *Tribune*, which agreed to set it in galleys and distribute it to other papers, promising to let Lincoln have it back in the late afternoon.

Having finally picked up their lecturer, the welcoming committee evidently liked him, for they offered to show him some of the town and included a publicity visit to the studio of Mathew Brady, pioneer portrait photographer. Brady studied his subject with care before deciding how his odd looks could best be made impressive. He tried to adjust the low collar and black ribbon necktie.

"Ah," said Lincoln, "I see you want to shorten my neck."

"That's just it," retorted Brady. Both of them laughed. The head clamp which was used to hold a subject still for long enough for the picture to "take" was not high enough for a man of six feet four, and Brady had to put a stool under it. Eventually he made the first of his many likenesses of Lincoln.

It was snowing on the evening of the Cooper Union lecture, but about fifteen hundred braved the weather, making a respectable, if not a packed, audience. Lincoln later admitted that as he came out to take his place on the platform, he felt as ill at ease as ever in his life. The new suit, crumpled from packing, was not a success. Lincoln was rarely conscious of what he wore, but the garments of the distinguished men who sat on the platform were of such a different order from his own that he realized at this unfortunate moment how he must look to them. William Cullen Bryant made his introduction with grace but all too briefly and sat down. It was Lincoln's turn.

Lincoln still felt embarrassed. Noah Brooks, later an intimate friend, says that he opened by addressing Bryant in his broad western accent as "Mr. Cheerman," which raised a titter. Lincoln was preoccupied by the fact that the right side of his coat collar flew up in an odd way when he lifted his arm to make a gesture. He started almost too quietly, being afraid that he might shout after speaking so often out of doors. All this produced an unimpressive beginning of what was planned as a skillful piece of exposition, Lincoln the lawyer making his case plain to a jury. "Old fellow, you won't do," murmured Brooks to himself. "It's all very well for the Wild West but this will never go down in New York."

It was not long, however, before the audience found itself interested in the subject. The founding fathers had voted this way or that on the following occasions, indicating that the following men took for granted the authority over the territories with regard to slavery which the Dred Scott decision had denied. Lincoln was developing a careful, logical, convincing case. The rhetoric, when at last it came, was simple, insidious, carefully developed. In view of the attitude of the founders it was the South, not the North, which was unfolding new doctrines. It was the South which was threatening to break up the Union unless it gained what it wanted, while at the same time it pretended that the crime of destroying the nation would rest on the North. "A highwayman holds a pistol to my ear, and mutters through his teeth, 'Stand and deliver, or I shall kill you, and then you will be a murderer!' "

What did the South really want from the people of the North? "This and this only: cease to call slavery *wrong* and join them in calling it *right*. And this must be done thoroughly—done in *acts* as well as in *words*." Swiftly Lincoln outlined the necessary acts, all unacceptable to his audience, as well he knew. They were aroused by now, and he could call on them to examine their consciences and stand by their plain duty without groping for a middle ground—"vain as the search for a man who should be neither a living man nor a dead man." He let that sink in for the sake of Greeley and others who had attempted to make a deal with the Douglasites. Then he came to his conclusion: "Let us have faith that right makes might, and in that faith, let us dare to do our duty as we understand it." That this amounted to a plea for war over the slavery issue if it should prove necessary, neither Lincoln nor the audience was disposed to consider. Like many a great declaration of war it brought people to their feet, cheering, waving handkerchiefs, and throwing hats in the air. "He's the greatest man since St. Paul!" cried Noah Brooks, totally converted.

The inner circle of the club carried Lincoln off to a supper and had a very good time. Only one had the courtesy to walk back with him to the Astor. Lincoln was limping and confided that his new boots hurt. They mounted a horsecar, and Lincoln's companion alighted at his own destination, merely saying the car was going right down by the Astor. There were no other passengers, and Lincoln looked to his backward glance both sad and lonely. Probably he was only suffering from reaction, but his escort reproached himself for having left him to make his own way back with a blister on his heel and a confused impression of people cheering, awkward clothes, a tactless question at supper: "Mr. Lincoln, what candidate do you really think would be most likely to carry Illinois?," for all the world as though there could be no possible question of Lincoln *of* Illinois being in the field.

Though they were looking for a candidate to replace Seward, the New Yorkers had not included Lincoln in their original program and showed no signs of having found more in him than a fine orator. Meanwhile, Lincoln had not quite finished his day. He found the *Tribune* office nearly opposite the Astor and climbed to the fourth floor to chat with the night editor while the galleys of his speech were being fetched. He put on his spectacles, checked the proofs carefully, and went away, leaving a manuscript which would have been priceless to later collectors for the editor to toss into his wastepaper basket.

It is by no means true that the Cooper Union speech converted Easterners to the idea of making Lincoln President. The publicity which he got from Greeley, however, and the text of his speech in various other papers did result in pressing invitations to speak throughout New England. On his way to Exeter, when he got there, and later in other parts of New Hampshire, he delivered a dozen addresses. Only in Manchester was he introduced as the "next President," which means that elsewhere the notion was too fantastic even for the exaggerations of exuberant politicians. "I have been unable to escape this toil," wrote Lincoln to Mary. "If I had foreseen it, I think I would not have come East at all. The speech in New York, being within my calculation before I started, went off passably well and gave me no trouble whatever. The difficulty was to make nine others before reading audiences who had already seen all my ideas in print."

Popular enthusiasm is often supposed to have no effect on political choices, but it does have an indirect one on politicians. Lincoln's friends in Illinois soon began to look on him less as a "favorite son" with a complimentary first vote from his own delegation than as a "dark horse," a runner who might just possibly be worth pushing to win. This attitude was only in part due to his oratorical successes, for an important question had been asked of him in December during the meeting of the legislature in Springfield. Prominent among the men who hoped for the Presidency was Simon Cameron, political boss of Pennsylvania, one of the four states which had voted Democratic in the last election and whose support was necessary if Republicans were to win in 1860. Cameron had an unsavory financial reputation, but many thought that his control of a doubtful state with fifty-four electoral votes was of crucial importance. Jackson Grimshaw of Quincy, Illinois, had been prominent in organizing Cameron-Lincoln clubs to push Cameron for President with Lincoln as his Vice President. Taking advantage of the opportunity afforded by the gathering of leading Illinois Republicans in Springfield, Grimshaw succeeded in organizing a confidential meeting.

Grimshaw's proposal was introduced with tact. Lincoln was asked if his name could be put in nomination for the Presidency, to which he consented after decent hesitation. This cleared the way for a further question which was, to Grimshaw at least, the point of the discussion. Suppose at the convention it became obvious that Lincoln could not win the nomination, would he accept the Vice Presidency? "No," replied Lincoln without hesitation, ruling out not only Grimshaw's proposition, but any other wire-pulling which might tend to a similar result.

From Lincoln's point of view, this answer had undoubtedly meant that his chief aim was to defeat Douglas the next time that he ran for the Senate, and that the Vice Presidency did not interest him for this reason. Its effect, however, was the formation of a Lincoln committee pledged to support him either for the Presidency or for nothing in 1860. Some of those involved were not yet ready to make more than a token effort, but others had come to the conclusion that it might be worth their while to gamble on him.

In March on his return from the East, Lincoln himself was unquestionably encouraged by his successes there. "The taste *is* in my mouth a little," he admitted to Senator Trumbull. In letters to other prominent men he discussed the chances of various candidates in Illinois. Seward of New York and Chase of Ohio were too radical and Bates of Missouri too southern to carry the state. McLean, a Supreme Court justice of seventy-five with a repellant manner, would be the best choice if he were not too old. Without mentioning himself, Lincoln knew how to make it look highly doubtful whether anyone else could carry the state against Douglas should the Little Giant become the Democratic champion. He did not need to add that the man who had beaten Douglas in popular votes for the Senate was the man who could do it again if he ran for the Presidency.

14

The Railsplitter

LINCOLN'S DRAWBACKS AS A presidential candidate were just as obvious to his friends as were his assets. What had he ever done except pass a couple of undistinguished years in Congress and fail to be elected senator? If the obscurity of his career had helped him to avoid making enemies, it had also failed to create admirers on a national scale. Plenty of presidential candidates without experience of office had been entered by parties before, and some of these had won. What they had possessed was emotional appeal. Since at that time a candidate was not expected to canvass personally, Lincoln's oratorical powers and capacity for making friends would not come into the campaign. He had to have, not a personality, but an image which would present him to the masses in a favorable light. It was a piece of good fortune for Lincoln that the arrangements for the state convention, which would elect delegates to Chicago, were in the hands of Richard J. Oglesby, who had natural talents as a publicity man.

The first task was to arouse a sense of the importance of the occasion. Chicago was completing a special building for the national convention which had been christened "The Wigwam." Oglesby determined to have his own Wigwam in Decatur, where state delegates were about to assemble. It was rather a hasty affair of logs and canvas, but it gave the meeting a revivalist atmosphere which promised excitement. While this was going up, Oglesby racked his brains for something which would make "Old Abe" a romantic figure, provide him with a nickname like "Old Hickory." Many a catchword had elected a President. Why not go back into Abe's pioneer background? That was something fading into a glamorous past in Illinois, but it evoked popular memories.

It happened that John Hanks, Lincoln's cousin, was living in Decatur. Oglesby went to see him and wanted to know the kinds of things Abe used to be good at. "Not much of any kind but dreaming," said John Hanks, evidently remembering the boy who tucked a book inside his shirt when he went plowing or interrupted the folk at harvest time with a political oration. "He did help me split a lot of rails when we made the clearing twelve miles west of here," said Hanks, ruminating. The comment suited Oglesby exactly. He drove Hanks out to where the rails had been, and rails of a sort were certainly still there. Hanks whittled off a few chips and found that the wood was black walnut and honey locust, just as he remembered it had been. Oglesby took a couple back to town slung under his buggy and found a sign-painter.

Illinois delegates came crowding into Decatur on May 9, only a week before the convention in Chicago. Their job was to choose candidates for state offices, including governor, and twenty-two delegates to the national convention, representing the Illinois electoral votes. Not all prospective delegates were for Lincoln, and most were unsure whether they ought not to decide where their votes were going after paying their opening compliments to Illinois' favorite son. If they had so decided, this would have been the end of Lincoln's chances as a candidate.

Proceedings began about half-past ten, but not until after lunchtime did the permanent officers get selected and the meeting was called to order. Up jumped Oglesby to announce: "I am informed that a distinguished citizen of Illinois

and one whom Illinois will ever delight to honor, is present;
and I wish to move that this body invite him to a seat on the
stand." He made a dramatic pause before shouting:
"Abraham Lincoln!" Lincoln, who was sitting near the back,
rose to his feet, but the assemblage was too tightly packed for
him to get through to the platform. Before he could object,
men had seized him and were passing him over their heads,
while those who could not reach him were cheering loudly.
They went on roaring as he tried to thank them, looking, as
a sympathetic spectator remarked, "one of the most diffident
and worst-plagued men I ever saw." Oglesby, who had not
finished with him yet, got up again to announce that an old
Macon County Democrat who had grown gray in the service
of his party wanted to contribute something to the meeting.

"Receive it! Receive it!" yelled the crowd, some of whom
had been primed beforehand.

Down through the center aisle marched old John Hanks
with a friend, each carrying a rail, between which hung a
banner saying:

ABRAHAM LINCOLN
THE RAIL CANDIDATE FOR PRESIDENT IN 1860

Two rails from a lot of 3,000 made in 1830
By Thos. Hanks and Abe Lincoln Whose
Father was the First Pioneer of Macon County

It did not matter that the sign painter had got John Hanks's
name wrong and that Thomas Lincoln was not the first pioneer of Macon County. The audience got the message and
nearly took the roof off the Wigwam. Hats, canes, books,
papers were tossed wildly in the air. The yell was heard for
miles around, and part of the awning fell in. The tumult went
on for fifteen minutes, at the end of which the perspiring
delegates discovered that they had created not a statesman,
not a man of genius, but a people's candidate, an Old Hickory,

a Tippecanoe, "The Railsplitter," a man symbolizing the success of free labor in the Land of Opportunity. Less than twenty-four hours later, after filling out the state ticket, they resolved, "That Abraham Lincoln is the choice of the Republican Party of Illinois for the Presidency, and the delegates from this State are instructed to use all honorable means to secure his nomination by the Chicago Convention and to vote as a unit for him." It was a notable victory, the more so as several of the delegates would, if left to themselves, have preferred Seward. The Lincoln boom had gained a head start on its opponents.

The moment that Chicago was announced as the site of the Republican National Convention, the leaders of that hustling town had determined to make something of it which had never been seen before. Five thousand dollars were subscribed to put up a special building designed to hold ten thousand people. Outside in Market Square, there was room for about thirty thousand more, who could be entertained by speakers sent out to give descriptions of the events within. Norman Judd persuaded some of the railroads, which in turn put pressure on others, to offer cut rates for fares to the convention. In fact it shortly dawned upon surprised Republicans that Chicago was inviting not merely the convention, but in effect the whole party.

It became necessary for those presidential aspirants who had well-drilled campaign organizations to send hordes of supporters to fill the Wigwam and even to yell in the crowd outside. Word was being passed around in Illinois that supporters of Abraham Lincoln could serve their candidate by merely appearing at the biggest, loudest, most spectacular spree ever held. Since most Illinoisians had been born out of state, groups were soon organized to mix with Republicans from their home states, offer hospitality, and talk about "the Railsplitter." Inside the Wigwam delegates were to be seated

on an enormous V-shaped platform faced by standing spectators on a gradually rising floor as well as by balconies above.
Each delegation had its own seating, to which Norman B.
Judd, chairman of the Illinois State Central Committee, had
given much thought. He was able to arrange things so that the
New York delegation, which had seventy votes and whose
candidate, William H. Seward, was expected to win, was
placed well off to the side, far removed from those delegations
which it most wished to influence. Illinois was unobtrusively
in a favorable position to talk with doubtful groups. Similarly
in the matter of tickets favoritism was blatant, yet not so great
that it would be objected to by New York, which might stand
to lose somewhat by raising the question.

The Lincoln committee took up headquarters at the Tremont House, Chicago's leading hotel. In outward showing
the group was not large, consisting only of David Davis,
wealthy judge of the Eighth Circuit, who was paying its expenses; Judge Stephen T. Logan, Lincoln's old partner; Jesse
K. Dubois, state auditor; and Leonard Swett, longtime political associate of Lincoln. There were not enough of them to
look formidable, but they had quantities of local help to call
on.

Far and away the favorite candidate among the bettors was
William H. Seward, who had served both as senator and governor of New York, besides being one of the early members
of the Republican National party. Seward was the political
protegé of Thurlow Weed, Republican boss of New York
State, whose control over his party machine was so absolute
that even Horace Greeley of the New York *Tribune* could not
get a place in the New York delegation and had been forced
to enter the convention as proxy for a friend in Oregon. In
person Seward was an odd-looking man with a thatch of
tow-colored hair, a nose like the beak of a parrot, and a reced-
ing chin. He was, however, both witty and intelligent, a

clever speaker, an influential senator, and a politician who had remained personally honest while profiting from the shamelessly corrupt Weed machine. He had been in effect leader of the party since its foundation and had very nearly gained the nomination in 1856.

There were really only three objections to Seward. The first of these was the Weed machine, which clearly intended to control the patronage which made the Presidency worth struggling for. The second was Seward's enlightened tolerance of Irish immigrants during his term as governor in New York. This had made him unpopular with the native American party which, after running Fillmore in 1856, had fallen to pieces. Victory in the coming campaign might easily depend on how many of these floating voters the Republicans could pick up. The third objection to Seward was really a flaw in the man himself. Either he talked more belligerently than he acted, or else he was a prey to strange impulses which contradicted his general policy. On the matter of slavery, for instance, he was as conservative as Lincoln, yet where Lincoln had challenged opinion with "A house divided against itself cannot stand," Seward, campaigning in New York State in that same fall of 1858, had spoken of two different labor systems in the country, slave and free, which were being brought into collision. He defined the situation as an "irrepressible conflict between opposing and enduring forces." Not only were these phrases stronger than Lincoln's, but they were uttered by a far more important man.

Among all the things which lost Seward the Presidency, those two words "irrepressible conflict" bulked very large. They marked him as a near-abolitionist, which he was not, and a man who looked forward to war, which he did not do. Such a position is easier to take up than to recede from. Seward made the effort in a great Senate speech in March, 1860, but his attempt to reassure moderates damped the enthusiasm of his extremist supporters without ever killing the suspicion that he stood too far left of center.

Being a candidate, Seward did not appear in person at Chicago, but Weed arrived with thirteen railroad cars full of supporters, tough-looking characters, it was noticed, and mostly drunk. These of course were merely the marchers and shouters, the men who were to be seen and heard to give the impression that the masses were overwhelmingly for Seward. Weed himself, disdaining the Tremont House, where most of the aspirants had set up headquarters, established himself at Richmond House, which was soon buzzing with Seward activity. Weed had offices to promise in Seward's government and hard cash to bestow as well. No man was better aware that more than noise and numbers were needed to nominate a President. The rumor was that delegations were falling like ripe blackberries into his outstretched hand. There would be no chance for Lincoln or indeed for anyone else if the Seward momentum could not be checked before the voting started.

The problem of a convention is really twofold. In the first place, it wants to select not the best future President, but the man who can win the election. In the second place, each state delegation wants to climb on the right bandwagon. This means that each wants to be close not merely to a man who can win the nomination, but to the one who actually does, expecting his gratitude to take tangible form in appointments for state leaders. Typical of this in 1860 was the attitude of the Indiana delegation. Indiana with twenty-six electoral votes was one of the states which had voted Democratic in the 1856 election and which the Republicans needed to carry if they were to elect a President who could not expect any support in the South. Each of the other three states in this position had its favorite son. Illinois had Lincoln. Pennsylvania, which had sent six hundred shouters to support its delegation, was fairly well under the control of the Cameron machine. New Jersey had William Dayton, who had run as Vice President on the 1856 ticket. Indiana alone had no presidential candidate and could, by throwing its large block of votes to any of the others, start a serious movement for some rival to Seward.

Indiana was for sale on its own terms, but had a preference for making a deal with Lincoln, since he had grown up in Indiana and had friends there. For this reason an official letter came to the Lincoln committee a short while before the Chicago convention opened. Twenty-six electoral votes were to be had at a price. Would Lincoln buy? Lincoln is said to have hesitated. Selling offices to get votes was not a new conception. The essence of political trading has always been that by making some concession, you try to gain a point more important to you. The question really was how far to go. Thurlow Weed, for instance, was known to have made so many promises of offices in Seward's name should he become President that there was little left for a latecomer. Seward's hands were effectively tied before he ever could be nominated. Lincoln evidently felt that Seward's position was wrong, but did that mean he should make no promises at all? If so, he had better get "the taste of it" out of his mouth with speed and disband his committee. Lincoln wrote to the Indiana men that Leonard Swett and Jesse K. Dubois would meet them in Chicago. In the event the Indiana delegation wanted the Secretaryship of the Interior for their leader Caleb B. Smith, and the Bureau of Indian Affairs for William P. Dole, an influential politician who had lately moved from Indiana to Illinois.

This secret bargain with Indiana had potential importance for Lincoln only if the Indiana delegates would keep it. It was known that many of them preferred Bates of Missouri to Lincoln, and until the showdown came, no one could be perfectly certain that the rank and file would stay in line behind their leaders. Bates was a sixty-six-year-old Missouri lawyer who still called himself a Whig and had not even voted Republican in 1856. His strength lay in his position in Missouri, a border slave-state. Bates had owned slaves in the past, and his anti-slavery sentiment was so mild that he looked more acceptable to some of the border states than anyone else. His candidacy was being pressed by Francis P. Blair, old intimate of President Jackson, and his two sons, one powerful in Missouri and the other in Maryland and Delaware. The Blairs were clannish and had many enemies. All the same it was obvious that the adherence of border states where slavery existed would make the Republicans less of a sectional party. The only questions were whether Bates and the Blairs could deliver these states, and if they did so, whether Bates would uphold Republican principles in office.

The convention was due to open on a Wednesday, and most of the visitors arrived on Monday or Tuesday. Included were the delegates and their trains of supporters, Illinoisians for Lincoln, newspapermen from all over the country, and onlookers simply coming for a spree. It was estimated that some fifty thousand visitors crowded into Chicago, very nearly half the number of its permanent inhabitants. Men were sleeping three in a bed, on billiard tables, on the floor. A few unlucky ones lay down on the wooden sidewalks, only to discover that Chicago's garbage collection system consisted of literally millions of rats who lived under the sidewalks and came out at night to see what there was to devour. Two thousand people were trying to get breakfast in the Tremont House on Tuesday morning.

David Davis, who had taken the precaution of setting up Lincoln headquarters before the crowd arrived, was deliberately playing an inconspicuous role. The shouting for Lincoln in the streets or the buttonholing of delegates by Lincoln men in bars had no discernible connection with the modest suite from which influential men found their way to other delegation headquarters.

On Monday, when the deal with the Indiana men was concluded, Lincoln had forty-eight votes. His committee calculated that they needed a hundred on the first roll call to show strength with as many more as possible ready to swing to Lincoln after complimentary votes to favorite sons. Some delegations had come instructed to vote as a unit; others had been tied to a particular candidate, as the Illinoisians had been to Abraham Lincoln. Most of the New Englanders were free to do what they wanted, which was, at least as far as rumor ran, to vote for Seward. Special emissaries went out at Davis' request to fish in these waters. Nor were they all men from Illinois. Henry S. Lane, gubernatorial candidate for Indiana, objected that it would not be worth his while to stand if Seward were nominated. The conservative Indiana vote would decide the issue in the state and would sweep the whole Republican state ticket away out of dislike for Seward. Lane was indefatigable at attending caucus meetings, insisting that Seward could not carry Indiana, or Illinois, or even Pennsylvania and New Jersey. Lincoln strategists were trying to draw these four states together, repeating that they would decide the election and should therefore select the candidate. In theory the four states agreed, but for the present the Pennsylvania machine demanded that the others rally behind Cameron, while the men from New Jersey preferred Dayton.

John A. Andrew, chairman of the Massachusetts delegation, was personally pro-Lincoln, though his followers wanted Seward. He helped to collect a group of New England Lincolnites who went in a band around uncommitted delegations, showing off their candidate's strength in an area which was supposed to be committed to Seward. The Connecticut delegation, uncertain whether to support Bates, was headed by Gideon Welles, to whom Lincoln leaders whispered of a cabinet job. A similar offer was made to the Blairs if they would switch to Lincoln when it became clear that Bates had little chance of nomination.

For two or three days and nights the Lincoln intriguers could not tell how matters stood. Bargains had been struck, but would they be honored? It might well be, for instance, that Indiana despite all her promises to Lincoln would embrace a more attractive offer from Weed. On Monday one of the Illinois delegates sent off a letter to Lincoln, who was in his office as usual, keeping up a conventional pretext that he did not want or expect the nomination. "Keep a good nerve —be not surprised at any result—but I tell you that your chances are not the worst." He added, significantly, "We are dealing tenderly with delegates, taking them in detail and making no fuss. Be not too expectant, but rely on our discretion."

Keeping a good nerve must have been a hard thing to do. Lincoln knew David Davis well, and he knew also the kind of promises that were made in conventions. If Davis were to outdo Weed, he must promise something besides what the Indiana delegation wanted. Lincoln, always a compulsive newspaper reader, was exposed to the guesses and hopeful schemes of editors who could watch people passing from one committee room to another and could pick up rumors without ever really knowing what went on. Even Greeley of the *Tribune,* who had foreseen this problem and got himself into the Oregon delegation, was shut out from the crucial deliberations of New York. As a Bates supporter Greeley was not trusted by the Lincoln men either, though they knew at a pinch he would vote for anyone who could defeat Seward. On the whole it is doubtful if Lincoln got much more sleep than the men in the Tremont House, still passing from one hot caucus room to another in the early hours of the morning.

Pennsylvania had fifty-four votes, but Cameron was getting nowhere outside his own state. His managers, having offered Vice Presidencies to other candidates in vain, despaired of his chances. Yet they represented one of the four doubtful states, actually bigger than Illinois and Indiana put together. If they were to switch from Cameron on the second ballot, they could at least sell him high. Davis, persistent in wooing Pennsylvania for Lincoln, was told that they would take nothing less for Cameron than the Secretaryship of the Treasury. Unfortunately it was precisely Cameron's financial deals which had made him unacceptable to those outside the control of his own machine. Even Davis perceived that this was a big promise to make in Lincoln's name without consulting him.

There are two stories about what happened, probably because days ran into nights in the Lincoln headquarters till the memories of exhausted men became confused. It is said that Davis telegraphed to Lincoln about Cameron and Lincoln telegraphed back. It is also said Lincoln read an article in a Missouri paper which, being presumably in favor of Bates, was attempting to spread a rumor that Lincoln was as radical as Seward. Rumors fly quickly in conventions and may be fatal. Lincoln sent his old friend Edward D. Baker, editor of the *Springfield Journal*, to Chicago with the article in question, noting in the margin where he agreed and where he differed from Seward's position. He added a sentence which may or may not have been written with knowledge of the Cameron deal and which may also have been sent up by telegraph. According to accounts the telegram said: "I authorize no bargains and will be bound by none." On the article was scrawled: "Make no contracts that will bind me."

These messages received at Lincoln's headquarters caused utter consternation. Dubois swore. Leonard Swett, ever polite, said, "I am very sure if Lincoln was aware of the necessities. . . ." Judge Logan spat into the cuspidor, growling, "The main difficulty with Lincoln is. . . ." Judge Davis closed the discussion with, "Lincoln ain't here, and don't know what we have to meet, so we will go ahead as if we hadn't heard from him, and he must ratify it."

Why did Lincoln, after authorizing the Indiana negotiations, after receiving a letter from a friend alluding to treat-
ment of delegates in terms which clearly indicated bargains,
send up instructions arriving the day before the voting
started forbidding these tactics? Indeed, why if he was not
prepared for what he knew must happen, did he authorize a
committee dedicated to winning the nomination? He could
have rested on his laurels as Illinois' favorite son for the first
ballot and waited to fight for the Senate four years later. As
so often, Lincoln does not explain his motives. It is possible
that he lost his nerve, particularly when the Cameron bargain
was put to him. If his managers would do that, what else
would they do? We think of Lincoln as a strong man, but he
was human. During his Presidency he was buoyed up by a
sense of duty to his office. Now at a moment of great suspense
he was a private person, still able to change his course if he
wished.

It is noticeable, however, that though Lincoln had given
Judge Logan a signed note withdrawing from the contest to
use if it seemed expedient at any moment, he did not now
require that it be produced. Though in effect withdrawing, he
still left his hat in the ring. It is this perhaps which gives
credibility to another explanation of Lincoln's conduct. He
knew Judge Davis well and might be fairly sure that his
reaction would be precisely what it was. His friends would
make promises because they must, but he would ratify them
only if he pleased. He wanted his committee to know this, but
did not think it would affect their actions. If he considered
what men might feel when promises were broken, he may
have been aware that more was always promised than could
be carried through.

The convention opened on Wednesday, but before the balloting started a presiding officer must be elected, a credentials
committee must pass on the delegates, and a platform must be

drawn up. These arrangements took two days and were chiefly notable for the way in which Seward's men controlled the meeting, surmounting easily such obstacles as arose. The platform, carefully phrased to include the special interests of the different groups which had united in the party, was adopted with enthusiasm on Thursday. The Seward men then pressed for a first ballot. They felt themselves in control and thought that if the business of the Thursday session could be prolonged, they would win at once. The opposition thought so, too, and wanted adjournment. It was nearly time for dinner. Seward's men hesitated, sure that they would win the next morning also. The clerk for the convention reported that the tally sheets for the ballot were not ready and would not be so for another half hour. There was the pretense of a vote on adjournment, but actually men started streaming out in search of dinner.

In this way there was time for one more night of meetings. Pennsylvania was still undecided. Weed was offering lavish campaign funds if they voted for Seward, but Andrew G. Curtin, their candidate for governor, was just as positive as Henry S. Lane of Indiana that Seward would lose, however backed, and would destroy the state ticket. It was after midnight before Pennsylvania agreed to vote first for Cameron and second for old Judge McLean, both complimentary votes which would give them a couple of chances to judge whether Lincoln was still in the running. If so, they would swing to him unless their resolution, which clearly required last-minute consultation, should falter.

Meanwhile New Jersey, the fourth crucial state, had favored Seward after its first-ballot vote for Dayton. Illinoisians had been working on them for days, and they were vulnerable to the notion that the four states should stick together. They too were thrashing the matter out on Thursday night, and the Pennsylvania decision was promptly reported to them. After much discussion New Jersey fell into line. The delegates would go for Lincoln after their first vote for Dayton—who was promised an important embassy by Lincoln's men.

Newspaper editors, who had been circulating amid the crowds for four or five days had been for some time reporting on surprising Lincoln strength, not only among the delegates, who in some cases kept their own counsel, but in the onlooking crowd. Chase of Ohio, perhaps the ablest of the candidates and certainly in appearance the most imposing, had expected that people would coalesce around him in opposition to Seward. This never happened, not only because Chase was too radical, but also because Lincoln took his place. Bates of Missouri, who had similar expectations, had also visibly lost ground to Lincoln. It was doubtful if anyone could beat Seward, particularly after the skillful way his men had handled the convention during its two opening days. If anyone possibly could, it was likely to be Lincoln.

In the Tremont House Lincoln's managers, counting anxiously on their fingers those crucial first ballots which were to make Lincoln the man who could challenge Seward, believed they had the hundred which they had aimed for. They did not, however, know precisely. Some delegations were divided. There was the danger that friends might talk the Lincoln men over. At the last minute, when the roll was being called, delegates might think Lincoln was not coming out as strongly as expected and switch their votes. The Lincoln management, leaving no stone unturned, wanted a frenzy of support from the audience to reassure these waverers. In the first two days of the convention Seward's supporters had lined up each morning outside the Richmond House a thousand strong and complete with brass bands and banners to march in procession to the Wigwam. If they could be crowded out before they arrived, it would be helpful.

Jesse W. Fell and a crony of Lincoln's, Ward Lamon, saw

to the printing of a large supply of extra tickets. A crew was called in to forge signatures on these and to distribute them among Lincoln men with instructions to be on the spot the moment the doors opened. A man said to have the loudest yell in Chicago was to be located in one strategic spot with a competitor in another. Both of them had a good view of delegate Cook of Illinois on the platform. When Cook took out his handkerchief, these two were to start yelling at the tops of their voices and to go on without stopping till he put it back again. Having made these simple moves to outshout Seward supporters, some Illinois men may have snatched a little sleep. Others were busy with Virginia, which had sold out so many times to different parties that nobody could guess where her vote would go. Pennsylvania had been promised by Weed "oceans of money" to win a campaign for Seward and might still go any way despite Curtin's efforts.

On Friday morning all went according to the Illinois plan. Seward's thousand followers with their brass bands and entrance tickets found no room. Some furious men struggled in, but the bulk were penned among the crowd outside, which was enormous because the balloting was due to begin.

The nominations went fairly fast, as it was not the custom for florid speeches to be made in favor of candidates. William M. Evarts of New York rose to say: "In the order of business before the Convention, Sir, I take the liberty to name as candidate to be nominated by this Convention for the office of President of the United States, William H. Seward." The tremendous shriek that arose from the audience proved that by no means all Seward supporters had been excluded by the bogus tickets. No sooner had it died away than Norman B. Judd was on his feet. "I desire, on behalf of the delegation from Illinois, to put in nomination, as a candidate for President of the United States, Abraham Lincoln of Illinois." This time the applause was even louder, outdoing the Seward men

without any question. Two more nominations were put in
without special incident, Cameron and Chase. Caleb B. Smith
of Indiana jumped up (as carefully planned at headquarters)
to second Lincoln's nomination. This showed him running
strong from the start with Indiana committed. The Lincoln
yell was described by reporters as "terrific."

Seward men were now on their mettle. Blair of Michigan
rose to second Seward's nomination and was applauded by
such a wild and frantic shriek that hundreds of persons were
said to have stopped their ears in pain. To men in the galleries
nothing was to be seen but thousands of hats flying up in the
air over a mass of human heads with mouths open. All around
the galleries, where ladies were sitting among the gentlemen,
hats and handkerchiefs were flying too.

The Lincoln men had a surprise waiting. Columbus Delano
of Ohio, "on behalf of a portion of the delegation of that
state," which belonged officially to Chase, begged also to second Lincoln.

"Imagine all the hogs ever slaughtered in Cincinnati,"
wrote a witness, "giving their death squeals together, a score
of steam whistles going. . . . I thought the Seward yell could
not be surpassed; but the Lincoln boys were clearly ahead,
and feeling their victory, as there was a lull in the storm, took
deep breaths all round, and gave a concentrated shriek that
was positively awful, and accompanied it with stamping that
made every plank and pillar in the building quiver.

"Henry S. Lane of Indiana leaped upon a table, and swing-
ing hat and cane, performed like an acrobat. The presumption
is, he shrieked with the rest, as his mouth was desperately
wide open . . . but his individual voice was lost in the aggre-
gate hurricane."

Pretty soon the roll began to be called, starting with Maine.
Maine was important because it was the first and because its
delegates were not committed, but had come to the conven-

tion inclining to Seward. Maine gave Seward ten and Lincoln six, not only showing Davis that bargains were being kept, but threatening Seward with the erosion of his supposedly solid New England vote. The thundering applause inside the Wigwam was an encouragement to New Hampshire, which came next. New Hampshire gave Seward one, Chase one, Frémont one, and Lincoln seven. The roll swept down through New England, picking up some votes for Seward and some for native sons, but unexpectedly and persistently a number for Lincoln. Next, however, it was New York's turn. Evarts stood up to say: "The State of New York casts her seventy votes for William Seward." This put Seward far ahead, as was to be expected. Now came a number of favorite sons, together with border-state support for Bates, with here and there a few votes for Lincoln, nearly all unexpected and likely to encourage the waverers still not called on. Virginia, expected to vote solidly for Seward, gave him eight and Lincoln fourteen. Kentucky and Ohio gave Lincoln some votes. Indiana and Illinois were solid for him. Most of the rest were for Seward with a minority for Bates. The count showed Seward 173 1/2, Lincoln 102, Bates 48, and a scattering of over a hundred votes for various others.

Lincoln men were jubilant. They had their hundred votes, enough to encourage the delegations pledged to switch on the second ballot. First of these to be called was Vermont, which gave its ten for Lincoln, a blow to Seward far beyond the actual numbers. The first ballot had shown that Lincoln, Cameron, and Bates, if put together, could defeat Seward. The second ballot indicated from the first that the opposition was concentrating around Lincoln. New Jersey did not fulfill its contract, but on the other hand Pennsylvania, reading the writing on the wall, forgot its second-round vote for McLean and handed Lincoln forty-eight out of its fifty-four. On went the roll, Pennsylvania's example giving courage to Lincoln

men, but some increases going also to Seward. Presently the
results were announced. Seward 184 1/2, Lincoln 181. Cook
presumably took his handkerchief out, for the yelling and
shouting went on until the convention secretary was forced
to plead for silence. Bates and Chase had diminished, others
were nowhere at all. Lincoln had gained seventy-nine votes
and Seward eleven. The third roll-call presented a chance for
those who were doubtful to jump on the Lincoln bandwagon.
Prominent among these were the Blairs, supporters of Bates,
who came over to Lincoln, on the chance of winning Mont-
gomery Blair a cabinet appointment. Ohio, perceiving that
their candidate, Chase, had no chance, partly came over, giving Lincoln twenty-nine votes. When it came to rewards,
Seward had been already committed by the Weed machine
long ago. It looked more likely that Chase could find a prominent post under Lincoln. After Ohio, whispers went around
that Lincoln would be nominated on this present ballot. People were totting up the score and finding that Lincoln had
two hundred and thirty-one and a half, one and a half short
of the majority he needed.

At the beginning of the day Joseph Medill of Illinois had
taken a seat among the Ohio delegation to encourage those
who were inclining to Lincoln. Opponents had tried to turn
him out, but Medill with no possible right to remain had
somehow stayed. At this moment Medill saw that it might not
be wise to risk a fourth ballot, in which anything might always happen. Before the clerk could announce the result of
the ballot, he turned to David K. Cartter, beside whom he was
sitting, and whispered to him: "If you can throw the Ohio
delegation to Lincoln, Chase can have anything he wants."
Cartter hesitated for a second. What authority had Medill? In
a flash he perceived that it was now or never and that Chase
really would have a claim. He jumped to his feet. "I-I a-a-rise,
Mr. Chairman," he said, struggling in vain with a stutter, "to

a-announce the c-c-change of f-four votes, from Mr. Chase to Abraham Lincoln." Out came Cook's handkerchief, and the Lincoln men exploded.

Not till the frenzy had died down inside the Wigwam could the man who had been stationed on the roof to signal results of the ballot to the waiting crowd outside discover what had happened. Frantically leaning over the skylight, he saw one of the secretaries of the convention with a tally-sheet in his hands, yelling up to him, "Fire the Salute! Abe Lincoln is nominated!" A cannon which had been hoisted up to signal the announcement went off with a bang. A roar arose outside of such dimensions that the subsequent bangs of the cannon were inaudible to delegates within. The thing was done.

15
Farewell, Springfield

———◆———

ABRAHAM LINCOLN OF ILLINOIS was nominated! Chicago exploded, parading everywhere with bands and victory yells. Men staggered out of the Wigwam so exhausted by their triumph that they walked as though they were drunk. Tears ran down the cheeks of Thurlow Weed as the New York delegation, facing the incredible fact with dignity, moved that the nomination be made unanimous. Far away in Auburn, New York, most of Cayuga County had gathered in front of Seward's house, bringing a cannon to fire when the expected news arrived. A messenger galloped up from the telegraph office with the first ballot showing Seward out in front, and everyone cheered. The second ballot arrived, announcing Lincoln only three votes behind. Seward could not believe this was significant because he knew himself far stronger than Lincoln. "I shall be nominated on the next ballot," he declared. Finally the third telegram arrived:

LINCOLN NOMINATED.

The New York senator stared at it, pale as ashes. The crowd melted away, taking the cannon, which was fired in downtown Auburn because after all the party had a nominee.

Why did they have Lincoln? History was to prove him the best man for the job, but why was he given it by a convention which was not looking for the "best man" and which had no reason to suspect that Lincoln would be he. Historians have thrown up their hands and talked about luck, which certainly was involved to some extent. If the convention, for instance, had not been in Chicago, it is unlikely that Lincoln could have gained the nomination. Others, weighing the matter, come to the conclusion that the convention did bumblingly choose the person whom they were seeking—namely, the candidate most likely to win the election.

It was a period when lack of enemies gained more votes for a man than a distinguished career. Lack of enemies had elected Pierce and Buchanan. The Republican party was a conglomerate of people who had sunk differences for the sake of resisting the spread of slavery. When it came to supporting individuals, however, these differences counted. Moreover, to win an election without any southern votes the party needed to attract northern members from uncommitted and usually moderate groups. Bates, an ex-slaveowner and conciliatory towards the South, would have been the choice of many who feared secession and war. In 1856, however, Bates had voted for Fillmore, candidate of the American party, or Know-Nothings. This made him obnoxious to the Germans and most of the foreign-born. Seward, on the other hand, was supported to the bitter end by German leaders, but had frightened precisely the people who might have voted for Bates. To Chase, an even more radical leader, Carl Schurz, most talented of the Germans, had said with a lack of political tact which was characteristic: "If the . . . Convention . . . have courage enough to nominate an advanced anti-slavery man, they will nominate Seward; if not, they will not nominate you." The convention did not have the courage, so that Chase and Seward were out of the question.

Lincoln meanwhile, though less conservative than Bates on the crucial issue, was considered far more so than Chase or Seward. Though he did not approve of Know-Nothing policies, he had not offended either native or immigrant groups. His argument against Fillmore in 1856 had mainly been that he could not be elected, but would take votes which should have gone to Frémont. Having held no office for the last ten years, Lincoln had not recorded votes or joined in debates which might have forced on him a feud with one or other of these sections. Except in the eyes of Southerners, he was that rare phenomenon in politics, a blameless man. Thanks to the inspiration of Oglesby, he was also "the Railsplitter," the people's choice. This might do him disservice with the intelligent voter by representing him as more of a rustic than he was. Since, however, the level of popular education was low, such prejudice did not count heavily. Finally he was "Honest Abe," free of connection with a corrupt political machine. It was possible to represent him as having been chosen in defiance of Weed's money and corrupt bargains. His nomination had in fact been achieved by making bargains, and it could not have been gained otherwise, but this was not spoken of by his supporters. Whatever had been promised, there really was a contrast between Abe with his lawyer friends and the Weed machine.

On that Friday morning when the crowds in front of Seward's house were waiting with their cannon ready to celebrate the news, Lincoln left home as usual to walk the few blocks to the square, but he could not work. Instead he went to the office of James C. Conkling, one of his friends who had been up to Chicago and had just got back by the night train. Lincoln lay down on the couch with his feet over the end and asked questions, but the chief news was that no ballot had been taken on Thursday and that the Lincoln managers, though weary, were not without hope.

Lincoln went off to find Edward D. Baker of the *Journal* whom he had sent up the day before with the message forbidding commitments. Possibly Baker described Davis' reaction.

He may have discussed Lincoln's chances of getting this delegation or that. If Lincoln did not like the way his cause was being handled, it was by now too late to object. The pair of them visited a bowling alley to pass the time, but it was full. They tried a saloon which had a billiard table, but it too was in use. They went back to the office of the *Journal*, hoping that a telegram might have come in. There was nothing. After hanging around till noon, Baker went off to lunch. Lincoln stayed, unable to drag himself away.

Quite shortly after twelve o'clock a messenger boy came panting in from the telegraph office with a telegram for Lincoln. "We did it," the telegram said. "Glory be to God." Other telegrams came quickly on the heels of the first one, so that the *Journal* office buzzed with the news. Men crowded around with congratulations, and there was a hubbub in the midst of which some heard Lincoln say, "I reckon there's a little short woman down at our house who would like to hear the news." He made his way to the door, but apparently was stopped again, for he repeated, "There is a lady over yonder on Eighth Street who is deeply interested in this news; I will carry it to her." Off he went for what was perhaps his last quiet moment.

Springfield, of course, lost no time in lighting bonfires. Stephen A. Douglas, hearing the news in Washington, had commented "there won't be a tar barrel left in Illinois tonight." There certainly were not many left in Springfield, where the inevitable brass band was playing on Eighth Street and a gathering crowd was calling for a speech. A hundred-gun salute began at one o'clock and went on for most of the afternoon. Church bells kept up a continuous jangling till dark. Lincoln, appearing on his front porch, told people that the honor was not given to himself, but to the representative of a great party. He refused to make a statement, adding that all might discover his political position by reading his already published speeches. He would have liked to invite everyone into his house if it had been large enough to hold them. "We will give you a larger house on the fourth of next March," somebody cried. It being impossible to accommodate all his good neighbors, Lincoln asked as many as he could to squeeze in. This invitation was accepted promptly, and the candidate stood his ground, heroically shaking all possible hands. It is not known what Mary did or what she said to torn curtains and broken bric-a-brac when the invasion was over. She, too, looked forward to a larger house in the near future.

The great Chicago convention had done its work, and as the delegates crowded into trains for home, a more exhausted group of combatants was never seen. Even the Illinois men were physically unable to raise a cheer for Old Abe at stations where tar barrels burned, drums rolled, and groups of people triumphantly paraded rails and posters. As for the Seward men, they did not try to cheer. They would, of course, work to get Abe elected, but they were appalled and embarrassed by the decision in which they had taken an unwilling part. Their attitude was well expressed by a Massachusetts politician who was asked to open a Lincoln Club in his home town. "You fellows at Chicago . . . knew that above everything else these times demanded a statesman, and you have gone and given us a *rail splitter.*"

Lincoln had been chosen not so much for his qualities as for his lack of them. What responsible office had he ever held? What things had he done? "Who is this huckster in politics?," demanded Wendell Phillips, Boston intellectual and abolitionist. "The Chicago Republican Convention is over," wrote the unsuccessful candidate Bates in his diary. "That party will henceforth, subside into weakness and then break into pieces. . . . Mr. Lincoln . . . has no general popularity, hardly a general reputation . . . His nomination can add no strength to the ticket."

So said the wise ones of the party and so undoubtedly felt

a good many of the delegates as they emerged from the excitement of the convention into the prosaic world of daily life. Notwithstanding, the thing was done, and the momentum of a great party had been set rolling. It would be sustained not only by the magic of a nominee who was a real "man of the people," but by the local ticket in every state, by Republican candidates whose success or failure must depend upon the image which they created of Abraham Lincoln.

Meanwhile in Springfield a ceremony was taking place. The nomination had to be offered by a committee chosen for the purpose, and formally accepted. Springfield Republicans, who had suddenly found their town the focus of the whole nation, determined to show that they were worthy of the honor. The celebrations of Friday afternoon and evening had been a spontaneous explosion. On Saturday when the train bearing the Committee of Notification puffed in, the Springfield Lincoln Club was on hand to greet them and had marshaled a welcoming crowd of citizens enlivened by the Young American Silver Band and the German Saxe Horn bands. There were cannons, rockets, banners and illuminations, and a fine procession, first to the Chenery House and then to the statehouse, where a reception for distinguished guests had been arranged. Luckily this last affair distracted public attention from the actual committee which, quietly leaving the Chenery House, made its way to Lincoln's home, where the candidate was waiting.

There had been an argument in the Lincoln house about refreshments. Mary Lincoln, on her dignity as future First Lady of the land, had provided sandwiches and champagne. A couple of political friends who had dropped by to give Lincoln a briefing had thought that champagne would not do. What would happen if some of the committee were temperance men? Mary was instantly up in arms in defense of her arrangements, but Lincoln, ever careful, did not like the risk of offending. He had always served water to his guests, he said, and he was not going to alter his ways at this moment. The champagne was removed.

A good many of the committee had never met Lincoln, who was dressed as badly and looked as awkward as ever. His parlor, decorated in conventional middle-class style, looked typically comfortable but provincial. Willie and Tad, hanging around the garden gate, appeared a brash pair of boys in sensible and by no means extravagant clothing. While absorbing these impressions, the group performed its little ceremony. George Ashmun, its leader, made a short speech and gave Lincoln a formal letter confirming his nomination together with a copy of the party platform. Lincoln answered briefly, but as all felt, appropriately, admitting that he could almost wish this great responsibility had fallen on one of the far more eminent men proposed to the convention.

The moment was over. With one of his sudden changes of expression, Lincoln beamed and wanted to shake his new friends by the hand. Sandwiches and water were consumed, and the committee took its leave, discussing impressions. Some thought the candidate was rather simple-minded and inexperienced, but all had liked him. William D. Kelley of Pennsylvania even conceded: "Well, we might have done a more brilliant thing, but we could hardly have done a better thing." He was exactly right.

While the tide of luck ran strongly in Lincoln's favor, that of Stephen A. Douglas was clearly running out. Charleston, South Carolina, had been agreed on in 1856 as the site of the next Democratic Convention. As the situation had developed over the intervening four years, a more unfortunate choice could scarcely have been made. Charleston, a handsome, residential town of about fifty thousand, was ill provided with hotels. These and the boarding-houses had made an agreement to charge five dollars a night, a price so outrageous that

Northerners, who were no longer welcome in private houses, were hard put to it to pay expenses. The Douglas committee hired a building, used the lower part for conferences, and put rows of cots upstairs. Washing facilities were minimal there, and Charleston was hot already, though it was April. The building in which the convention met held only three thousand and was almost unbearably airless when it was filled. Thus, though it was obvious from the first that Douglas had a majority of the delegates, the atmosphere in Charleston was unfriendly and daily became more so as northern visitors began running out of cash and going home.

A southern minority encouraged by the Buchanan administration was determined not to have Douglas. If southern leaders had simply refused to accept him, it is possible that another candidate might have been agreed on. They concentrated, however, on the platform, into which they were determined to write a clause enjoining Congress to pass a code of laws protecting slavery within the territories. The Dred Scott decision, which had forbidden Congress to exclude slaves, had not deprived it of the duty to protect private property according to the southern argument. Since slavery required special laws to maintain it, Congress must pass them.

It was known that Douglas could not accept a platform which ran counter to his doctrine of popular sovereignty. It was clear also that the Douglas forces were too strong for the adoption of this offensive clause. The response of the minority was that they would leave the convention unless they got their way. Douglas men paid little attention to this threat because they imagined that only a few states would withdraw, after which Douglas might find it easier to get the two-thirds majority which by the rules of the convention he needed to win. In the event, what with the heat, the atmosphere in town, and the departure of so many northern supporters, the split widened. Douglas was left without the necessary two-thirds of those who had been seated when the convention opened. There was nothing to do but adjourn to Baltimore a few weeks later. It was hoped that wiser counsels would prevail in the southern states so that fresh delegations with a less extreme point of view would consent to attend.

On the whole, while the Chicago convention was being held in May, it had looked as though Douglas must triumph. This being the case, the argument for Lincoln had been strengthened because Douglas was very powerful in the North. When Lane and Curtin had insisted that Indiana and Pennsylvania could not be carried by Seward, they were thinking that they could not be carried by Seward against Douglas.

The convention in Baltimore was able to nominate Douglas, but only at the expense of a permanent split in the party. Douglas himself, offering to make way for a compromise candidate, was told by his supporters that no one else could carry the North and in particular the Northwest against Lincoln. Knowing the truth of this, he was forced to stand firm, while the southern states, holding their own convention, nominated Breckinridge of Kentucky on a pro-slavery platform.

Appalled by the split in the only national party which had cemented the Union together, a fourth well-meaning group calling itself the "Constitutional Union Party" had put up Bell of Tennessee, seconded by Everett of Massachusetts with no platform save that of loyalty to the Union. This group gained inspiration from elderly conservatives who would on most occasions have voted Democratic. Its strength was in the border states, where it drew off votes from Breckinridge and Douglas. There were thus four contending parties, those of Breckinridge and Lincoln frankly sectional, while Bell and Douglas, though claiming national strength, had yet to demonstrate that they could assert it.

It was soon clear that Bell and Everett could not. These were respected statesmen of the second rank whose platform, "The Constitution," begged the question which divided North and South—namely, how this same Constitution was to be interpreted. Bell and Everett did not even agree on this point, since Bell sounded like a slavery man to Massachusetts, while Everett looked like an abolitionist in Tennessee. They had little in common but their concern to save the Union. Their attitude was shared by many, but particularly by comfortable, bedrock conservatives, who were ready to vote but not to get out and work hard.

Douglas was not well, exhausted by the continuous strain he had been under. Once again he was drinking a good deal. He saw that his candidacy had little chance, but feared that the men behind Breckinridge might carry the South, including the border states of Maryland and Virginia. They might then, whatever the result, declare Breckinridge elected and in collusion with Buchanan's southern cabinet seize Washington and set up their government there. The Little Giant lacked cash and support for the coming campaign, but he never lacked courage. He spoke all over the border states, less to carry them himself than to make it possible for Bell and Everett to do so. His own position was that secession was not justified and that were it attempted, it would be the duty of the President of the United States to break it up. After uttering these defiant words, which were reported all over the South, he made a swing through the Northwest, his own territory and Lincoln's.

It happened that in a few states, elections for the state ticket preceded the presidential one. Maine and Vermont had gone Republican in September, and in October Pennsylvania and Indiana did likewise. "Mr. Lincoln is the next President," commented Douglas when he heard the news. "We must try to save the Union. I will go South."

To Georgia and Alabama he promptly went by way of Tennessee. He was worn out by travel and by the effort of speaking as often as three times a day. His life was threatened, and several efforts were made to derail his train, but he persisted, finding large audiences who shared his concern for the Union.

In contrast, the Republican leaders with victory in sight were far less conscious of the dangers threatening the federal Union. Lincoln, as was customary at that time, made no contribution to the campaign. Mail and visitors poured into Springfield, forcing him to give up his law practice and accept an office in the statehouse, where with a single secretary, John G. Nicolay, who had been lent from the governor's staff, he composed bland letters telling all inquirers that his opinions were to be found in his published speeches and that he had nothing to add. Towards visitors he was equally elusive. He was always glad to see them and gave no indication of impatience or boredom at having become a circus exhibit. No one, however, could bring him to the point of expressing opinions. He always had a little story to tell which kept the conversation firmly on innocuous lines. The party had chosen him, had created the Railsplitter and Honest Abe, the candidate selected without bribery or shady deals. It was for the party to put its man across.

Perhaps Lincoln was wise to follow the general practice of earlier candidates, perhaps not. It is true that whatever he said would have been misrepresented in all the newspapers of the South. It is also true, however, that while Northerners were deluged with pamphlets, extracts, campaign biographies, and editorials all calculated to introduce the unknown Lincoln, these did not circulate in the South, where a "Black" Republican as Southerners had christened their opponents went literally in fear of his life if he were discovered. Southerners were free to call Lincoln the aboriginal ape and to distort him in any way they chose. It was clear that in parts of the South persecution mania was running rampant. Strangers suspected of being northern agents were lynched. Rumors were afloat of another John Brown foray, of terrible slave conspiracies, of a trail of arson in Texas. Men flocked to vote for Breckinridge, angrily resolved to secede rather than submit to rape, arson, murder, and all the consequences of Black Republicanism. The person who above all others should have attempted to allay their fears was President Buchanan, but he, intent on his party feud with Douglas, was committed to Breckenridge, acquiescing in whatever his southern cabinet did without a protest.

The Republican party was on the move. Early in that year Republican clubs had adopted a new fashion of making themselves visible. Oilcloth was cheap and could be had in gaudy colors. It was easy to make uniform capes and top them with some sort of uniform hat. Republican groups, calling themselves Wide Awakes, were drilling and marching, as fascists about three-quarters of a century later were to do in Europe. Truth was that the Land of the Free was singularly lacking in the colorful festivals, religious processions, and traditional ceremonies which added interest to the life of the European peasant. Wide Awakes with shiny cloaks and flaring torches, with bands and drums and rockets gave people something which was otherwise missing from the American scene. There were catchy Republican songs to well-known tunes:

"Ain't you glad you joined the Republicans, Joined the Republicans, Down in Illinois?"

Railroads helped these displays, as they were to help fascists later. Ninety thousand Lincoln men poured into Springfield for a "grand rally of the banners of light," in other words a gorgeous torchlight procession with fireworks and transparencies all down the route.

Though Lincoln was silent, other Republican speakers

were busy. Seward, mindful of what had lost him the Presidency, was so conciliatory that one might almost have fancied that his heart was with the South. Extreme abolitionists had luckily got together, subscribed a war chest of fifty dollars, and nominated for the Presidency Gerrit Smith, one of the financial backers of John Brown's raid on Harper's Ferry. This idiotic act allowed Republicans to dissociate themselves from their own extremists. It is true that the German orator Carl Schurz and others brought up in Europe put freedom ahead of any constitution and continued to make extremist statements. Native Americans, exposed to milder language, were not aware that the South had anything to be frightened of.

Another thing which obscured the danger of secession was the fact that the contest in the North was not entirely concerned with slavery. The Republican platform, carefully drawn up to please all groups, supported tariffs for manufacturing interests, a homestead law to relieve debt-laden farmers, and recognition of the immigrant's right to vote. Many debates on these issues as well as on slavery were held in the North. This happened the more often because though the moral difference between the positions on slavery of Lincoln and Douglas had been outlined in the great debates, the practical difference as things at that moment stood was not large. Popular Sovereignty was destroying slavery in the territories nearly as effectively as outright prohibition. It was well understood that the South objected to the tariff and had no interest in most of the economic issues dealt with in the platform, but differences on these points did not seem worth seceding about. Nor was it to the interest of Republican speakers to emphasize the dangers of victory. They wanted votes.

Lincoln has been blamed for giving the party no leadership at this moment. His long absence from the national political scene accounts for the fact that he did not recognize the danger which was so plain to Stephen Douglas. He was aware that the South had been uttering threats of secession at intervals ever since the time of Jackson. For years the South had bullied the more populous North into making concessions. Southerners had obtained control of the administration during a large part of the history of the Republic. Lincoln was merely at one with the North in insisting that this situation had to be changed some time or other, and the consequences must be faced by the South. Northerners knew themselves in every way the stronger group and did not reflect on the strategic advantages which the South would enjoy if it came to a conflict. Lincoln's view accordingly was that the southern people would not follow their extremist leaders out of the Union. The audiences that Douglas was obtaining in the deep South seemed to prove this point. If any states did try to secede, Lincoln did not imagine that they would form a group of sufficient size to resist the pressure which it would be his presidential duty to apply. Finally, his political sense may well have told him that he was not yet ready to assume leadership of a party which hardly knew him and whose natural leaders were all jealous.

These seem to have been Lincoln's reasons for inaction. It is certainly difficult to believe that he could have altered the course of history by taking a prominent part in the election. It is arguable, however, that the task of a leader is to lead and that Lincoln ought to have tried, even at the risk of making the situation worse. Whether we condemn him or not, the choice is characteristic of Lincoln. Douglas, charging into every fight and calling upon his supporters to follow, resembles the popular concept of a hero far better than Lincoln, whose instincts were all the other way. He did not want to move out ahead of the people. His approach to leadership was always cautious, and he took time to make up his mind. Such persons are at a certain disadvantage in new situations because they do not leap to their feet and make decisions. Lincoln's slowness had always annoyed his partner Herndon and was to irritate a number of the men with whom he worked in the war years.

Lincoln spent most of election day in the governor's office which had been lent to him since his nomination. He chatted away with his callers and watched his opportunity to slip over to the polling place at a time when it was not crowded and vote for the local ticket after cutting his own name and those of his electors from the ballot sheet. The afternoon wore slowly on until the first telegram came in about seven from Decatur, showing large Republican gains since 1856. By this time, of course, it was dark, and crowds of Republicans were gathering in the statehouse to hear the bulletins as they arrived. By nine the suspense was too much for Lincoln, who decided to walk over to the telegraph office with a few friends. At ten a reassuring telegram came in from Pennsylvania, but there was no definite news from crucial New York. It had been evident for some weeks that the New York vote would make the difference and that it was not going to be as easy for Lincoln to carry the state as it would have been for Seward. A couple of long hours passed bringing inconclusive news. Lincoln, with iron self-control, expressed as much interest in the fortunes of his friends as in his own. About midnight he was invited to a supper spread for him and important friends by Springfield women. Hardly had the guests been seated when a messenger burst in with the long-awaited telegram. New York was safe!

Someone started up singing, "Ain't you glad you joined the Republicans?" Back in the statehouse men worked off their pent-up feelings by hugging each other, throwing up their hats, even rolling on the floor. Lincoln stayed through supper, went back to the telegraph office, where more confirmations had come in, and walked soberly home. It is unlikely that he slept, not only because the burden of the responsibility was heavy, but because Republicans all over town were parading, yelling, being glad they "joined the Republicans," and firing off cannon.

At the other end of the country, in Mobile, Alabama, Stephen A. Douglas heard that Lincoln was elected . It was no more than he had expected personally, but the attitude of the South, which he had been seeing at first hand, was on his mind. He too walked home, his secretary observing that he was "more hopeless than I had ever before seen him."

The news also came to Washington, where Buchanan, seventy and ailing, had four months more of his Presidency ahead of him, knowing that all his appointees would be out of office at the end of that time and that a policy of any sort would be difficult to pursue. If he ever thought of talking over his problems with the future President, he dismissed the notion. With a Black Republican, with an ape, a railsplitter, a seedy local politician, there was nothing he could discuss, no matter what happened.

The news came, too, to Charleston, South Carolina. Within a few hours the palmetto flag was hoisted above the offices of the Charleston *Mercury* amid wild cheers from an onlooking crowd. The local federal judge and collector of taxes at the port of Charleston had already resigned. The legislature could not act quite so fast, but within a few days it had appropriated a hundred thousand dollars to buy arms. South Carolina's senators in Washington were coming home. South Carolina had exploded like a powder keg. Elsewhere in the South matters went a little more slowly, but with no less enthusiasm. Militia and "minute men" were busy drilling, while the States Rights flag, a red star on a white ground, was fluttering everywhere.

This crisis came to Lincoln before he, so to speak, came to

it. Four months would have to pass before he was actually the President of the United States. He had no cabinet and very little assurance that Republicans in Congress at the moment would ask what his wishes were or listen to his advice. One way of estimating his position in the country is to look at the electoral figures. He had won a total of a hundred and eighty electoral votes with a popular vote of a million eight hundred thousand. Stephen Douglas, running second in the popular vote with a million three hundred thousand, had only twelve electoral votes. Breckinridge, coming third with less than nine hundred thousand, had seventy-two electoral votes from the lower South. Bell, polling under six hundred thousand, had thirty-nine electors from three border states. In other words, Lincoln, though a clear and legal winner over all the others combined, polled only about one-third of the popular vote. This had happened previously and was to happen again, but the Constitution which made it possible and legal had produced this result at a singularly awkward time.

In view of these figures, we do not need to wonder why Lincoln did not stride into the limelight while the break-up of the federal Union went on. The real change in his position was that as President-elect, he was going to have to choose a cabinet, appoint diplomats, and distribute patronage which reached, as we have seen, into every hamlet in the land. Until he made some moves to settle these questions, he could hardly even be said to have a party. What was to be done about promises made by his managers? What was to be done about Seward, who still considered himself the Republican leader in everything but name? The ruin of the Democratic party had come about through a split between Buchanan, its titular leader, and Douglas, its ablest statesman. The Democratic party had a long tradition, the Republicans a short one. Differences of opinion within the coalition which called itself Republican were great.

Lincoln faced a difficult task, made more complex by an enormous increase in his visitors. Some were country people who just wanted to look at their new President. Some were old friends. There were also men like Thurlow Weed, who wanted to be certain they could pull the strings which made this Lincoln puppet dance. There were representatives from the Land of Enterprise who wanted office, high or low according to what they thought their merits, and supposed the best way to get one was going to the top. Lincoln, who never turned anyone away, was forced to make secret appointments if he wanted to talk with certain men and to transact other business, including the answering of letters, in the middle of a hubbub.

He did not make many public pronouncements, though he assured individuals who questioned him that he had no intention of appointing Northerners to federal offices in the South or of trying to interfere with the southern way of life. He insisted that the duty of a President was to maintain the Union, but he expected to accomplish this by peaceful means. Though it was not for him to criticize the inadequacies of Buchanan, it did become obvious that he ought to make a statement of some sort before open conflict began. Congress was trying to devise a compromise, and Lincoln needed to give some idea of his own attitude. On November 20 Senator Trumbull was due to speak at a grand celebration in Illinois at which Lincoln would be present. The general opinion was that Trumbull's speech would reflect Lincoln's views. It was a moderate speech in which Lincoln consented to insert a couple of paragraphs appealing to the moderate men of every state to preserve the Union. The speech received wide publicity, but as Lincoln observed, no newspaper previously opposed to the Republicans used it to quiet public anxiety. On the contrary, northern Democratic papers hailed it as an attempt on Lincoln's part to betray the platform on which he had been elected, while southern papers called it a declaration of war. This experience reinforced Lincoln's resolve to make no public pronouncements until he was in power.

While Lincoln gave little direction to the public, Buchanan gave less, neither appealing to the loyalty of the masses nor adopting a firm policy towards seceding states. For some time he retained secessionists in his own cabinet. Congress, attempting to fill the vacancy caused by the weakness of the Chief Executive, discussed compromise. The leaders of the lower South were not, however, in a mood to make concessions. On the other hand Republicans who knew the mind of Lincoln were aware that he felt the question of slavery in the territories had been settled by the election and must not be reopened. To do so would not bring peace, but merely raise another quarrel over the acquisition of Cuba or territories to the south.

No President of the United States had ever been elected with so little experience either in government or at least in military affairs. The translation of Lincoln from a good but by no means remarkable lawyer to the Chief Executive of his country consumed the time from his nomination in May till the following March. This may seem extraordinarily long when we consider what was taking place in the South while he remained in Springfield, as it were in a chrysalis state. Fundamentally, however, Lincoln's quiescence was not due to inexperience or weakness, nor even to a serious struggle with Seward who wanted to control his cabinet. In Seward's mind the future of his country depended on his being the power behind the inexperienced Lincoln, so that the mastery of the party and the government was at stake. Nevertheless Lincoln's inaction was not paralysis, but policy. He did sincerely believe that the mass of the people was loyal to the Union, even in the South. He was waiting, in other words, for a reaction against secession.

Seven slave states of the fifteen soon left the Union, but eight remained, all showing encouraging signs of loyalty, including the vitally important state of Virginia. Indeed for the moment the danger appeared to lie less with the loyal slave states than in the weakness of Buchanan, which might encourage secessionists to attempt a coup in Washington or block by violence the inauguration of Lincoln. As long as power could be transferred quietly to the legally elected President, there was much ground for hope. The thing to avoid was any incident leading to war. Being absent from the Washington scene and without influence on Buchanan, Lincoln relied on Seward to keep an eye on the administration, both by contact with old General Scott, commander of the Army, and with Edwin M. Stanton, now Attorney General, who was still freely referring to Lincoln as the Aboriginal Ape, but was a strong man in Buchanan's cabinet and vigorously loyal to the Union.

The position of a President-elect is always awkward, especially when the new administration is of a different party from the old one. As Lincoln waited, negotiating quietly behind the scenes lest pressure be put on him to change his mind, he was publicly harried by office-seekers of every sort to whom he could not deny entry without giving offense to party members. In outward manner he appeared exactly the same as he had always been, both to old country friends from the Eighth Circuit and to Springfield neighbors. He gave strangers the impression that he was glad to see them, never betraying the strain his constant visitors put him under. To those who knew him well, however, there were some changes. He looked haggard, as well he might; and he was growing a beard, apparently to look more dignified. He made no change in the nature of his costume, but older clothes seem to have been quietly retired. The greenish umbrella was laid aside, and criticism of his appearance by strangers began to center not on how badly his clothes fitted, but on how awkwardly he wore them. Mary Lincoln made a big shopping trip to New York with the intention of showing the Washington world that a lady brought up in Kentucky and used to the best society in Springfield could hold her own with anybody in the land. Lincoln's little changes were more unobtrusive. Tad and Willie still dashed in whenever they pleased, interrupting conversations with demands for a dime or some other thing which for the moment seemed important. Neither they nor their father thought this inappropriate, as indeed it was not considering how complete strangers intruded upon him.

The New Year came and went, so that eventually Lincoln began work on his inaugural speech, in which he was at pains to be as conciliatory to the South as he could manage. Suitable garments were acquired in Chicago for the inauguration, which included a shiny new top-hat and a stick with a gold knob. In Washington old General Scott was taking precautions against any attempt at assassination or interference with the ceremony. The Lincoln house had been rented, and packing was started. The plans for an eleven-day journey were drawn up to include official receptions and speeches all along the way. The presidential party included two secretaries as well as Elmer E. Ellsworth, a young protegé of Lincoln's; an old friend, Ward H. Lamon, armed to the teeth; and a more official and soldierly bodyguard. Robert, dubbed by the papers to his obvious embarrassment the "Prince of Rails," was with his father. Some pressure was apparently put on Mary Lincoln to travel separately with Willie and Tad by a shorter route, but suspicious of possible danger to her husband, she insisted on sharing the trip and joined the party next day in Indianapolis.

All these arrangements were duly made, but Lincoln had one or two private matters to deal with in which even Mary had no share. His stepmother, Sarah Lincoln, had remained in the old cabin on Goose Nest Prairie built by Thomas Lincoln. She was, however, by now seventy-two, fairly old to be in the country alone, especially in winter. It is said, moreover, that the cabin chimney had recently collapsed and needed repair. At all events, she was staying in Farmington, not too far from Charleston, with her daughter Matilda Moore, now for the second time a widow. It becomes a little more understandable that Mary Lincoln had never seen her when we realize that Lincoln caught a morning train from Springfield, changed at Tolono and once again at Mattoon, from which he had to go on in the caboose of a freight train which unceremoniously set him down in the mud and slush outside the railroad platform in Charleston after a journey of about eight hours and a half. He spent the night in Charleston with friends and drove out along a bad country road the next morning in a two-wheeled buggy with Augustus Chapman, who had married the daughter of Dennis Hanks who had lived eighteen months with the Lincolns. They got to Farmington about two hours before midday dinner. Apparently their coming was a surprise. At all events the neighbors, highly excited and honored, made dinner a party, after which they retired to leave Lincoln with his family. He had brought old Sarah a fur cape as a going-away present, and it seems likely that she went back with him and Chapman in the buggy to spend the night with the Chapmans, getting up very early to say good-bye to her boy the following morning. Poor old Sarah must have known that it was likely that four or even eight years would go by before Lincoln could come this way again. But someone had frightened her by talk of threats against his life, so that what she said to him was not that she would die before she saw him, but that his enemies were going to kill him.

"No, no, Mama," he comforted her. "They will not do that. Trust in the Lord and all will be well."

A little more than four years later, Dennis Hanks rode out from Charleston one day to the Goose Nest Prairie cabin, where Sarah still lived with one of her grandsons.

" 'Aunt Sairy,' sez I," runs Dennis's account, " 'Abe's dead.' "

" 'Yes, I know, Denny, I knowed they'd kill him. I ben awaitin' fur it,' an' she never asked no questions. She was gettin' purty old, an' I reckon she thought she'd jine him. She never counted on seein' him agin after he went down to Washington, nohow." Poor old Mama had somehow not trusted in the Lord, despite the assurance of the "best boy in the world."

There was one more private parting in which Mary had no share. Lincoln went up to the office on the afternoon of his last day in Springfield, ostensibly to discuss unfinished business with Billy Herndon. Mostly he just lay on the old couch and talked. Perhaps there was a worry in his mind about how Herndon would make out in Springfield without him because he asked directly, as he had never done before, how many times Billy had been drunk, adding that other lawyers had tried to persuade him to dissolve the partnership. He got up in the end and picked up an armful of books which he wanted. Herndon walked down the stairs with him for the last time, and they stopped to look up at the sign which said "Lincoln & Herndon." "Let it hang there undisturbed. Give our clients to understand that the election of a President makes no change in the firm of Lincoln and Herndon. If I live, I'm coming back some time, and then we'll go right on practicing law as if nothing had ever happened." They shook hands on it, but both of them must have known that a great deal was bound to happen. A stage in life had come to an end and could not ever go on without interruption. Herndon managed pretty well during Lincoln's life, and the partnership was not severed. Later he began to drink more, and his end was unhappy. We are grateful to him for timely research on the details of Lincoln's early life, but his feud against Mary caused her a great deal of sorrow after her husband's death. This would have terribly distressed Herndon's friend and partner.

There was not much more to be done. The Lincolns had leased their house, sold their furniture, and given their dog to a neighbor. They were waiting at the Chenery House for their departure. Lincoln had roped their trunks himself and addressed them to "A. Lincoln, The White House, Washington, D.C."

February 11 was a cold and drizzling morning. Everyone who assembled in the small brick railroad station appeared gloomy as the President-elect and his party clambered aboard the special train, consisting of a single passenger car with engine and baggage wagon. People gathered on the rear of the platform, huddled under umbrellas as Lincoln stood on the open entry of the car, leaning against the end rail. It was the moment to say good-bye to much, and he found words for it as follows: "My friends, no one, not in my situation, can appreciate my feeling of sadness at this parting. To this place and the kindness of these people I owe everything. Here I have lived a quarter of a century, and have passed from a young to an old man. Here my children have been born, and one is buried. I now leave, not knowing when, or whether ever, I may return, with a task before me greater than that which rested upon Washington. Without the assistance of that Divine Being who ever attended him, I cannot succeed. With that assistance I cannot fail. Trusting in Him who can go with me, and remain with you and be everywhere for good, let us confidently hope that all will yet be well. To His care commending you, as I hope in your prayers you will commend me, I bid you an affectionate farewell."

Index